The Anthropology of Postindustrialism

T0331312

This volume explores how mechanisms of postindustrial capitalism affect places and people in peripheral regions and deindustrializing cities. While studies of globalization tend to emphasize localities newly connected to global systems, this collection, in contrast, analyzes the disconnection of communities away from the market, presenting a range of ethnographic case studies that scrutinize the framework of this transformative process, analyzing new social formations that are emerging in the voids left behind by the deindustrialization, and introducing a discussion on the potential impacts of the current economic and ecological crises on the hypermobile model that has characterized this recent phase of global capitalism and spatially uneven development.

Ismael Vaccaro is Associate Professor at the Department of Anthropology and the McGill School of Environment at McGill University.

Krista Harper is Associate Professor of Anthropology and the Center for Public Policy and Administration at University of Massachusetts Amherst.

Seth Murray is Director of the Program in International Studies and Teaching Associate Professor in the Department of Sociology and Anthropology at North Carolina State University.

Routledge Studies in Anthropology

The Anthropology of Postindustrialism

Ethnographies of Disconnection

Edited by Ismael Vaccaro,
Krista Harper, and Seth Murray

Routledge
Taylor & Francis Group

NEW YORK AND LONDON

First published 2016
by Routledge
711 Third Avenue, New York, NY 10017

and by Routledge
2 Park Square, Milton Park, Abingdon, Oxon OX14 4RN

First issued in paperback 2017

*Routledge is an imprint of the Taylor & Francis Group,
an informa business*

Library of Congress Cataloging-in-Publication Data
The anthropology of postindustrialism : ethnographies of disconnection /
    edited by Ismael Vaccaro, Krista Harper and Seth Murray.
        pages cm. — (Routledge studies in anthropology ; 27)
    Includes bibliographical references and index.
    1. Deindustrialization—Social aspects.   2. Industrialization—
Social aspects.   3. Shrinking cities—Social aspects.   4. Cultural
landscapes.   I. Vaccaro, Ismael, editor.   II. Harper, Krista,
editor.   III. Murray, Seth, editor.
    HD2329.A584 2016
        306.3'4—dc23   2015021681

ISBN 13: 978-0-8153-4736-1 (pbk)
ISBN 13: 978-1-138-94364-3 (hbk)

Typeset in Sabon
by Apex CoVantage, LLC

Contents

Figures

Foreword

Industrialization (with its associated rapid expansion of production, waged employment, and market integration) has long been treated as a universal process—a recognizable if complex set of transformations that presents certain regularities and patterns, even as it takes different, "path-dependent" forms in different times and places. Thus, we have become familiar with the topic of industrialization as a rich field for comparative inquiry, with the familiar (and often intellectually very productive) dialectic between sweeping big-picture narratives proposed by "grand theory" and the closely observed qualifications and counter-narratives generated by ethnographers.

In contrast, deindustrialization (and its associated processes of market de-linking, mass layoffs, and economic decline) has tended to appear as a kind of terrible accident—an interruption, an exception, or a temporary aberration. Perhaps as a result, we have nothing approaching the sort of comparative literature that is associated with the topic of industrialization. Rich literatures exist, to be sure, on the social suffering caused by such processes, and on specific egregious forms of disinvestment (such as "red-lining"), but we have for the most part not framed deindustrialization, disconnection, and decline themselves as central and general topics for anthropological investigation.

This volume is an attempt to alter this state of affairs. Disinvestment, deindustrialization, and economic decline, the editors point out, have long been important features of the uneven global landscape of capitalist development. Far from being accidental blips, such processes are essential to the process of capitalist accumulation, a process in which the withdrawal of capital from some sites and its entry into others are two sides of the same coin. What is more, the editors suggest that the current moment, in which a global "free trade" regime often allows capital to move from one nation or region to another more quickly and easily than in the past, is one in which disinvestment and deindustrialization are becoming both more important and more visible features of global capitalism.

If this is so, then the time is surely right for increased comparative attention to such processes, with an eye both to identifying patterns and regularities that cut across cases, and to recognizing how specific histories and sociocultural contexts inform the way that disconnection and decline are experienced and responded to. The contributors to this volume are in this respect exemplary, attending as they do to the local specificities of their ethnographic cases while convincingly relating them to other phenomena that are less place-bound (but equally particular), such as capital flows and global commodity markets.

One especially valuable aspect of this volume's contribution is its recognition that zones of disinvestment and deindustrialization are always sites not only of loss and suffering but also of innovation and creativity. There is sometimes a perception (not least among the people who must live through such difficult times) that a time of decline and abjection involves simply "falling back"—returning to a backward past while losing a more stable and secure recent past (and perhaps also an anticipated prosperous future). Yet as the editors emphasize in their introduction, the transformed social, physical, and ecological landscapes of failed or aborted industry offer no possibility of really "going back." Instead, the interruption of the plotline of industrial development always opens up a new space, within which, as they put it, "something new has to emerge" (1). Here ethnography has a special role to play in tracing the emergence of these various forms of "something new." And as the contributions to this volume show very well, people make their way in these new landscapes both by improvising new sorts of livelihoods (ranging from the respectable provision of tourism services to quite dodgy or illegal forms of "informal economy") and, equally importantly, developing new forms of social and political mobilization that allow them to make new sorts of claims on resources (which again can take a range of forms, all the way from lobbying state agencies for subsidies to violent predation on the part of those experiencing economic exclusion).

As a final thought, I would like to suggest that both such new, improvised livelihoods and new mobilizations around the issue of the distribution of resources may become even more important in the years to come. One reason for this is what seems to be, in much of the world, a certain decoupling of economic growth from employment. The cases treated in this book, like most of the other literature on the topic of economic decline, deal mostly with industries that have declined or closed down, and with capital flows that have withered or dried up. Such withdrawals of capital, as the editors note, have long been a fundamental feature of global capitalism, with its characteristic "cycles of capitalist investment and disinvestment." There is another process, though, that can have equally devastating results without being balanced by any countervailing cycle. That is the process through which new capitalist investment itself (and not disinvestment) renders people "redundant," unemployed, and cast off. In South Africa, for instance, capital investment in mining and agriculture has in recent years facilitated not increased employment, but mechanization and modernization that has put hundreds of thousands out of work. Here, as in some other world regions, it is a certain kind of transformative economic investment, not disinvestment, that is casting people adrift or rendering them "surplus" (Li 2010; Ferguson 2013). And the fact that deprivation and decline (for communities that formerly depended on a regular demand for low-skilled manual labor) are unfolding in the very midst of expanded production (and indeed enhanced prosperity for many) renders the sorts of new social and political mobilizations traced in this volume especially important, part of what I have termed a "new politics of distribution" (Ferguson 2015).

As we try to think through such new developments, we will need good ethnographic accounts that can track the ways that people in a range of different settings are actively responding to predicaments of disconnection and abandonment, creating that "something new" that may show us the way to something more hopeful. This volume provides us with such accounts. In doing so, it makes a valuable contribution to an area of investigation that could hardly be more timely or more important.

James Ferguson
Palo Alto, California
April 30, 2014

REFERENCES

Ferguson, James. "Declarations of Dependence: Labor, Personhood, and Welfare in Southern Africa." *Journal of the Royal Anthropological Institute* 19 (2013): 223–42.
———. *Give a Man a Fish: Reflections on the New Politics of Distribution.* Durham: Duke University Press, 2015.
Li, Tania. "To Make Live or Let Die? Rural Dispossession and the Protection of Surplus Populations." *Antipode* 41 no s1 (2010): 66–93.

1 The Anthropology of Postindustrialism
Ethnographies of Disconnection

*Ismael Vaccaro, Krista Harper,
and Seth Murray*

THE POSTINDUSTRIAL MOMENT

How do the economic mechanisms of capitalism, characterized by a hyper-mobility of flows, affect actual places and people? The principal motivation or rationale that underlies these mechanisms is a quest to increase profits through market expansion, establishing favorable terms of trade, or cost reduction. This is most easily and commonly achieved by rapid relocation from place to place in search of a labor force with cheaper costs, new pools of resources or raw materials, or sites with weak environmental regulations. It is in this sense that mobility and commodification—be it of people, cor-porations, goods, or ideas—becomes the fundamental framework through which to understand late modernity, its new economic articulations, and their associated sovereignties (Steinberg 2009). Anthropology has often dis-cussed and theorized the impact of market integration on local communities across the world (Ensminger 1992). This volume, in contrast, analyzes the disconnection of a community away from the market.

The goal of this collection is to create a framework through which to understand places affected by disinvestment after a period of capitalist integration, as well as the radical transformations resulting from indus-trialization and abandonment. How do communities respond to cycles of connection and disconnection from the markets that pushed their industri-alization? Peripheral locales are radically transformed by sudden integra-tion into an economic framework characterized by mass extraction and transformation of natural resources (Pels 1997; Peters 1994). In other cases, industries draw people into urban centers that decline within a generation or two as investors seek new fast-growth locales. Disconnected communities cannot go back to the world as it once existed, as society and environment have forever changed. Yet the model provided by the market integration becomes obsolete. In its place something new has to emerge, even if this means an abandoned landscape, a legacy of pollution, or the informaliza-tion of employment.

Our anthropology of postindustrialism examines how the retreat of market-oriented mass production produces diverse, but repeated patterns in places around the world. Scholars have used the term "postindustrial" in a number of ways to characterize economic and social reconfigurations. Initially, "postindustrial" referred to a transition from manufacturing to service industries (Bell 1973). Many viewed this shift with optimism about the growth of skilled jobs in the new "knowledge economy" (Drucker 1994). Bluestone and Bennett viewed deindustrialization and postindustrialism more pessimistically, with industrial collapse leading to the decline of stable, unionized, and well-paid employment in manufacturing (1984). Others criticize the term "postindustrialism" because it seems to imply that the industrial era of capitalism is over, when in fact manufacturing continues to take place on a massive scale—in other places than Western "industrialized nations." Contributors in this volume, however, demonstrate that communities around the globe are confronting uneven development (Smith 2008), industrial booms and busts, and their attendant social dislocations. More popularly, "postindustrial" refers to the traces of previous industrial development and labor that appear in infrastructure, social relationships, and memory—a sense that we are living in postindustrial times (Ringel 2014). Scholars today are writing about postindustrial landscapes, archaeology, and heritage (Cowie and Heathcott 2003; Dawdy 2010; Edensor 2005; Storm 2014).

As with most anthropological definitions, we use the term postindustrialism more flexibly, as an entry point to comparisons that may trouble earlier, more evolutionary definitions. Katherine Verdery harnessed ethnography to the field of "postsocialism" as a way of deconstructing mainstream transitology and the idea that "shock therapy" could lead to a smooth and predictable transition to free markets (Verdery 1996). In Verdery's spirit, we use the term "postindustrial" not to refer to a predetermined development trajectory but as a way of imagining "what comes next" in different places facing the social, economic, and ecological legacies of prior industrial development that continue to influence people's present-day lives.

Regardless of terminology, the human burdens of disconnection and industrial transformation are unequally shared across people and places (Doussard et al. 2009). We discuss how communities are drawn into the mobile uneven networks of capitalism. Drawing from political ecology, we explore how industrialization and deindustrialization transform nature and landscapes. We then move to the scale of everyday life: how people experience "postindustrial time" (Ringel 2014) and space. Finally, we present several postindustrial pathways that resonate with the ethnographic case studies presented in this book.

MOBILE UNEVEN NETWORKS

The anthropology of disconnection is the study of the local impacts of the capricious unraveling of uneven transnational networks. This asymmetrical unfolding is best understood through the lens of uneven development, in which volatile transnational networks spatially restructure economic and social life (Castells 1996; Harvey 2001; Smith 2008). Neil Smith points to the ways that unequal power relations fundamentally regulate these processes:

> The logic behind uneven development is that the development of one area creates barriers to further development, thus leading to underdevelopment, and that the underdevelopment of that area creates opportunities for a new phase of development. Geographically this leads to the possibility of what we might call a "locational seesaw": the successive development, underdevelopment, and redevelopment of given areas as capital jumps from one place to another, then back again, both creating and destroying its own opportunities for development. (Smith 2008: 151)

These pages describe a global network in a perpetual state of change and in which peripheries and centers are continuously made and unmade.

We present cases of rural and urban postindustrial regimes alongside one another. The central nodes of the networks tend to be cities because the gravitational pull of larger markets dominates network flows (Appadurai 1988; Bestor 2001; Freidberg 2001). But not all urban areas are created equal in the global capitalist system. Cities, or even sections of cities, might get disconnected from other cities and segments of the global networks of production and consumption. The auto-producing midwestern United States became the Rust Belt as Japanese car companies started to distribute equivalent and cheaper products in America and as American car companies started to outsource parts manufacturing to Mexico and other countries (Dudley 1994; High 2003; High and Lewis 2007). Parts of that industry then returned to the United States—not to Detroit, which remained in decline, but to lower-wage regions in the Appalachian states from whence an earlier generation of Detroit workers had come (Kingsolver 2011). The post-socialist industrial areas of eastern Europe also faced pressures following the end of state socialism. Heavy industrial regions like northern Hungary were consciously developed and integrated in state-planned economies (Burowoy and Lukács 1992). After 1989, the privatization of state-owned firms produced a landscape of small cities with unemployed workers and quiet, empty factories stripped of their machinery, which was sold and shipped to other regions (Harper 2012; Pickles and Smith 1998).

We also see the effects of rural disconnection in industrial agricultural and extractive sectors. Vaccaro's field site in the Catalan Pyrénées in the early twentieth century offered cheap coal, yet most mines closed as Spanish power plants switched to cheaper South African coal (Vaccaro 2006). Timber mills all over North America were outcompeted and abandoned due to the massive flows of transoceanic processed wood (Clark 2001; Power 2006).

Fish processing towns became ghost towns when processing ships took over and delocalized the fishing industry (Marchak et al. 1987; Sepez et al. 2007; see also Acheson and Acheson in this volume). Others have documented disconnection due to ecological destruction in the form of depleted fishing stocks resulting in abandoned canneries and quiet fishing ports (Schrank 2005; St. Martin 2005) or deforested and impoverished timber country (Mattey 1990; Raffles 1999). Social scientists have also examined plantation economies suffering the vagaries of the market (Mandle 1974; Wiley 2008) and decapitalized industrial farming economies (Dudley 2000; Tauxe 1993). In all these cases, the hypermobility of capital, people, information, commodities, ideas, and energy has had an important transformative effect on communities, landscapes, and regions all over the world (Inglehart 1997; Sivaramakrishnan and Vaccaro, 2006). When the strategic advantage of one such rural area disappeared, the productive activity vanished with it, leaving abandoned landscapes and communities behind.

These phenomena are not exclusive to the internal peripheries of the global North. Ferguson's *Expectations of Modernity* tracks how this process affected the Zambian copperbelt when extraction costs rose and global prices dropped (1999). The Amazonian rubber tapper industry evaporated once someone learned to cultivate the rubber tree and opened plantations in Asia (Dove 2002). The economies of entire countries in the global South collapsed when their main export markets failed because of significant shifts in global supply (Frynas et al. 2003).

The events studied here are not ontologically new: as E. P. Thompson observed, industrialization created similar boom and bust cycles all over the English countryside in the nineteenth century (Thompson 1968). The novelty lies in their frequency, speed, and range. The cases presented here look at how, on a local level, economic systems, institutions, demographic patterns, and individual and collective identities are reshaped in the conflictive process of connection and disconnection to and from productive and consumptive processes at a regional and global level. Each site faces well-known socioeconomic processes: market integration, expansion, hypermobility, abandonment, or reinvention (Charles and Lipovesky 2005; Hannerz 1996; Pred and Watts 1992). Financialization is also a fundamental feature of the current model, contributing to the speed and spread of speculative markets (Ho 2009; Holmes 2009; Van der Zwan 2014; Palomera 2014).

What happens with localities and their people that, after a period of capitalist integration and connection, suddenly find themselves on the wrong end of the seesaw? Usually, there is a crisis of social reproduction as material conditions and the range of possible livelihood strategies and life trajectories are recast. Industrialization requires higher densities of labor for the factories, which in turn increases the level of consumption in absolute terms due to the sheer number of people required and in relative terms due to the development of new needs associated with modern life. These needs are covered by a continual flow of cheap commodities produced elsewhere in other peripheral nodes of the networks controlled from the urban centers. When mass production moves away from a given location, local communities tend to have reached dimensions beyond the carrying capacity of their local environments and are no longer self- sufficient productive regimes. At that point, however, nobody is interested in providing these community members with the products they have grown to desire because the community members no longer have wages to pay for them. In addition, the expectations, the perceived quintessential needs, the imagined futures of these postindustrial populations cannot be covered by the preindustrial local mode of production, which is neither developed nor diverse enough to do so.

Emerging postindustrial modernities, thus, are characterized by restructuring and, more often than not, different levels of scarcity and crises. As the global stock-market crash of September 2008 and the subsequent U. S. governmental plan to salvage the market should have proven to the last believers of the free market, state and big corporations work and exist in close articulation. Public national interest, as defined by the national centers of power, directs governmental agency. The achievement of the highest possible margin of economic benefit in the shortest possible time directs capital investment. We can only comprehend the paths taken by postindustrial locales by attending to the agency of state and major economic actors in shaping territories and resources.

POSTINDUSTRIAL POLITICAL ECOLOGY

While trying to understand a globalizing modernity through the idea of disconnection we are forced to unpack the workings of the late capitalistic territorial logic. The point of such logic is the generation of maximum profit by extracting or processing at the cheapest possible location with the goal of sending it for consumption to often distant affluent markets. Mainstream economists championed this model as an export-led development strategy for decades (Giles and Williams 2000). Other scholars have drawn attention to the vulnerabilities of this model: market crashes and ecological destruction (Boyce 2002; Martinez Alier 1991). The last thirty years of environmental social sciences have been devoted to the understanding of the interaction between production and consumption as well as its local social and ecological consequences. Because an important part of this research—i.e., political ecology—occurred initially in the global South where rampant spoliation and ecological collapse have been not uncommon, these questions were identified as postcolonial (Bryant and Bayley 1997): that is, that the rationality behind the inequalities, behind the exploitation, was mostly understandable as an outcome of the legacies of colonialism, of the tensions between metropolises and colonies. This tension, following the "world system" model provided by Wallerstein (1974), was articulated around the center and periphery axis in which countries or regions were more or less connected with capitalistic centers that coincided with the old and new colonial centers.

Prior to co-editing the present volume, the three co-authors had separately conducted fieldwork in various locations in Europe. Our field research shared the grounding of a political ecology framework, and we had invariably encountered instances of inequality and dispossession that paralleled in many notable ways scenarios familiar to us from the anthropological literature focused on the global South (Bryant and Bailey 1997; Escobar 2008; Godoy 2001). However, as our analyses could not rely as unconditionally on colonial or postcolonial tensions to strengthen our explanatory frameworks, our interpretations of the territorial "behavior" of late capitalist modernity seemed to require something with a wider explanatory potential (McCarthy 2002). First of all, the old colonial capitalistic centers were quite heterogeneous, and a quick review of those countries' histories unveils radical processes of internal expropriation, rebellion, and repression as turbulent as anywhere else (Hobsbawn 1975, 1987; Thompson, 1968). Instead, the fault line that seemed to connect conflicts in the global South and North alike was the tension between resource-hungry capitalistic and urban populations and the disempowered rural hinterlands (Cronon 1991; Gandy 2002).

Postindustrial landscapes are often characterized by depopulation and economic recession, and, consequently, important ecological transformations are associated with these changes based on the variations of the level of human pressure. Idealized versions of culture and nature emerge in this situation. The state expands the idea of national patrimony to the realms of nature and culture, allowing for public agency intervention. Nature is culturalized through conservation as it becomes a symbol and a commodity. Culture is naturalized through its preservation and consumption as an ideal form in museums and other cultural heritage sites (Vaccaro and Beltran 2007). This patrimonialization happens in parallel to a commoditization of the environment. The enjoyment of the environment has become a multimillion-dollar business, sustained on the consolidation at all strata of western society of post-materialistic values (Inglehart 1997). Even the environmental discourse has become a commodity in itself, just another link in the mass consumptive behavior of enlightened contemporary households (Guha 2000; Santamarina 2006). In many rural peripheries affected by depopulation and economic crises, the revalorization associated with patrimonialization and commoditization has opened new venues to market integration, in order to reconnect with different regional, national, or international networks (Escobar 2008; Zanotti 2009; Zimmerer 2006).

This revaluing of nature and landscapes has a history. During the nineteenth century, industrial elites reinvented the concept of leisure (Plumb 1973; Veblen 1998), turning non-productive activities into an identity marker, a distinction that is part of a habitus (Bourdieu 1984). The consumer preferences, cash availability, and easy mobility enjoyed by the urban masses made it possible for more people to become "nature lovers" (Carr 1999; West et al., 2006). The enormous creation of wealth associated with the consolidation of post-World War II capitalism resulted in the spreading out of post-materialistic values from the elite to the rest of the social structure (Galbraith 1958; Inglehart 1997). In this way, leisure then became a quintessential post-materialistic economic sector that was expanded as a social and cultural right across western societies (Galbraith, 1993). The consumptive domains were expanded because of new leisure preferences. In the post-scarcity society that consolidated during late industrial capitalism, leisure became a central social domain (Giddens 1995; MacCannell 1999; Nazareth 2007). The consolidation of post-materialistic values and leisure as an economic sector have had a fundamental influence on the paths taken by many rural areas experiencing the decay that follows industrial abandonment.

The economic and cultural shifts that accompanied the unfolding of modernity became associated with important new legislative developments as well. The construction of the idea of national interest, the public good that characterizes the emergence of the modern states, and their consecution of the governmental and coercive monopoly (Dean 1999; Foucault 2007) evolved to include environmental protection (Gottlieb 1993; Guha 2000) and cultural collective heritage. This new type of governmentality began to be implemented at the end of the nineteenth century with the first territorially based protected areas (United States in 1872, Canada in 1885, and South Africa in 1902–1926). Since then it has become a massive worldwide phenomenon. The increased value attributed to nature as a space of contemplation and leisure has gone, thus, hand in hand with increased penetration of public agency into environmental protection. In 2005, 6.1 percent of the world, 1,506,436 hectares, was under some level of IUCN protection. This process has resulted in the conversion of the environment into public patrimony (Cooper 2000). The intellectual introduction of the environment into the realm of the public dominion prepares the redefinition, via conservation, of landscape and territory from private (individual or communal) to public, thereby making it susceptible to being expropriated by governmental agencies (Agrawal 2005; Haenn 2005; Hayden 2003, Li 2007).

Nature, as a hot commodity, has paid off in numerous locales across the globe that are transitioning away from an industrial, mass-oriented, productive system. In the Spanish Pyrenees, the closure of mines and factories, combined with the near-disappearance of traditional mountainous agro-pastoralism, resulted in a process of accelerated depopulation and reduced human pressures on the environment. Ironically, depopulation and environmental recovery set the stage for social and economic revival. The landscape, with its natural values and beauty, became the next commodity that these areas could offer to the urban customers (Vaccaro and Beltran 2010). Protected areas, ski resorts, and second residences became powerful economic forces in the renewal of mountain economies.

Not everyone benefits from the shift to nature tourism, however. In South Africa, former Afrikaans farms around Kruger National Park have been converted into thriving safari enclosures in which the veld—the bush—is recreated, and wild animals are unleashed for the pleasure of European and American tourists or hunters. The social impacts of such shifts are numerous, however. Game farms require a smaller labor force from neighboring Black communities than did industrialized farms. These new, smaller productive units produce money (remunerated services) instead of food that could fulfill basic household needs in the area.

Citizens around the world are starting to question the wisdom of the current economic model as a result of the global financial crisis, the volatility of energy prices, and the visible consequences of climate change. Serious consideration of relocating productive centers has coincided with the consolidation, in the West, of a pool of consumers interested in high-quality local food, *terroir* products, and organic agriculture (Welch-Devine and Murray 2011). These trends may yet alter the global economic market and provide incentives for the relocation, once again, of the productive poles closer to their markets.

AT LIFE SCALE: ETHNOGRAPHIES OF EVERYDAY EXPERIENCE

As ethnographers of postindustrial contexts, we must simultaneously attend to temporal and spatial scale. In the previous section, we presented how communities and regions embedded in national- and global-scale political economic processes experienced industrialization and de-industrialization over the course of time. The rise of industries and the new connections they foster across global space are often strikingly visible in new buildings and industrial complexes, consumer goods from faraway places, and influxes of workers from other places. The process of deindustrialization can be seen in abandoned landscapes and depopulated homes, but the evidence of disconnection can be more difficult for scholars to discern. At this scale, the analytic task is to render the connections and disconnections occurring across space and generations visible. As Friedman and Ekholm Friedman write, "Ordinary lives do not confront the global as such. They face more immediate issues" (2013: 249). Ethnographers come to understand cultural change across geographic distance and time by attending to people's everyday practices and sense-making.

Spatial scales become visible in everyday life in many forms: in the built environment and infrastructure where people live and work; in the goods they consume; and in people's consciousness and ways of thinking about connection to "other places." Roads and railroads, factories and warehouses, workers' neighborhoods with homes and public spaces—all these facilitate some kinds of connections while discouraging others. Infrastructure communicates spatial connections that encompass but also exceed production. In Harper's field site in northern Hungary, railroads carried materials into the state-socialist era glass factory and transported finished products out. Locals took pride in the fact that people throughout the country used jars and glasses produced there. But the factory and railroads facilitated other spatial connections as well: ethnic Hungarians worked alongside Roma from the "Gypsy Row" on the other side of town, and factory workers competed in integrated boxing and football leagues against opponents from other counties. Following the collapse of state socialism, the factory closed and residents without motivation or means to travel beyond their neighborhoods now live in ethnic segregation (Harper 2012; Szelenyi and Ladanyi 2006). This is in fact an example of disconnection, not only from a market perspective, but also from the state apparatus, which has its own set of social and ecological consequences.

In the United States, Carbonella looks at infrastructure through the history of Fordist workers' housing projects built by industrialists. These developments elevated an idealized form of the "New England village" as a model for garden cities but eliminated public buildings, such as union halls, that characterized many historical New England mill towns with histories of labor activism (Carbonella 2006). In today's deindustrializing cities, the project of Fordist urban planning and garden cities is over. Some cities and regions have converted industrial workspace into postindustrial leisure space—Manchester United fans now may watch televised games at pubs overlooking the city's late nineteenth century canals built to transport cotton to the textile mills. Many deindustrializing cities, however, have not made the shift to the postindustrial service and information economy that Bell (1973) predicted. Economist Edward Glaeser has proposed that cities like Buffalo and Detroit should stop building infrastructure and instead aim for "shrinking to greatness," even if it means encouraging residents to leave (Glaeser 2007). Yet even in the fastest-shrinking cities, some residents stay on, struggling to endure in the places that are most meaningful to them (Ringel 2014).

In everyday life, one also experiences spatial scales through consumption. Ferguson's "ethnography of decline" pays close attention to the forms of cosmopolitan consumption and sociability adopted by Zambian mineworkers, and their sense of loss when their urban livelihoods collapsed. The Zambian economy of the 1960s and 1970s had been a model of national modernization via export of a single commodity, copper. Zambian mineworkers migrated to the city, where they worked in unionized enterprises and became accustomed to middle-class consumption patterns—wearing British suits, enjoying international jazz and blues music during leisure hours, living in city apartments with electricity and running water, and eventually, moving through an expanding range of city spaces after the end of colonial rule. All this ended during the 1980s due to a worldwide bust in copper prices and exports. The emergent Copperbelt urban society collapsed, too, and the cosmopolitan networks connecting Zambian workers to the global economy were gradually severed. Retired and laid-off mine workers were forced to reconnect with the rural areas from which they had originally come in order to secure access to local sources of food. The country shifted from being an emerging modern nation to an aid-dependent postcolonial nation subject to structural readjustment. Lacking alternative commodities attractive to the global market, Zambia entered, in Ferguson's words, into an era of global disconnect. Individual miners experienced this shift as abjection, as they lost the daily comforts, mobility, health, and intellectual stimulation that shaped their everyday lives (1999).

Finally, spatial scales reverberate through people's ways of thinking about connection to "other places." People imagine spatial affinities in numerous ways: through producing products to be used in other places, as in the Hungarian glass factory (Harper 2012), or through consuming music and products from far away, as Ferguson describes in Zambia (Ferguson 1999). In these cases, deindustrialization marked a turn away from the national and global connections. But in some cases, translocal affinities arise to fill the vacuum left by fleeing industries. Kristen Ghodsee studied an Alevi Muslim community in a post-socialist Bulgarian mining town as the national mining sector entered into decline. Residents' allegiances shifted when an Islamic charity from the Gulf States built a beautiful new mosque. Young people, influenced by new non-profit organizations promoting religious education, began to criticize their elders' "Bulgarian" clothing and way of life forged over years of negotiating a way to be Alevi under the Bulgarian communist system (Ghodsee 2004). In other instances, working-class communities have responded to disconnection from markets by organizing translocally to fight the global "race-to-the-bottom" for their product. Charles Menzies' ethnography of a Breton fishing community traces its history of national-level labor activism as a response to the rise of large-scale trawl fisheries (Menzies 2011). Today, these artisanal fishworkers are forming alliances beyond France with fishing communities in India through the International Collective in Support of Fishworkers (ICSF) (Menzies, n.d.).

Ethnographers must also move between temporal scales—from historical shifts to daily life—as we study postindustrialism in specific places. British cultural theorist Raymond Williams reflects on the difficulty of representing individuals' experience in light of economic formations. Williams identifies the problem of the "habitual past tense" of political economic analysis, in which the analyst is only able to see clearly those aspects of social life that have crystallized into institutions and fixed forms (Williams 1977: 128). Williams instead draws our focus to moments in the individual's micro-scale of everyday life when accepted common-sense beliefs brush against practical experience. These moments allow us to discern emergent "structures of feeling" embedded within larger historical processes (Williams 1977).

"Structures of feeling" include ways of thinking about time. Under industrial regimes, individuals come to experience their days divided into units determined by clock time (Attali 1985, Thompson 1967). Clock time, whistles, and bells are applied to other parts of social life, such as education, even as individuals devise ways to "poach" time back from these institutions (De Certeau 1984, Scott 1976). On a longer scale, individuals learn to think about their lives and their families' lives as temporal trajectories: ideally, these stories center upon the "hope of a better life" in which hard work pays off, if not for the workers, then for their children (Narotzky and Besnier 2014). These aspirations shape what people do and their sense of what futures are possible—as well as people's ability to mobilize around those hopes.

The postindustrial moment is represented in popular discourse through temporal metaphors. These may evoke decline and decay, or through the rosier lenses of the "knowledge economy," an evolutionary process of economic change. Christine Walley observes:

> Deindustrialization, then, is not so much about evolutionary historical transformations in which . . . one abstracted kind of economy (an industrial one) turns into another (a service-and knowledge-based one). Rather, it's about the reworking of social relationships in moments of historical flux in a way that benefits some at the expense of others. (Walley 2013: 82)

Every massive economic transformation comes with an attached new framework of individual and collective positionalities that articulate identity and rights. By replacing the previous socioeconomic model, this new framework leaves a generation of already socialized individuals "offside," unable to play by rules that are no longer valid. The local moral economy is challenged by these massive and successive alterations (Polanyi 1944; Scott 1976; Thompson 1968).

In industrialized locales, entire generations were raised to fit a way of life intensively connected to urbanization patterns, wage economies, and market-regulated distribution of resources. Peasants and tradespeople became workers: miners, fishermen, loggers, factory workers, plantation laborers, or monoculture farmers. They developed occupational and political identities, friendships, forms of knowledge, and patterns of work and leisure around these new economic activities (Vaccaro 2008). The collapse of the industrial complexes and infrastructures that sustained these "structures of feeling" left these emergent ways of life stranded with nowhere to go. This disintegration resulted in cultural and economic dislocations as the expectations of modernity created by the economic boom failed with the bust (Ferguson 1999). This seems to suggest that the reconfiguration of economic structures seems to occur at a faster pace than the equivalent redefinition of local collective and individual identities. These undigested transformations result in cultural "disenchantments" or "reroutings" associated with cycles of failed expectations (Holmes 1989, Kalb 2009).

As the speed of industrial change increases, people are now expected to reinvent themselves several times in their lifetimes or else be left behind in the world of wage labor (Newman 1988; Urciuoli 2008). Richard Sennett refers to this emergent postindustrial process as the "specter of uselessness" (Sennett 2006). Workers must successfully re-skill to new industries as their previous jobs become automated, de-skilled, or obsolete. Sennett notes: "'Skill' became defined as the ability to do something new, rather than to draw on what one had already learned to do" (2006: 98). Bell and others forecasted that postindustrial capitalism would shift work away from the easily automated skills of the manufacturing economy to the cognitive skills and "good jobs" of the information age. Firms then developed strategies to automate, de-skill, and outsource many of these service economy jobs. In light of these volatile, unpredictable shifts, Sennett pinpoints "the capacity to surrender, to give up possession of an established reality" as a key characteristic of flexible, postindustrial workers (2006: 98). However, skills alone cannot guarantee "good jobs," which history has shown are only created and maintained through political struggle.

PREVIEW OF THE VOLUME

How do individuals and communities respond to the massive ruptures, dispossession, and human suffering that happen when capital moves on to more profitable places? Imagining futures without the security of industrial workplaces—which may be a romanticized security that looks best in hindsight—can be a scary business. After all, as Narotzky and Besnier remind us, "the economy is about projecting into the future" (2014: S10). The close-up lens of ethnography allows us not only to understand how people make sense of the world through structures of feeling—we also can see how people plan and act in response to change.

The chapter contributors show community responses to the postindustrial crisis unfolding along four different pathways: ghost towns, collective action aimed at the state, reconnection, and the search for alternatives. These four pathways might occur in isolation or in different combinations in any given place. In the first response, residents migrate away from an industrial center as factories close and the state starts to neglect infrastructure, creating ghost towns. The residents who remain must find ways to cope with reduced services and public amenities. Even in ghost towns, life goes on, and ethnography helps us to see the webs of remittances, non-market economic practices, and household strategies through which people endure. The second pathway is mobilizing and petitioning the state to remake local economies through state subsidies and reconfigurations of value. Often this means revaluing a natural resource in terms of payment for ecosystem services (Rosa et al. 2007). A third pathway is reconnection—identifying and exploiting a new, substitute commodity that is currently valued in the global network. Finally, some people respond to crisis and uncertain futures by attempting to develop local community alternatives to the capitalistic framework (Gibson-Graham 2006). The seeds of renewal may be found in non-market activities that already exist, submerged but allowing people to survive in the current system. Or communities may creatively invent new, cooperative ways to organize livelihoods. Several ethnographers in this volume have taken a participatory action research framework in which community members and researchers join together to cultivate emergent economic subjectivities and practices (Cameron and Gibson 2005; Gibson-Graham 2008; Kingsolver 2010, 2011).

The chapters of this volume all explore community responses to disconnection from the global capitalist market and its supporting centers of power. Each examines different facets and angles at a local level of this global transformative process, analyzing new social and ecological formations that are emerging in the voids left behind by the absconding industries. Through the lens of ethnography, contributors develop a broader, comparative frame for the anthropology of disconnection in postindustrial regimes.

For more than two decades, development on the Pacific island nation of Papua New Guinea has been largely dependent on natural resource extraction, namely oil, timber, and mining. Although operations such as the well-known Porgera gold mine have the potential to integrate local communities into the global marketplace and could ostensibly benefit indigenous groups, Jerry Jacka argues that the development of resources and the distribution of wealth has been markedly uneven: only a few customary land-owning groups were compensated for land lost or damaged by mining activities, and few individuals are directly employed by the mining consortium. Even the development of a coffee-growing scheme that was intended to help local farmers as a corporate social responsibility outreach program has failed, and the reality is that the prospective mining wealth has bypassed most people of Porgera. Jacka's chapter shines a light on a dark side of postindustrialism: many young men in Porgera now work in the "life market," which entails attacks and extortion by those marginalized from the benefits of the gold mine on groups receiving benefits such as royalties from mining proceeds. Within this context, the "value of labor-less wealth" has destabilized social network ties and directly contributed to the resurgence in tribal warfare in the highlands of Papua New Guinea.

Ann Kingsolver's chapter follows the industrial and postindustrial transformations of Nicholas County, Kentucky, a part of Appalachia that has witnessed the rise and fall of tobacco, coal, and textile industries. Kingsolver characterizes the rural region's history within global capitalist networks as a 200-year "cycle of abandonments by single commodity industries." She traces how these cycles shaped the landscape and infrastructure of the region through externally focused capital investments that simultaneously facilitate the movement of goods and the isolation of populations. Residents experience the ongoing recession of each industry as a series of "everyday disasters." Today, Nicholas County looks to the internet-based service economy as a way out of the latest cycle of industry abandonment, with Amazon distribution warehouses and call centers as pathways for reconnecting, even though many residents of this rural area remain unconnected in a "Broadband Desert." Kingsolver examines the diverse economic strategies that Kentucky's women and men have used to endure as their labor has been commandeered by absentee capitalists for decades. These strategies, much like those of the "life market" described in Jacka's chapter, include illegal and informal cash economies—from alcohol distilleries and bootlegging during the Prohibition era to today's trade in powerful prescription painkillers. More positive contemporary strategies involve collective action and civic organizations that promote youth development, environmental sustainability, local community media, and rural tourism.

Elena Khlinovskaya Rockhill's chapter offers us a particular version of disconnection in the far northeastern Russian territory of Magadan, or Kolyma, an area replete with natural resources that was occupied in the early twentieth century following a state-sponsored project of colonization and development. The collapse of the Soviet Union and the costs of maintaining this northern frontier resulted in a punctuated disconnection, not necessarily from the market itself, but from the state structures, which until then had sustained the area's model of exploitation and production. The area went through a rapid and intense process of depopulation, leading to social atrophy and the outright abandonment of some communities. The traumatic disconnection from its initial network of institutional support is being currently replaced by a new set of private commercial initiatives, both local and global in origin, that are reconnecting the region to global markets.

James Acheson and Ann Acheson focus on the ephemerality and mobility of market-oriented industries, such as timber and fisheries, in the state of Maine during the last three centuries. The geographical and chronological scale of their analysis creates an image in which mass extraction or production is in permanent mobility: one industry replaced by a new one due to the obsolescence of the product, the discovery of cheaper sources elsewhere, or the decimation of the local resource. The authors also track the impacts of these economic changes on the historical micro-demography and social vitality of areas of the state that experience fleeting golden eras followed by abandonment, or areas that have experienced cycles of economic collapse and recovery as they have been economically reinventing themselves for centuries.

Vanesa Castán Broto identifies a pollution landscape in and around Tuzla, Bosnia and Herzegovina, one that is specifically attributed to coal ash pollution from power plants. She discusses how the long-term presence of pollution in Tuzla leads local inhabitants to incorporate pollution as a ubiquitous feature of their daily lives, shaping both individual and collective experiences. Drawing from Heidegger and Ingold's ideas on the politics of dwelling, Castán Broto suggests that a polluted landscape is not automatically stigmatized if a mode of production is created within this landscape, or if one persists in place. In this post-conflict instance, the appropriation and cultivation of a wasteland is a paradoxical process that enhances people's livelihoods by expanding their possible resource base while simultaneously increasing their exposure to pollutants and related health problems. Castán Broto examines how community members come to accept life in a polluted landscape rather than mobilizing the state for compensation and clean-up.

In her research with informal electronic waste (e-waste) recyclers in China, Anna Lora-Wainwright problematizes the distinction between industrialism and postindustrialism. She writes: "Situated as it is at the intersection between production of goods and provision of services, manufacturing and de-manufacturing, recycling is both industrial and postindustrial." China's e-waste "scalvagers" treat the discarded products of the information economy—mobile phones, computers, and monitors—as a resource to be mined in cottage industries. Recycling the flood of e-waste reuses rare minerals and metals that would otherwise rot after just a few years of consumer use. At the local level, however, the economic opportunities provided by e-waste processing come hand in hand with serious environmental and occupational hazards. Responding to media reports on the pollution created by e-waste recycling, the Chinese government is attempting to curtail informal scalvagers and to create its own large-scale facilities for e-waste processing. While these state policies may improve environmental oversight, informal scalvagers see them as an infringement on their autonomy as small producers. Lora-Wainwright's chapter offers a provocative lens on the uneven coexistence of industrial and postindustrial regimes within China's rising economic center.

Dawson's chapter discusses the collapse of an industry, such as sugar cane in northeast Brazil, with an extremely deep social and ecological footprint, as the result of the combination of global processes (competition) and national transformations (slavery abolition). This collapse in the nineteenth century looked different in the state capital than in the surrounding areas, where the old plantations and mills were once sited. This disconnection was accentuated by the loss of political centrality of this region due to the growth of the urban and industrial centers of the South of the country. Dawson also discusses how the capital, Salvador de Bahia, is currently experiencing a process of reconnection to national and global markets thanks to the oil industry and tourism. In other words, he provides an example of how increasing political marginalization, market shifts, and cultural transformations have resulted in a succession of historical disconnections and reconnections of Salvador de Bahia to the national and global economies.

Veronica Davidov writes about the world of urban explorers, or "urbexers," who explore industrial ruins as a hobby. Davidov sheds light on how abandoned industrial buildings around the world have become subcultural spaces. She explores the meanings urban explorers attribute to deserted factories, hospitals, schools, and other once-thriving buildings: curiosity, nostalgia, heritage salvage, and the adventure of going "off-limits." Davidov holds that urbex, as "pursuits involving abandoned urban spaces utilized and valued in ways that run counter to the conventional allocation of use-value in the late-capitalist city," is a leisure form that poses an implicit and sometimes explicit critique. Urban explorers are attracted to industrial ruins as potentially emancipatory spaces because they show how much work and investment it takes to maintain the appearance of modernity and order, and how quickly rust, vines, and entropy set in without the resources and labor of day-to-day production. These ruins have a special pathos because they show the wastefulness of industrial systems: the abandonment of places, buildings, and tools that become mysterious artifacts when removed from use. Davidov maintains that urbexers create new forms of aesthetic, heritage, and leisure value in conventionally de-valued and abandoned spaces.

Nitzan Shoshan's chapter focuses on one East Berlin *Plattenbauten*, or socialist-era high-rise residential neighborhood, which is portrayed in the national media as an urban ghetto devolving into a neo-Nazi zone. Shoshan interrogates these representations, placing them in conversation with residents' perceptions of changes in the neighborhood. He contextualizes the neighborhood's transformation in terms of the spatial reorganization of workplaces, cultural life, and participants' expectations of a better life under state socialism and reunification. This reorganization of urban space and economy has rendered what was once a well-located neighborhood of residents who worked together in nearby socialist industrial firms into a distant urban periphery populated by *Wendeverlierer* (transition losers).

Janet Newbury and Katherine Gibson take a look at residents' responses to changes coming to Powell River, British Columbia, once a "model company town" that was home to the world's largest newsprint mill. With the decline of Canada's paper industry in the 1990s, the paper mill provides fewer and fewer jobs to Powell River, and residents and policymakers are debating strategies for the town's future. Drawing from geographer J.K. Gibson-Graham's "community economy" approach, Newbury and Gibson have been carrying out participatory activist research in Powell River, eliciting citizen conversations about the role of diverse economic practices in possible "postindustrial pathways" for the town and region.

All of these chapters, with all their diversity and complexity, help us to reflect on the inherent temporal nature of industrial transformations, as well as on the impacts that this ephemerality has on the communities that experience the hypermobility of late capitalism. This compendium of study cases allows us to see the form in which the uneven networks that the contemporary economic system builds across continents grow and wither. Most importantly, these ethnographies show us how communities that struggle after industrial abandonment cope with that dramatic contextual change and seek more just, hopeful, and livable futures.

REFERENCES

Agrawal, Arun. *Environmentality: Technologies of Government and the Making of Subjects*. Durham: Duke University Press, 2005.

Appadurai, Arjun. *The Social Life of Things: Commodities in Cultural Perspective*. Cambridge: Cambridge University Press, 1988.

Bell, Daniel. *The Coming of the Post-Industrial Society*. New York: Basic Books, 1973.

Bestor, Theodore. "Supply-Side Sushi: Commodity, Market and the Global City." *American Anthropologist* 103 no 1 (2001): 76–95.

Bluestone, Barry and Bennett Harrison. *The Deindustrialization of America: Plant Closings, Community Abandonment and the Dismantling of Basic Industry*. New York: Basic Books, 1984.

Bourdieu, Pierre. *Distinction: A Social Critique of the Judgment of Taste*. London: Routledge, 1984.

Boyce, James K. *The Political Economy of the Environment*. Northampton, MA: Elgar Publishing, 2002.

Burowoy, Michael and János Lukács. *The Radiant Past: Ideology and Reality in Hungary's Road to Capitalism*. Chicago: University of Chicago, 1992.

Bryant, Raymond and Sinéad Bailey. *Third World Political Ecology*. London: Routledge, 1997.

Cameron, Jenny, and Katherine Gibson. "Participatory Action Research in a Post-structuralist Vein." *Geoforum* 36 no 3 (2005): 315–31.

Carr, Ethan. *Wilderness by Design: Landscape Architecture and the National Park Service*. Lincoln: University of Nebraska Press, 1999.

Castells, Manel. *The Rise of the Network Society*. Malden, MA: Blackwell Publishers, 1996.

Certeau, Michel de. *The Practice of Everyday Life*. Berkeley: University of California, 1984.

Charles, Sebastien and Giles Lipotevsky. *Hypermodern Times*. New York: Polity, 2005.

Clark, Charles. "Stability and Moral Exclusion: Explaining Conflict in Timber-Dependent Communities." *Human Ecology* 8 no 1 (2001): 13–25.

Cowie, Jefferson and Joseph Heathcott, eds. *Beyond the Ruins: The Meanings of Deindustrialization*. Ithaca: Cornell University Press, 2003.

Cronon, William. *Nature's Metropolis: Chicago and the Great West*. New York: Norton, 1991.

Dawdy, Shannon Lee. "Clockpunk Anthropology and the Ruins of Modernity." *Current Anthropology* 51 no 6 (2010): 761–93.

Dean, Mitchell. *Governmentality: Power and Rule in Modern Society*. London: Sage, 1999.

Doussard, Marc, Jamie Peck and Nik Theodore. "After Deindustrialization: Uneven Growth and Economic Inequality in 'Postindustrial' Chicago." *Economic Geography* 85 no 2 (2009): 183–207.

Dove, Michael. "Hybrid Histories and Indigenous Knowledge among Asian Rubber Smallholders." *International Social Science Journal* 173 (2002): 349–59.

Drucker, Peter F. *Post-Capitalist Society*. Oxford: Butterworth Heinemann, 1994.

Dudley, Kathryn. *The End of the Line: Lost Jobs, New Lives in Postindustrial America*. Chicago: University of Chicago Press, 1994.

———. *Debt and Dispossession: Farm Loss in America's Heartland*. Chicago: University of Chicago Press, 2000.

Edensor, Tim. *Industrial Ruins: Spaces, Aesthetics, and Materiality*. New York: Berg, 2005.

Ensminger, Jean. *Making a Market: The Institutional Transformation of an African Society*. Cambridge: Cambridge University Press, 1992.

Escobar, Arturo. *Territories of Difference: Place, Movements, Life, Redes*. Durham: Duke University Press, 2008.

Ferguson, James. *Expectations of Modernity: Myths and Meanings of Urban Life on the Zambian Copperbelt*. Berkeley: University of California Press, 1999.

Foucault, Michel. *Security, Territory, Population: Lectures at the Collège de France 1977–1978*. New York: Palgrave MacMillan, 2007.

Freidberg, Susanne. "On the Trail of the Global Green Bean: Methodological Considerations in the Multi-Site Ethnography." *Global Networks* 1 no 4 (2001): 353–68.

Friedman, Jonathan, and Kajsa Ekholm Friedman. "Globalization as a Discourse of Hegemonic Crisis: A Global Systemic Analysis: Globalization as a Discourse of Hegemonic Crisis." *American Ethnologist* 40 no 2 (2013): 244–57.

Frynas, George, Geoffrey Wood and Ricardo Soares de Oliveira. "Business and Politics in Sao Tome e Principe: From Cocoa Monoculture to Petro-State." *African Affairs* 102 (2003): 51–80.

Galbraith, John Kenneth. *The Affluent Society*. New York: New American Library, 1958.

———. *The Culture of Contentment*. Boston: Mariner Books, 1993.

Gandy, Matthew. *Concrete and Clay: Reworking Nature in New York City*. Cambridge: MIT Press, 2002.

Ghodsee, Kristen. *Muslim Lives in Eastern Europe: Gender, Ethnicity, and the Transformation of Islam in Postsocialist Bulgaria*. Princeton: Princeton University Press, 2004.

Gibson-Graham, J.K. *A Postcapitalist Politics*. Minneapolis, MN: University of Minnesota, 2006.

Gibson-Graham, J.K. "Diverse Economies: Performative Practices for 'Other Worlds'." *Progress in Human Geography* 32 no 5 (2008): 613–32.

Giddens, Anthony. *Affluence, Poverty and the Idea of a Post-Scarcity Society*. UNRISD Discussion Papers 63, 1995.

Giles, Judith, and Cara L. Williams. "Export-Led Growth: A Survey of the Empirical Literature and Some Non-Causality Results. Part 1." *The Journal of International Trade & Economic Development* 9 no 3 (2000): 261–337.

Glaeser, Edward. Can Buffalo Ever Come Back? *Cities Journal* 17 no 4 (2007): 94–99.

Godoy, Ricardo. *Indians, Rain Forests, and Markets: Theory, Methods, and Analysis*. New York: Columbia University Press, 2001.

Gottlieb, Robert. *Forcing the Spring: The Transformation of the American Environmental Movement*. Washington, DC: Island Press, 1993.

Guha, Ramachandra. *Environmentalism: A Global History*. New York: Longman, 2000.

Haenn Nora. *Fields of Power, Forests of Discontent: Culture, Conservation, and the State in Mexico*. Tucson: Arizona University Press, 2005.

Hannerz, Ulf. *Transnational Connections: Culture, People, Places*. London: Routledge, 1996.

Harvey, David. *Spaces of Capital: Towards a Critical Geography*. Edinburgh: Edinburgh University Press, 2001.

Hayden, Cori. *When Nature Goes Public: The Making and Unmaking of Bioprospecting in Mexico*. Princeton: Princeton University Press, 2003.

High, Steven. *Industrial Sunset: The Making of North America's Rust Belt, 1969–1984*. Toronto: University of Toronto Press, 2003.

High, Steven and David Lewis. *Corporate Wasteland: The Landscapes and Memory of Deindustrialization*. Ithaca: Cornell University Press, 2007.

Ho, Karen Zouwen. *Liquidated: An Ethnography of Wall Street*. Durham: Duke University Press, 2009.

Hobsbawm, Eric. *The Age of Capital: 1848–1875*. New York: Vintage, 1975.
———. *The Age of Empire: 1875–1914*. New York: Vintage, 1987.
Holmes, Douglas. *Cultural Disenchantments: Worker Peasantries in Northeast Italy*. Princeton, NJ: Princeton University Press, 1989.
———. "Economy of Words." *Cultural Anthropology* 24 no 3 (2009): 381–419.
Inglehart, Ronald. *Modernization and Postmodernization: Cultural, Economic, and Political Change in Forty-Three Societies*. Princeton: Princeton University Press, 1997.
Kalb, Don. "Conversations with a Polish Populist: Tracing Hidden Histories of Globalization, Class, and Dispossession in Postsocialism (and beyond)." *American Ethnologist* 36 no 2 (2009): 207–23.
Kingsolver, Ann E. " 'Like a Frog in a Well': Young People's Views of the Future Expressed in Two Collaborative Research Projects in Sri Lanka." *Human Organization* 69 no 1 (2010): 1–9.
Kingsolver, Ann E. *Tobacco Town Futures: Global Encounters in Rural Kentucky*. Long Grove, IL: Waveland Press, 2011.
Li, Tania Murray. *The Will to Improve: Governmentality, Development, and the Practices of Politics*. Durham: Duke University Press, 2007.
MacCannell, Dean. *The Tourist: A New Theory of the Leisure Class*. Berkeley: University of California Press, 1999.
Mandle, Jay. "The Plantation Economy and its Aftermath." *Review of Radical Political Economics* 6 no 1 (1974): 32–48.
Marchak, Patricia, Neil Guppy and John McMullan, eds. *Uncommon Property: The Fishing and Fish-Processing Industries in British Columbia*. Toronto: Methuen Publications, 1987.
Martinez-Alier, Joan. "Ecology and the Poor: A Neglected Dimension of Latin American History." *Journal of Latin American Studies* 23 (1991): 621–39.
Mattey, Joe. *The Timber Bubble that Burst: Government Policy and the Bailout of 1984*. New York: Oxford University Press, 1990.
McCarthy, James. "First World Political Ecology: Lessons from the Wise Use Movement." *Environment and Planning A* 34 (2002): 1281–1302.
Menzies, Charles R. *Red Flags and Lace Coiffes: Identity and Survival in a Breton Village*. Toronto: University of Toronto, 2011.
———. "Global Forces and Global Struggles: Linking the Bigoudennie to the Global Fishers' Movement." Unpublished manuscript, n.d.
Narotzky, Susana and Niko Besnier. "Crisis, Value, and Hope: Rethinking the Economy: An Introduction to Supplement 9." *Current Anthropology* 55 no S9 (2014): S4–16.
Nazareth, Linda. *The Leisure Economy: How Changing Demographics, Economics, and Generational Attitudes Will Reshape Our Lives and Our Industries*. Ontario: John Wiley and Sons, 2007.
Palomera, Jaime. "Reciprocity, Commodification, and Poverty in the Era of Financialization." *Current Anthropology* 55 no S9 (2014): S105–15.
Pels, Peter. "The Anthropology of Colonialism: Culture, History, and the Emergence of Western Governmentality." *Annual Review of Anthropology* 26 (1997): 163–83.
Peters, Pauline. *Dividing the Commons: Politics, Policy and Culture in Botswana*. Charlottesville: University Press of Virginia, 1994.
Pickles, John and Adrian Smith, eds. *Theorizing Transition: The Political Economy of Post-Communist Transformations*. New York: Routledge, 1998.
Plumb, John Harold. *The Commercialization of Leisure in Eighteenth Century England*. Reading: University of Reading, 1973.
Polanyi, Karl. *The Great Transformation*. New York: Holt, Rinehart and Winston, 1944.

Power, Thomas. "Public Timber Supply, Market Adjustments, and Local Economies: Economic Assumptions of the Northwest Forest Plan." *Conservation Biology* 20 no 2 (2006): 341–50.

Pred, Allan and Michael Watts. *Reworking Modernity: Capitalisms and Symbolic Discontent*. New Brunswick: Rutgers University Press, 1992.

Raffles, Hugh. "'Local Theory': Nature and the Making of an Amazonian Place." *Cultural Anthropology* 14 no 3 (1999): 323–60.

Ringel, Felix. "Post-Industrial Times and the Unexpected: Endurance and Sustainability in Germany's Fastest-Shrinking City: Post-Industrial Times and the Unexpected." *Journal of the Royal Anthropological Institute* 20 (2014): 52–70.

Rosa, Herman, Deborah Barry, Susan Kandel and Leopoldo Dimas. "Compensation for Environmental Services and Rural Communities: Lessons from the Americas." In *Reclaiming Nature: Environmental Justice and Ecological Restoration*, edited by James K. Boyce, Sunita Narain, and Elizabeth Stanton, 237–58. New York: Anthem, 2007.

Roura-Pascual, Nuria, Pere Pons, Michel Etienne and Bernard Lambert. "Transformation of a Rural Landscape in the Eastern Pyrenees between 1953 and 2000." *Mountain Research and Development* 25 (2005): 252–61.

Santamarina, Beatriz. *Ecología y poder: el discurso medioambiental como mercancía*. Madrid: Catarata, 2006.

Schrank, William. "The Newfoundland Fishery: Ten Years after the Moratorium." *Marine Policy* 29 no 5 (2005): 407–20.

Scott, James. *The Moral Economy of the Peasant*. New Haven: Yale University Press, 1976.

Sepez, Jepez, Cristina Package, Patricia Malcolm and Amanda Poole. "Unalaska, Alaska: Memory and Denial in the Globalization of the Aleutian Landscape." *Polar Geography* 30 nos. 3–4 (2007): 193–209.

Sivaramakrishnan, Kalyanakrishnan and Ismael Vaccaro. "Postindustrial Natures: Hyper-mobility and Place Attachments." *Journal of Social Anthropology* 14 no 3 (2006): 301–17.

Smith, Neil. *Uneven Development: Nature, Capital and the Production of Space*. Athens: University of Georgia Press, 2008.

Steinberg, Phillip. "Sovereignty, Territory, and the Mapping of Mobility: A View from the Outside." *Annals of the Association of American Geographers* 99 no 3 (2009): 467–95.

St. Martin, Kevin. "Mapping Economic Diversity in the First World: The Case of Fisheries." *Environment and Planning A* 37 (2005): 959–79.

Storm, Anna. *Post-Industrial Landscape Scars*. New York: Palgrave Macmillan, 2014.

Tauxe, Caroline. *Farms, Mines and Main Streets: Uneven Development in a Dakota County*. Philadelphia: Temple University Press, 1993.

Thompson, E.P. "Time, Work-Discipline, and Industrial Capitalism." *Past & Present* 38 (1967): 56–97.

———. The *Making of the English Working Class*. London: Peter Smith Publisher, 1968.

Urciuoli, Bonnie. "Skills and Selves in the New Workplace." *American Ethnologist* 35 no 2 (2008): 211–28.

Vaccaro, Ismael. "Post-Industrial Valleys: The Pyrenees as a Reinvented Landscape." *Journal of Social Anthropology* 14 no 3 (2006): 361–76.

———. "Cornellà through the Looking Glass: Stories, Knowledge, Society, Ecology and Change." *Journal for Cultural Research* 12 no 2 (2008): 151–65.

Vaccaro, Ismael and Oriol Beltran. "Consuming Space, Nature and Culture: Patrimonial Discussions in the Hyper-Modern Era." *Journal of Tourism Geographies* 9 no 3 (2007): 254–74.

———. "Livestock Versus 'Wild Beasts': The Contradictions of the Natural Patrimonialization of the Pyrenees." *Geographical Review* 99 no 4 (2009): 499–516.

———, eds. *Social and Ecological History of the Pyrénées: State, Market and Landscape.* Walnut Creek, CA: Left Coast Press, 2010.

Van der Zwan, N. "Making Sense of Financialization." *Socio-Economic Review* 12 no 1 (2014): 99–129.

Veblen, Thorstein. *The Theory of the Leisure Class.* New York: Prometheus Books, 1998.

Verdery, Katherine. *What Was Socialism, and What Comes Next?* Princeton Studies in Culture/Power/History. Princeton, NJ: Princeton University Press, 1996.

Wallerstein, Immanuel. *The Modern World-System I: Capitalist Agriculture and the Origins of the European World-Economy in the Sixteenth Century.* New York: Academic Press, 1974.

Walley, Christine. *Exit Zero: Family and Class in Postindustrial Chicago.* Chicago: University of Chicago, 2013.

Welch-Devine, Meredith and Seth Murray. " 'We're European Farmers Now': Transitions and Transformations in Basque Agricultural Practices." *Anthropological Journal of European Cultures* 20 no 1 (2011): 69–88.

West, Paige, James Igoe and Dan Brockington. "Parks and Peoples: The Social Impact of Protected Areas." *Annual Review of Anthropology* 35 no 1 (2006): 251–77.

Wiley, James. *The Banana: Empire, Trade Wars, and Globalization.* Lincoln: University of Nebraska Press, 2008.

Williams, Raymond. *Marxism and Literature.* New York: Oxford University Press, 1977.

Zanotti, Laura. "Economic Diversification and Sustainable Development: The Role Non-Timber Forest Products Play in the Monetization of Kayapo Livelihoods." *Journal of Ecological Anthropology* 13 no 1 (2009): 26–41.

Zimmerer, Karl. *Globalization and New Geographies of Conservation.* Chicago: University of Chicago Press, 2006.

2 Working in the "Life Market"

Gold, Coffee, and Violence in the Papua New Guinea Highlands

Jerry K. Jacka

INTRODUCTION

On 30 March 2012, the Papua New Guinea *Post-Courier* featured the image of a burned and battered Toyota Land Cruiser under the headline "Illegal Miners Attack Porgera Mine." Scorched car parts and shattered glass litter the ground around the destroyed vehicle. While the charred, hulking remains of the car are now windowless, the cages that once covered them to protect the passengers from stone throwers remain intact. The driver's side door hangs open trailing singed weather stripping, providing the image of the driver beating a hasty retreat from an enraged mob of illegal miners. The picture of a burned, cage-covered car conjures *Mad Max*-like scenarios of a post-apocalyptic future where roving bands of humans battle over the world's few remaining resources. This is not the future, though, this is the stuff of everyday life for people living around one of the world's largest gold mines, the Porgera mine in highlands Papua New Guinea. And this is not a story of a post-apocalyptic landscape, but rather a more complex story of how global capitalist resource extraction and uneven development (Smith 1984) can simultaneously, albeit paradoxically, produce industrial and postindustrial regimes adjacent to one another in both time and space.

The word "postindustrial" conjures images of rusting and abandoned factories in the desolate wastelands shaped by global capitalist production. However, I want to think about the possibilities of broadening how we define postindustrialism by engaging with Ferguson's (2006) concept of the "extractive enclave" in which capital does not "flow" or "encompass" a region but is often concentrated in razor-wire-fenced and policed compounds at mineral and petroleum extraction sites. Unlike earlier forms of development in the developing world that were "socially *thick*"—i.e., had larger social projects in mind (cf. Ferguson 1999; Scott 1998)—contemporary neoliberal resource extraction is "socially *thin*" and "depends ever less on wider societal investments" (Ferguson 2006: 36, his emphases). It is the very nature of the extractive enclave that allows for an industrialized core, such as a mining camp with electricity, running water, and other amenities, to be surrounded by a nonindustrialized periphery of plywood shanty towns and bush-material village houses with none of the conveniences of modern life. An important question, though, is how do we get from the nonindustrial to the postindustrial?

In most cases, it is impossible for the extractive enclave to be a true fortress, ensuring that some benefits do not seep out into the surrounding communities. Starting in the late 1990s with the rise in internet-based information sharing regarding global corporate activities, there were new responses by resource extraction companies purporting to be concerned not just with economic profit, but also with social and environmental sustainability—what in the parlance of green development has come to be called "the triple bottom line" or "corporate social responsibility" (CSR). Recent anthropological analyses of corporate social responsibility (Rajak 2011; Reed 2009; Welker 2009), however, question the moral intent of these endeavors. Writing about Angolan oil extraction, Reed (2009: 175) argues that Chevron's philanthropic undertakings "are not random acts of kindness. . . . CSR responds to shareholder interests, deflects the demands of international watchdog groups and local activists, and creates a more stable, profitable operating environment." In order to better understand the discourses and practices surrounding "socially thin" development, we need to pay attention to the ways that corporate and state-corporate joint ventures pursue social and environmental sustainability programs in resource extraction areas.

It is the twin processes of making extractive enclaves and half-hearted corporate social responsibility programs that generate the transition from a nonindustrial periphery to new kinds of postindustrial landscapes. They allow industrialization and postindustrial "abjection" (Ferguson 1999) to occur in the same area. Through maintaining oppressive regimes of governance around the enclaves, resource extraction companies try to ensure that capital does not flow out to surrounding communities but "hops" (Ferguson 2006: 38) from the extractive zone to the centers of finance in the developed world. At the same time, though, CSR programs keep local people expectantly waiting for the promises of development that in most cases arrive in insufficient amounts or fail to materialize at all. Communities surrounding extractive sites thus become "resource frontiers" (Tsing 2005), places where promising booms on the not-so-distant horizon become daily lived busts for the hopeful and expectant. The people in these settings are postindustrial, for they have imagined (and in many cases, seen first-hand) the material wealth that industrialization will bring, but are all too often left with the pollution and broken dreams of a postindustrial society. Many individuals, too, live postindustrial livelihoods. Once flush with cash from jobs at the mine, many former workers now pursue subsistence horticulture. Some left work tired of the constant demands from relatives for money and assistance, others were forced to quit for fear of crossing enemy clans' lands en route to work in the ever-present milieu of tribal fighting. For most of these men (mining jobs being predominantly held by males), the promises of development that have come and gone in a matter of a decade and half or so arouse strong feelings of resentment, which often find outlet in inter-group conflicts and everyday forms of violence.

Extractive development is complicated in PNG (and the rest of Melanesia) by the fact that approximately ninety-seven percent of the nation's land base is owned by customary groups. While the state does hold title to the sub-surface mineral rights, national law ensures that landowners affected by development will receive monetary compensation for lands lost or damaged by mining activities and will receive a portion of royalties as well. In Porgera, landowners also received relocation houses and promises for preferential hiring and business contracts (Filer 1999). Porgerans whose lands did not fall within the boundaries of the Special Mining Lease (SML) were not entitled to the same slew of benefits that their neighbors were. Nevertheless, plans were made to create a township with retail and educational facilities that would benefit all. In addition, alternative income generating activities were on the agenda for communities outside the SML boundaries. In the eastern Porgera Valley, where I have conducted sixteen months of social and ecological research since 1998,[1] coffee growing was promoted as the "green gold" that would sustain the local economy in the post-mining years.

In the remaining sections of this chapter, I explore the promises and failures of mining and coffee development for the people of Porgera. Mining and the extractive enclave it has created and coffee development as corporate social responsibility both depend upon forms of limited connection as a means of engaging with the community. I argue that Porgerans have never been fully connected to, nor completely disconnected from, global economic systems. Instead, the connective structures that link the various development projects and people are partial constructs that are shaped and reshaped by discourses of modernization, incomplete knowledges, and differing social and economic motives of the different actors (Jacka 2005). The paradoxical outcome of all of this is that people negotiate diverse terrains of industrial and postindustrial life in their daily perambulations depending upon kin group, geography, and historical circumstance. In the following section, I examine the social history of mining and its intersection with kinship and land tenure. Then I turn to the development of the Maliapaka Coffee Plantation among non-SML landowners. After this, I describe the resurgence of violence in Porgera in the mid-2000s—a social development that many young men describe as working in the "life market," or in other words, pursuing tribal warfare as a form of redistributive economic exchange. In my conclusions, I explore the consequences of working in the life market on the society and ecology of Porgera.

MINING, KINSHIP, AND LAND TENURE

Since the late 1950s, gold has been the "second garden" of the Porgera people (Biersack 2006). Sweet potatoes (*Ipomoea batatas*) and, to a lesser extent, taros (*Colocasia esculenta*) comprise their main gardens. Living and farming in the montane tropics (between 1,600 and 2,400 meters above sea level) requires a diversity of landholdings for gardening purposes in order to mitigate the climatic and geological catastrophes, such as torrential rainfall, droughts, frosts, and landslides, that frequently impact household production. Households gain access to these various garden lands through the recognition of flexible membership in several different clans (more technically, sub-clans). Upon birth, every Porgeran acquires the rights to affiliate with eight different sub-clans, four from their father's grandparents' paternal clans and four from their mother's. After a person gets married and begins to raise children, the expectation among their kin members is that they will "come and go" (*pu ipu* in Ipili). Coming and going involves building houses and planting gardens on their various sub-clans' lands and helping with group affairs with their sub-clans. With a married couple having the possibility of affiliating with sixteen different sub-clans (eight from each spouse), it would be nigh impossible to realize this full potential. Instead, most couples maintain between two and four houses and about double that number of gardens on their various sub-clans' lands. Aid in bridewealth payments, other important exchanges, and warfare are offered to as many of their other groups as they can manage.

One of the ways that Porgerans characterize their land and social groups is through the statement that "the land is big, and the groups are small." As such, they are intent on recruiting kin members with promises of land so that group size is increased. Large group size has the advantage of being able to marshal more resources during exchanges and to provide sufficient warriors to either defend the group during tribal fights or, as most people hope for, to deter conflict altogether. There are also mechanisms to recruit non-kin, which all involve providing land for gardening and houses for varying lengths of time. The goal of bringing non-kin to a group's land is to eventually turn them into kin by marrying them into the group, or by marrying their children into the group when they come of age.

In addition to these local mechanisms of promoting flexible membership within clans, Porgerans also cultivated long distance exchange networks with high altitude dwelling Enga speakers to their southeast. Porgera serves as a refuge during major frost events, which are often associated with El Niño, that destroy gardens region wide at altitudes above 2,400 meters (Waddell 1975). After such calamitous events, Enga migrate en masse with their pigs to lower altitude areas and live with their Porgeran hosts. Porgerans are especially welcoming because pigs from the high altitude swamplands to the southeast are considered a delicacy and are renowned for their massive size. As well, they welcome the extra people that swell the ranks of their group's population. Maintaining connections with multiple groups in the valley and the larger region has a social importance in addition to the ecological factors just discussed. One of the most important social functions of multiple group affiliation is to provide places to migrate to during times of warfare when people feel unwilling to support their group's martial projects. Porgerans don't expect all the members of their clan to support them, especially when conflict breaks out with a neighboring group with which some of the clan's members are actively gardening and interacting. In such cases, individual clan members will migrate to one of their third or fourth clans to maintain neutrality. It is also critical to note that warfare is a very common occurrence in Porgera. Porgera is one of six districts in Enga Province, and across the province as a whole, between 1991 and 2010 there were 500 wars fought in which 4,816 people were killed (Wiessner and Pupu 2012: 1652, Table 1).

In a preindustrial, pre-hard rock mining era, this system of high mobility and the recruitment of outsiders worked well to promote household and group resilience against frequent social and ecological upheavals. Moreover, during the colonial era—1961 to 1975 for Porgera—warfare was suppressed by the Australian colonial government. During this brief, fourteen year interbellum period, given the wide kinship networks, around seventy-five percent of the male populace in Porgera was involved with alluvial mining at some time during the year, truly making gold a second garden for most Porgeran households. In a 1986 study of alluvial mining in Porgera, researchers counted between 700 and 800 people mining every day, and estimated that small-scale gold mining contributed between 3.5 to 5 million kina (approximately US$4.2 to 6 million) to the local economy annually, with individuals earning between K300 and K1000 monthly (Handley and Henry 1987: 9–11). With an estimated population of around 7,000 people in the mid-1980s,[2] this means that about ten percent of the total population was mining daily, and annual incomes varied between $4,000 and $14,000. Given that the World Bank calculated PNG's 2011 GNI per capita at $1,480, these 1980s figures are truly remarkable indicators of the wealth that small-scale mining generated for Porgerans.

In a recent analysis of rubber production in Borneo, Michael Dove (2011) presents a model of the elimination of smallholders in productive systems in which state and corporate interests realize a profit can be made. Arguing that non-timber forest products should be more accurately called "non-valuable forest products" because there is no large profit in their extraction, Dove illustrates how capitalist ventures attempt to encompass smallholder production once markets and substantial profit margins can be realized by these larger entities. The same mechanisms were at play for gold production in Porgera. The 1970s and 1980s saw a number of commercial gold ventures come and go in Porgera. The area was too remote and the price of gold too low to justify the efforts at large-scale extraction. However, with the demise of the gold standard in 1971 and the meteoric rise in gold prices (from $35/ounce in the 1960s to over $600/ounce by 1980), commercial production became a more promising notion. By 1987, the development of the Porgera Gold Mine[3] officially began, with production planned to begin in 1990.

The shift from alluvial to hard-rock mining radically altered social and economic relations in the Porgera Valley (see Biersack 2006 for an in-depth overview). The largest source of alluvial gold lies in the middle reaches of the Porgera River in an area Porgerans call Lower Porgera. Where the mine was to be built, however, was in the upper tributaries of the Porgera River on the lands of completely different sub-clans than the ones who owned land in the Lower Porgera. With the flexible social relations, one might wonder if this was not to be a problem though. Wouldn't mining proceeds flow widely through the broad kinship networks? In total, twenty-three sub-clans in seven different clans owned lands within the boundaries of the Special Mining Lease. With approximately seventy named clans living in the valley, only ten percent were designated as SML landowners by the conditions of the Mining Act. However, the amounts of land held by each sub-clan were significantly different, which meant that just a few sub-clans have received the bulk of mining proceeds that come from compensation. Royalties are also paid on the basis of land owned within the SML to 192 agents from the twenty-three sub-clans who are then supposed to distribute the money to individuals, although it is widely reported that big men retain most of the cash. Therefore, to a large extent, money has not flowed with the same ease and freedom along the kinship networks through which formerly people, pigs, and shell wealth did flow relatively unrestrictedly. Moreover, while it was fairly easy to gain access to the alluvial gold fields by activating a distant kinship link, it required a person's labor to extract wealth from the land. In the era of hard-rock mining, wealth comes without work for the SML landowners and there is less of an emphasis on sharing access to wealth than there was in the alluvial mining era.

The development of a large-scale mine also reconfigured regional social relations. Prior to when the mine opened in 1990, most of the valley was occupied by Ipili speakers. After 1990, when compensation and royalty money started to be paid to SML landowners, the more populous Enga to the east and Huli to the south started to move onto the lands of SML sub-clans. These migrations were supported by their Ipili hosts, as they both mirrored preindustrial exchange and climate migration routes and increased group size and strength. With SML clans growing in size and potential strength, non-SML Ipili clans started to also actively encourage Enga and Huli kin to settle among them as well. What has ensued has been a population explosion and demographic transition in Porgera. From 9,255 people counted in the 1990 census, the 2000 census recorded over 22,000 people, and there are estimated to be over 50,000 people in the valley today. From 1980 to 2000, the annual population increased by over eight percent annually. The demographic transition has resulted in young people in their teens and twenties who are nominally Enga or Huli, but who have never lived outside of the Porgera Valley.

This confluence of shifting fortunes surrounding mining wealth, local political factionalization, and shifting land tenure regimes is ripe for an analysis grounded in political ecology. Blaikie and Brookfield provide the classic definition, in which political ecology "combines the concerns of ecology and a broadly defined political economy . . . [which] [t]ogether . . . encompasses the constantly shifting dialectic between society and land-based resources, . . . within classes and groups within society itself, . . . [and] a concern with the role of the state" (1987b: 17). In the next section, I explore the shifting dialectic between and among non-SML landowners and sub-clan estates in the context of a state/corporate-sponsored alternative economic development scheme, the Maliapaka Coffee Plantation.

COFFEE AND "GREEN" GOLD

Since opening in 1990, the Porgera Gold Mine has remained one of the most productive mines in the world, with annual production averaging over 900,000 ounces of gold. During the lead-up to mining development in the late 1980s, Porgera was hailed in development circles as constituting a new kind of mining project through the inclusion of local stakeholders upon whose land the mine was being built. During development negotiations, local stakeholders were guaranteed a range of monetary and other benefits: an equity share in the mine (currently two and a half percent), a share of royalty proceeds (currently one percent of the value of quarterly mine output), compensation for lands lost, preferential hiring and granting of business contracts, and in some cases relocation houses. There were also indirect benefits promised that would include improvements in health, education, and infrastructure services. Many of these projects were to be overseen by an entity called Porgera Development Authority (PDA), which is a quasi-governmental organization that receives its funding from a portion of the mine royalty payments to the SML landowners and from annual grants from the provincial government (Jackson and Banks 2002: 161, 303). One of the major undertakings of the PDA was the building of a town to service the mine. By the end of the 1990s, the town, Paiam, was mostly completed and at that time had an international primary school, a high school, a hospital, a grocery store, a radio station, rugby fields, a market, a Toyota dealership, and a number of homes to house the families of non-local workers at the mine (Jacka 2001 and 2007).

The Porgera benefits package was negotiated in the shadow of the Panguna mine on Bougainville Island, North Solomons Province, which was shut down by landowner protests in 1989 over environmental damages and unequal intergenerational compensation practices (May and Spriggs 1990). As a consequence, mining development at Porgera was negotiated in the hope that money and services would accrue to the greatest possible number of people. Mining officials voiced the opinion that, since the Ipili were "an exchange-based society," mining money would move extensively throughout the kinship network. Yet, for the most part, money from mining royalties and compensation has not been shared widely. The concept that wealth from hard-rock mining was not making its way into outlying communities was well known by the local-level government. In 1998, local officials began discussions with a vociferous group of non-SML landowners in the eastern Porgera valley in an area called Tipinini who were upset over "eating the dust of the mine, but not eating any of the money," as one leader put it to me. The discussions between the government officials and the residents of Tipinini were over the planned development of a pilot project that was to create interest in an alternative income generation scheme. The project was to be a coffee plantation and nursery which would serve as a demonstration center/coffee plant source for local farmers.

Despite coffee being one of highland PNG's most important export crops (West 2012), with a gold economy Porgerans never became overly involved in coffee growing. In a 1998 census leading up to the coffee development talks, government workers in the Department of Primary Industries (PNG's agricultural department) reported to me that the census indicated that in the Tipinini area (comprising three of Porgera's ten census wards), only seventy-nine households were growing coffee, and that there were only 6,950 trees in the area (about eighty-eight trees per household, although the range per household was from 2–811). Given that the soils and climate were obviously suitable for coffee growing, the district government launched a two-pronged initiative to promote coffee production. The first was to encourage every household to plant and look after 500 coffee trees. The second initiative was to develop a 165-hectare for-profit coffee plantation that would serve as a resource center for meeting their first initiative. At the plantation, farmers would learn how to grow and harvest coffee, and the plantation would also have a nursery that would sell coffee plants to local farmers. The exciting thing for the government was that the plantation would be a partnership between local landowners in Tipinini and the Porgera Development Authority. The landowners would supply the labor and the land, and the government would oversee the money that would be provided by the PDA for the plantation development.

In 1999, because I was living in the Tipinini area conducting research for my dissertation, the PDA asked if I would be willing to work as a paid consultant for two months in order to conduct a baseline socioeconomic survey, assess attitudes about cash cropping and coffee growing, and survey opinions about the plantation in the three census wards where the coffee development would be occurring. With my two research assistants, who had already been working with me for several months, we developed a questionnaire and randomly administered it to thirty individual household heads in each of the three different census wards (ninety total). We also held two gender segregated focus groups in each of the three census wards to understand differing male and female perspectives on cash cropping and socioeconomic services, and then had the groups rank the respective services in order of preference. We also held semi-structured interviews with (a) some of the current coffee producers, (b) key landowners in the proposed coffee plantation area, and (c) the elected councilors in each of the three wards.

From this research, we saw the incredible need for an alternative income-generating mechanism in the eastern Porgera valley. Paralleling a 1992 study conducted by the mining company, it was apparent that mining wealth was barely making inroads into outlying communities. The 1992 study found that the average amount of mining wealth (from royalties) in one SML community was K1,906 per month per household, while in Tipinini it was it K0 (Banks 1999: 113, Table 3.8). The amounts earned per household from cash cropping were, respectively, K35 and K71. In our study, when we examined monthly incomes (excluding households whose members worked at the mine), the average monthly income was reported to be just over K28 (about US$9 in 1999). This number is somewhat artificially lowered by the fact that one of the census wards (one-third of our sample) is in a very remote area of the Porgera valley and there is no cash-cropping, the only money comes from remittances from friends and kin. The average monthly income in the data from the wealthiest census ward was just over K62 (about $20).

There were also a couple of findings from the research that gave us doubts about the long-term viability of the project. The first concern was lack of market access. There was only a footpath to the coffee plantation, and the government had neither plans nor money to build a road. Road maintenance is a constant issue in the highlands of PNG given the constant rain and geological instabilities. In fact, through an instrument called the Tax Credit Scheme (TCS), the mine had taken over many of the government services in Enga Province, such as road building and maintenance, in lieu of some of its tax burden paid to the state. TCS money had already been spent in the area around the plantation on housing for the elementary school teachers as well as on rain catchment tanks at the school, and the mine was unwilling to put more money into the area for a road. The second concern was the location of the coffee plantation in regards to traditional land holdings. The plantation was to straddle the lands of two clans (technically, four sub-clans, two from each clan), the Pakoa and Yawanakali, who were long-term enemies. There were a number of deaths that had occurred on both sides within the last decade that had still not been compensated. As a consequence there was much distrust between the principle landowners involved in the project. The final concern was the lack of the PDA's willingness to sign any sort of agreement with the landowners about compensation for the land or profit sharing. Over all the years of alluvial and hard-rock mining, Porgerans have come to appreciate formal, written documentation surrounding agreements about land tenure, land use, and appropriate compensation for lands taken out of horticultural production for development purposes. That the PDA was unwilling to do this is, I argue, a larger-scale mechanism by which funding partners appear to be interested in corporate social responsibility, but intend to never fully follow through with their plans. Moreover, an institution like the PDA complicates the very nature of what "corporate social responsibility" even is. In essence, it provides the mine a way to show shareholders and mining critics that it cares about social and economic welfare through some of its profits going to the organization, but doesn't have to be involved in the messy day-to-day affairs of ensuring that the money actually makes a difference in the lives of local people. In addition, even when the PDA funds projects, Porgerans always say that "the mining company built it."

Despite these concerns, the government and the PDA were keen to get the plantation started. Ten contracts were issued to clear one hectare of primary rain forest each. The funders wanted the land cleared quickly, so the holders of the contracts hired between twenty and forty of their group members to help them cut down trees and brush and burn the slash piles. With the contracts priced at K1,000, each person received no more than K50 (about $17) for their efforts. As one worker commented to me later, "There wasn't even time to save the economically valuable trees. It was just cut and burn, cut and burn." The plan was to clear and plant coffee on fifteen hectares the first year (despite there only being contracts to clear ten hectares), and then to continue to clear and plant another ten hectares every year after that, so that the 165-hectare plantation would be complete once mining ended. Over the next few weeks, teams of contracted workers (mostly men) planted over 25,000 coffee plants on the ten hectares. Excitement in the surrounding hamlets about the coffee development was high. Extra plants were being bought for about US 10 cents apiece and planted around people's households. I bought 100 plants for each of my two research assistants after they complained that they were missing out on the future wealth from the green gold.

Coffee takes about three years before it starts to produce cherries, so after a few weeks, the excitement died down and people went back to their sweet potato gardens to await their future wealth. A few months after the plantation was planted I returned to the U.S. In the next section, I describe my return to the Porgera Valley six years after I left and recount the dismal events surrounding the demise of the Maliapaka Coffee Plantation.

WORKING IN THE "LIFE MARKET"

In November 2006, Epe Des, the former councilor of Tipinini #1 census ward, and I stood on the high ridge separating the western part of the Porgera valley, with the mine, from the eastern part of the valley, where the coffee plantation was located. In the far distance, on the other side of the coffee plantation, we could see the sun glinting off of a small metal roof. "That's my brother-in-law's grave,[4] I just buried him last month," Epe reflected. Pius, Epe's brother-in-law, had been shot in the middle of the night during a tribal fight. A devout Seventh Day Adventist, Pius had apparently thought a pig was in his garden, but stumbled upon a group of warriors who mistook him for the man they had come to kill in Pius's village. In 1999, during the coffee plantation study, I had slept several nights at Pius's house, as he was one of the key Pakoa landowners, and the thought of him dead in the prime of his life saddened me deeply. Oddly enough, the events that led to Pius's death in 2006 started in 1999 with another killing, and in some ways this first death set the preconditions for the failure of the coffee plantation a few years later.

Around the same time the coffee plantation was being developed, an argument over some land along the main road broke out between two cousins. The argument turned ugly and one of the men smashed his cousin over the head with a stick, killing him. A fight broke out between the two men's clans, but because many of the combatants were relatives the conflict was resolved in a few months. In 2003, however, the killer's brother was shot in the chest with a shotgun in broad daylight in a trade store in Tipinini. Everyone in the Tipinini area assumed that the killing was a revenge murder for the 1999 killing. The killer, meanwhile, had escaped through the rainforest in the direction of Lese, where the Pakoa landowners affiliated with the coffee plantation lived. The deceased man's clan and his wife's clan (upon whose lands the killing happened) set out the following day to Lese to find the killer. When they arrived in Lese, the killer had left, but to punish the Pakoa (who were unaware of the murder), they burned every house in the village down and chopped down all of the trees (a common warfare tactic in Porgera). Next the deceased man's two clans moved on to the Maliapaka Coffee Plantation and started chopping down the coffee trees. Over the next few months a large-scale conflict broke out in the eastern Porgera valley, which engulfed all of the stakeholders in the coffee development project. Two of the prominent landowners in the coffee project, Pius, and a Yawanakali clansman named Was, moved into the plantation to try and protect the remaining trees, yet were ultimately unsuccessful. Between the 2003 killing and Pius's killing in 2006, seven different conflicts broke out in the eastern Porgera valley that were in some way linked back to the initial killing in 1999. In each conflict, the coffee trees were a target for destruction, as Porgeran warfare seeks to damage the productive resources upon which enemy clans are dependent. By the time I arrived in late 2006, depending upon whom I talked to, either "all" or "most" of the coffee plantation had been destroyed during fighting.

In 2006 I was unable to travel to the coffee plantation to assess for myself how much, if any of it, remained. Another conflict had broken out in September of that year, and just a week before my arrival in Porgera, two women and a man were gunned down on the footpath to the Tipinini area from the main road by one of the warring clans. In fact, due to the daily battles in this conflict, I was unable to even visit the area where I had lived for fourteen months during my dissertation research. I eventually lived in the nearest village I could with some of my earlier informants and friends, such as Epe, who were refugees from the fighting. This latest conflict was also instigated by the same man who had killed the man in the trade store in 2003. A few days after I arrived in Porgera, I interviewed him, a bittersweet task as both he and the man he killed had been close friends of mine during my earlier research period.

This man, whom I will call by the pseudonym Kangi, had been a cook at the mine and a relative of the man killed in 1999. After this event, he was forced to quit his job, as the mining company doesn't provide housing for Porgeran employees and he would have been forced to travel through enemy lands en route to work—one of the main reasons why many Porgerans have quit working at the mine. When I knew Kangi in 1999, he had a Tok Pisin (Melanesian Pidgin) name, but now had changed his name to an Ipili word that means "it is burning." When I asked why he had changed his name, he replied, "After I had to quit, I knew I wouldn't see money anymore. I was just going back to live in the fucking bush. I didn't want to be reminded of anything modern, so I got rid of my Tok Pisin name." He laughed and said, "I've got a good name now, because now all I do is fight."

This latest conflict (September 2006) came from the perceived uneven distribution of a compensation payment from the mining company for a landslide that had occurred in connection with road maintenance. A very small portion of the land covered in the landslide was part of land held by Kangi's clan, but the mine provided no compensation money to them, so Kangi and his brother argued that the compensated clan should provide their clan with some of the money. When the compensated clan refused, as there had been no improvements made to Kangi's clan's land, Kangi and his brother rushed their leader and attacked him with machetes, killing him.

A few weeks before I interviewed Kangi, I was walking around the charred remains of the Porgera Elementary School, which had been burned down in December 2005. From out of the surrounding forest a man with a pair of binoculars and an AR-15 assault rifle stopped me. When he saw that I wasn't an enemy combatant and after learning I was a university professor researching in Porgera, we went to his house for tea. He recounted how his clan—whose land the school was on—had received a significant compensation payment from the mine for some land destroyed during mining operations. A neighboring clan demanded some of the money from his clan and when his clan refused a fight broke out and eventually, to disgrace his clan, the opposing clan burned down the elementary school. Almost a year later, nothing had been rebuilt, as the mine and the Porgera Development Authority were waiting for hostilities to be settled before embarking on the construction of a new elementary school. To make matters worse, the PDA building was ransacked and burned in 2006 by angry Porgerans after a drunken policeman (funded and housed by the mine) shot and killed a high school student.

The uneven distribution of benefits from mining wealth has created new prospects for a warfare economy in Porgera. There is a long-standing association between warfare and economics in Porgera, expressed in the Ipili phrase "*yanda takame*," which means "war is wealth." Explaining this term to me in 2000, an elder remarked that in the short-term, fighting is bad, as people might die, but in the long-term, compensations flow back and forth between combatant groups, and eventually due to the compensations the groups start to intermarry and live among one another. But by 2006, this association between war and wealth had radically altered. Talking with a group of young men from Kangi's clan who were involved in fighting, they said that now they use the Tok Pisin term "*wok long laip maket*," or "working in the life market," to characterize conflict. One of the young men said, "I'm just a bush man, I can't get a job at the mine, I don't have money for school. It's better for me to go to work in the life market. Before, when our ancestors fought, few people died and most were just wounded, then in 2003 we started using guns to fight. Now, when you go to fight, you either live or you die, it's one or the other in the life market." Moreover, fighting today is not about generating the long-term benefits captured in a concept like "war is wealth," as much of the fighting is generated from dissatisfaction with uneven development and oriented toward short-term monetary gains. Moreover, when many of these young men aren't working in the life market, they sneak into the open pit mine and conduct "illegal" mining (from the state and corporate perspective, but not their own), and become entangled in the violent kinds of clashes that resulted in the torched Land Cruiser discussed at the beginning of this chapter.

CONCLUSIONS: POSTINDUSTRIAL LANDSCAPES IN THE MIDST OF THE MINING INDUSTRY

The hope that Paiam, the mining town, would serve as a model of the indirect benefits that mining can offer to a community has not materialized. In 1999 and 2000, while many non-SML landowners in Porgera called Paiam "the landowners' town," many people were still hopeful that Paiam would serve as an industrial catalyst for the valley by bringing in expatriates and high-paying jobs, and would be a place where they could spend the money they generated from coffee growing. At the end of 2006, I walked around Paiam with many of the same people who were so hopeful for the town's future back in 1999, looking over the developments and discussing them. The few expatriates who had bought homes in Paiam lived in a gated compound surrounded by eight-foot-tall corrugated iron walls topped by double strands of razor wire. Due to the constant violence, the bank and the Toyota dealership had closed. Despite the enormous amounts of wealth in the valley, the nearest bank was in the provincial capital, Wabag, a four- to five-hour bus ride away through a region renowned for highway robberies and rapes. The hospital and grocery store were, and are, still in operation, although the prices keep all but the wealthiest out of them. Paiam and the coffee development project remain half-promises offered by state and corporate social responsibility undertakings. While remaining perpetually underfunded and half-supported, these projects allow for the publication of glossy brochures demonstrating resource extraction partners' "commitment" to social, environmental, and economic sustainability to international agencies and shareholders.

The phrase "working in the life market" highlights the complex ways that obtaining "wealth without work" (Reed 2009) play out in the PNG highlands. Social ties used to have value in Porgera in terms of the production and reproduction of society. The new value of social ties in Porgera concerns money. For Marx, "money is a representation of socially necessary labor time" (Harvey 1996: 152). In Porgera, though, the value of labor-less wealth results in social disruption and conflicts over land and resources. As David Harvey remarks,

> [Money] fails as a central value system to articulate human hopes and aspirations in collective terms. Money is what we necessarily aspire to for purposes of daily reproduction and the realization of individual desires, wants, and needs. In this sense money does indeed become the community; but a community emptied of any particular moral passion or of humane meanings even though it engages human passions in furious and obsessive ways. (Harvey 1996: 156)

For Kangi and the other men working in the life market, money that seemed to be within everyone's reach through alluvial mining networks, coffee development schemes, and wage-paying jobs seems now more elusive, and it requires novel, albeit violent, social projects to capture it. The "furious and obsessive ways" that these endeavors are pursued, though, threaten both the mining and coffee economies upon which they are dependent. Yet they are continually fueled by the fact that these men, living in the midst of an industrial mining center, daily experience the abjection of feeling relegated to living postindustrial lives. As several men and women have poignantly asked me, "How can we go back to living like our ancestors?" I don't need to tell them the answer, though, for as one older woman answered her own question, "No money, no clothes, no rice, no medicine, just nothing, just nothing."

NOTES

1. From December 1998 to February 2000, I conducted research for my dissertation in anthropology. In November and December 2006, I spent an additional two months conducting research in Porgera.
2. The 1980 census listed a total of 5,011 people in Porgera, while the 1990 census listed 9,255.
3. The Porgera mine is run by a consortium called Porgera Joint Venture. Initially ninety percent of the consortium was owned equally by three mining

companies and ten percent by the PNG state with Placer Dome, Inc. working as the operating partner. Five percent of the state's share was split between the Enga Provincial Government and the Porgera landowners, who had an option in the future to buy the other five percent. They declined this. In 2006, Barrick Gold Corp. had acquired Placer (which had a fifty percent share at that time), and since that time has increased its holdings to hold a ninety-five percent equity in Porgera Joint Venture.

4. Since converting to Christianity in the 1960s, Porgerans started to build roofed structures over the graves of the deceased to keep their souls from getting wet in the constant rains.

REFERENCES

Banks, Glenn. "The Economic Impact of the Mine." In *Dilemmas of Development: The Social and Economic Impact of the Porgera Gold Mine, 1989–1994*, edited by Colin Filer, 88–127. Boroko, PNG: The National Research Institute, 1999.

Biersack, Aletta. "Red River, Green War: The Politics of Nature along the Porgera River." In *Reimagining Political Ecology*, edited by Aletta Biersack and James B. Greenberg, 233–80. Durham: Duke University Press, 2006.

Dove, Michael R. *The Banana Tree at the Gate: A History of Marginal Peoples and Global Markets in Borneo*. New Haven: Yale University Press, 2011.

Ferguson, James. *Expectations of Modernity: Myths and Meanings of Urban Life on the Zambian Copperbelt*. Berkeley: University of California Press, 1999.

———. *Global Shadows: Africa in the Neoliberal World Order*. Durham: Duke University Press, 2006.

Filer, Colin, ed. *Dilemmas of Development: The Social and Economic Impact of the Porgera Gold Mine, 1989–1994*. Boroko, PNG: The National Research Institute, 1999.

Handley, G., and D. Henry. "Porgera Environmental Plan: Report on Small Scale Alluvial Mining." Unpublished manuscript, Porgera District Administration archives, 1987.

Harvey, David. *Justice, Nature, and the Geography of Difference*. Cambridge, MA: Blackwell Publishers, 1996.

Jacka, Jerry K. "Coca-Cola and *Kolo*: Land, Ancestors, and Development." *Anthropology Today* 17 no 4 (2001): 3–8.

———. "Emplacement and Millennial Expectations in an Era of Development and Globalization: Heaven and the Appeal of Christianity among the Ipili." *American Anthropologist* 107 no 4 (2005): 643–53.

———. "Whitemen, the Ipili and the City of Gold: A History of the Politics of Race and Development in Highlands New Guinea." *Ethnohistory* 54 no 3 (2007): 445–71.

Jackson, Richard, and Glenn Banks. *In Search of the Serpent's Skin: The Story of the Porgera Gold Project*. Port Moresby, PNG: Placer Niugini Ltd, 2002.

May, R.J., and Matthew Spriggs, eds. *The Bougainville Crisis*. Bathurst: Crawford House Press, 1990.

Rajak, Dinah. *In Good Company: An Anatomy of Corporate Social Responsibility*. Stanford: Stanford University Press, 2011.

Reed, Kristin. *Crude Existence: Environment and the Politics of Oil in Northern Angola*. Berkeley: University of California Press, 2009.

Scott, James. *Seeing Like a State: How Certain Schemes to Improve the Human Condition Have Failed*. New Haven: Yale University Press, 1998.

Smith, Neil. *Uneven Development: Nature, Capital, and the Production of Space.* New York: Blackwell Publishers, 1984.

Tsing, Anna. *Friction: An Ethnography of Global Connections.* New Haven: Princeton University Press, 2005.

Waddell, Eric. "How the Enga Cope with Frost: Responses to Climatic Perturbations in the Central Highlands of New Guinea." *Human Ecology* 3 no 4 (1975): 249–73.

Welker, Marina. "'Corporate Security Begins in the Community': Mining, the Corporate Social Responsibility Industry, and Environmental Advocacy in Indonesia." *Cultural Anthropology* 24 (2009): 142–79.

Wiessner, Polly, and Nitze Pupu. "Toward Peace: Foreign Arms and Indigenous Institutions in a Papua New Guinea Society." *Science* 337 no 6102 (2012): 1651–4.

3 When the Smoke Clears

Seeing Beyond Tobacco and Other Extractive Industries in Rural Appalachian Kentucky

Ann Kingsolver

Thousands of sheep grazing the steep hillsides, artisan cheese and maple sugar producers bartering with weavers in a local economy, distinctive distilleries, and tons of hemp grown for the global market: this is not only a vision you might hear articulated in a sustainable agriculture class about the post-tobacco, post-textile, post-coal future of rural eastern Kentucky. It is also a very accurate description of my home community, Nicholas County, Kentucky, two hundred years ago. The tension between extractive single-commodity economies and diverse livelihood strategies is not new to Appalachian Kentucky. The region has been intensely engaged with global capitalist networks for centuries, and that engagement has in fact shaped the very landscape, which in turn results in its being mistakenly imagined as left behind by global economic development busy-ness. Rather than a new abandonment by industry, there has been a cycle of abandonments by various single-commodity industries in rural eastern Kentucky, and there has always also been simultaneous assertion of diverse livelihood possibilities within the region.

Because the global industrial organization of eastern Kentucky's landscape has been less visible *as industry* than urban smokestacks, although the dust and scarring from blasting zones in coal-producing counties are no doubt visible from space, deindustrialization has also been less visible, at least in culturally recognizable ways. Empty factories, tobacco warehouses that are razed or turned into storage units, and truck cabs sitting in front yards rather than hauling trailers of t-shirts or loads of coal are some signs of the downturn in the production of major commodities that dominated the landscape in the twentieth century. In the nineteenth century, Appalachian Kentucky had global economic activity in the form of salt mines, iron production, coal mines, logging of giant chestnut trees for transatlantic ships' masts and railroad ties, and even a gold rush that predated the 1849 gold rush by twenty years (Lewis 2004). The ruins of iron furnaces serve as tourist attractions now, and the strong contributions of the region to the U.S.'s international capitalization were largely erased in popular imagination by subsequent literary and media portrayals of the region as temporally, spatially, and culturally isolated from national development and the global market.

If we think about rural communities as dynamic and constantly constructed through interactions of varying range, rather than static in both population and on the landscape, then it is possible to imagine how the trades in specific global commodities have contributed to the very fabric of towns, rivers, mountains, roads, fields, and forests that comprise an experience of region. During the British colonial period in what is now known as the United States, tobacco served as a currency (Goodman 1993), and it was produced not only in coastal plantations: the burley variety of tobacco was grown in central Appalachia and made its way to market via river travel. Cattle and tobacco production in the colonial era was not solely the province of stereotypical Euro-American planters and homesteaders. The British Royal Proclamation of 1763 meant that Native Americans controlled land use in the central Appalachian Mountains, and colonists could not cross that line to the west. Cherokee capitalists produced the cattle and turkeys, sometimes with enslaved African labor, that supplied meat to the plantations on the eastern coast of North America and in the Caribbean (Dunaway 1995). Daniel Boone, portrayed in what amounts to nearly a whole genre of painting focused on his eighteenth-century pioneer spirit, did not bring the first agriculturalists through the Cumberland Gap as the myth of homesteading on the frontier implies. Instead, Boone measured out the land for the foreign investors that George Washington and other planters used to raise capital for their newly established nation (Dunaway 1995 and 1996).

The tracts of land bought by international investors through land companies were large and the absentee owners paid little to nothing in local taxes, which set up a persistent pattern of exploitation of natural resources in the Appalachian region of the U.S., primarily lumber and coal, for capital that accumulated elsewhere, leaving ecological, monetary, and social debts accumulating at the locus of extraction of those resources. On the western edge of Appalachian Kentucky, where the mountains become hills, there were smaller land grants claimed by veterans of the recent Revolutionary War and various smallholder tenant arrangements with absentee landowners. Virginia's western territories became the state of Kentucky in 1792, and Kentucky's early counties were subdivided into, eventually, 120 counties. These counties, each a political entity with an elected judge-executive, are much smaller than counties in the surrounding states and tend not to collaborate across county lines. Residents, I have found, tend to identify more by county identity than by state-imposed identities such as the Appalachian Regional Commission's recognition of Appalachian counties or multi-county area development districts (created for the purpose of applying for community development block grants and other public funds, as well as marketing the locality to international corporations looking for factory sites).

In this chapter, the story of extractive industries in Appalachian Kentucky is followed in scale from county to region, and through commodities from tobacco to coal, and the mosaic of livelihood strategies always in counterpoint to those extractive industries is traced simultaneously. The conversation about diverse economies in the face of abandonment is not a new one in the region. Extractive industries are understood here to encompass more than the clear cut trees or the coal separated from the bedrock; repetitive growing of tobacco with heavy chemical use on the arable land in river bottoms or on the tops of ridges has taken its extractive toll from the soil. Extraction of low-wage and nonwage labor has also been a strategy of largely absentee capitalists. Enslaved African workers were significant members of the labor force of central Appalachia in the nineteenth century, and in the twentieth century there was an industrial strategy of extracting low-wage, non-unionized gendered labor through small garment factories. These factories were constructed in very rural areas where women were assumed by industrial recruiters and investors to be an available labor supply because they were in households with male workers. In turn, these male workers were assumed to be tied to the landscape because of proximity to underground or strip mining jobs or through the federal system of tobacco allotments in which the amount of tobacco allowed to be grown, or the "base," was tied to land deeds (Kingsolver 2011). In all cases, from tobacco to textiles to coal, the majority of profits from these commodities have not been reinvested in the communities generating them.

Centuries of intense engagement with global capitalist markets have shaped Appalachian Kentucky's landscape, placing communities and transportation networks at the convenience of commodity production for export (e.g., salt, lumber, tobacco, coal, garments, and cattle), and have also shaped its population. The diverse histories of Appalachian residents themselves defy stereotypes of white, isolated communities because of that very production over several centuries for a global market, including Native Americans producing cattle to support coastal plantations; African Americans producing tobacco and building infrastructure for railroads, lumber and coal camps, and mines, especially in the period between the Civil War and World War I; and miners being recruited from many nations by coal companies as a strategy to suppress labor organizing. There have been labor migrations continually into Appalachia and out of it, so that no rural Kentucky community has ever been isolated in terms of population or global market engagement. Isolation in Appalachian Kentucky, if it is a consideration at all, would be more an artifact of the infrastructure being established for purposes of commodity extraction rather than for purposes of community economic development.

Nicholas County, which was founded in 1799 and through which the Licking River flows, is a county on the western edge of Appalachian Kentucky. It has an area of just under 200 square miles, and the population dropped from around 12,000 at the beginning of the twentieth century, when tobacco production was booming, to nearly half that by the end of the century, when both the tobacco and textile industries in the region were in crisis. I grew up just outside the county seat of Carlisle, and have heard stories all my life that gave glimpses of earlier landscapes of production and a larger population. I would run across foundations in the woods, or millstones near a creek, from phantom communities and industries, and wonder about them. Jane Nadel-Klein has written that "global processes call localities into existence, but make no commitments to their continued survival. . . . An explicit link between place and political economy enables us to see how localism remains a highly salient, creative category, not merely a plaint to be invoked on behalf of those who live in out-of-the-way places" (1991: 502). One way of looking at how Carlisle, Morning Glory, Bald Eagle, Barefoot, Mexico, and other settlements in Nicholas County came to be on the landscape at all is through the lens of the global commodity, tobacco. The transportation infrastructure of the new state of Kentucky was river travel, and the orientation of that travel was west, not east. River arks carried 1,200 pound hogsheads of tobacco down the Licking and other rivers to the Ohio River, and from there to the Mississippi to New Orleans. In the early 1800s, that amounted to a $2.25 million commodities trade that was so important to Kentuckians that they considered seceding from the U.S. and joining Spain to facilitate their global trade through the Spanish-controlled port of New Orleans (Clark 1977: 15).

Each investment in transportation infrastructure in eastern Kentucky for the production of a commodity for the global market—an investment made largely by those absentee capitalists who profited from its markup and sale—over the last two centuries has rendered it particularly unsuited to the next wave of development. For tobacco production, when tobacco was still a currency, river travel and port cities were the cutting edge of organizing the landscape and the economy. East of Nicholas County, in the mountainous zones of Appalachia, railroads were the next infrastructural emphasis, to facilitate large-scale logging. Once the land was logged, the same owners of the land and infrastructure for logging (labor camps, mills, loading platforms, company stores, payroll management, and post office concessions) often turned to the extraction of coal, hauling it out by railroad. The point of the tracks across the land was getting the coal to global markets, not connecting existing towns for the purpose of diverse regional economies. Carlisle, in Nicholas County, was one of the towns built with its orientation along the railroad rather than the river. In the early twentieth century there were three large tobacco warehouses in Carlisle, with platforms for loading the tobacco onto railroad cars (two of them were called the People's Warehouse and the Red Star Warehouse, indicating the agrarian populism of that time). Later, all three tobacco warehouses were torn down, farmers hauled their tobacco to other counties by wagon on roads to sell it, and the railroads were company tracks for the coal passing through on its way to Maysville, on the Ohio River. I was told as a child that coal was going to the Ohio River, the Atlantic, and finally to Italy, where it would be burned. That global connection to the railroad track we played near was mystifying to me then. Why did the coal, in the mountains since the tree ferns stood there, need to ride on a barge to Italy? It seemed like a lot of energy going into energy.

During the U.S. War on Poverty, in the 1960s, highways, not railroads, were promoted as the key to economic development in rural east central and eastern Kentucky. The Appalachian Regional Commission, a partnership between federal and state governments formed for the purpose of economic development and poverty alleviation, provides grants for infrastructural development, mainly roads and hospitals. The new system of roads and highways was, in turn, used by state chamber of commerce and other industrial development promoters to attempt to attract corporations outside the region to build factories in the region, where they were promised an affordable and non-unionized workforce. Textile and apparel plants came, and coal trucks, tobacco wagons, parts trucks, and trucks full of freshly sewn underwear—an abundance of it, mostly with Jockey and Fruit of the Loom labels—traveled the results of the road improvement investments.

The expiration of the Multi-Fibre Arrangement in 2005 made the infrastructure for the garment industry obsolete, because the last of the factories that had not already moved south or offshore closed with the locus of production shifting to the PRC and Bangladesh. The multinational goose had been invited to each county to lay the golden egg of a factory in the empty nest of an industrial park, conveniently located somewhere near a highway. But, before the last development plan could be fully implemented and the industrial parks filled with factory employers, there was a new development infrastructure to be left behind in: Internet-based employment. Amazon warehouses and call centers started sprouting on the landscape near affordable and imminently available workforces in some regions of Kentucky, and telecommuting seemed a possibility for those who wanted to stay in, or move to, rural areas and have Internet-based jobs. But the rivers, railroads, and not-yet-completed highway transportation networks have been supplanted as the relevant infrastructure in discussions of economic development: now it is the digital highway. Access to Internet-based employment is limited to where there is access to the Internet, and like the other forms of industrial infrastructure, it is very uneven in the region. There is a Broadband desert in parts of eastern Kentucky, most prominently in what the Appalachian Regional Commission classifies as "economically distressed" counties, the lowest ten percent of U.S. county economies by multiple performance indicators. As James Ferguson said of the Zambian Copperbelt supplanted by its own success as copper-facilitated telephone networks led to fiber optic cables and satellite-based communications in the shifting sands of modernity:

> What we have come to call globalization is not simply a process that links together the world but also one that differentiates it. It creates new inequalities even as it brings into being new commonalities and lines of communication. And it creates new, up-to-date ways not only of connecting places but of bypassing and ignoring them. (Castells 1998, in Ferguson 1999: 243)

In eastern Kentucky, broadband access is an example of a new way of being bypassed, even as its ubiquity is assumed. Unemployment checks and other disbursements to citizens are now being distributed through online banking, even though many residents cannot use online services. This lack of access can be a source of further marginalizing those left unemployed by the single-commodity industries decamping from the region in the twenty-first century: tobacco, textiles, and coal. The appearance of being the last reached by global capitalist markets—reinforced in stereotypical portrayals of Appalachia as a region "out of time" (othered through, as Fabian would put it, denial of coevalness) or lagging in modernity—is, ironically, due to the region's having been caught up in global capitalist processes for far too long.

As Jane Collins describes deterritorialization, "it is a strategy of minimizing long-term commitments and investments, maintaining labor as a variable cost, and enhancing the flexibility of the firm at the expense of workers' security" (2002: 153). Each of these extractive industries has had no accountability to the region. There have been moments, over the past century, when workers attempted to change that. The tobacco growers' strike organized against the American Tobacco Company (ATC) in 1908 began in Nicholas County and led to 35,000 farmers refusing to plant burley tobacco because of ATC's monopoly pricing. Tracy Campbell (1992: 77) has called that action "the only large-scale agricultural strike in America." Anti-trust legislation passed then, and the Depression-era farm stabilization programs, brought some protection to tobacco farmers from the vagaries of the global market. The 1998 Master Settlement Agreement and the Fair and Equitable Tobacco Reform Act of 2004 ended the tobacco program; this was supposedly to reduce the damaging effects to health of tobacco use, but as Benson (2012) documents, the tobacco companies long influenced government regulation of the industry to their benefit. There are still as many tobacco products marketed, to new global consumers, and as much tobacco produced, by new global producers, and U.S. producers take all the risks of production, as they did before the anti-trust legislation a century before (Kingsolver 2011).

The image of Appalachian Kentucky as a region of independent agrarian homesteaders, promoted through local color literature after the Civil War when the area was actually being heavily industrialized (Ledford 1999), obscures the role of absentee land ownership and the early dominance of extractive industries with profits going outside the region (Billings and Blee 2000). Even in the 1800 census for Nicholas County, in which agricultural diversity was richly recorded, one lodger recorded his occupation as "capitalist." Wilma Dunaway wrote about the infrastructure of Appalachia having always favored commodity pathways moving profits out of the region and decreasing economic diversity within the region, saying "the export sector drains off labor and capital from subsistence producers to augment production for external markets. Moreover, infrastructure and state priorities are directed toward expansion of external trade, to the neglect of local roads and services. Progress in the export sector, therefore, blocks economic growth in local market activities" (Dunaway 1996: 232). She also pointed out that "the Appalachian mountains were not formidable obstacles that locked communities away from the world. Instead, the system of interconnected gaps, trails, roads, turnpikes, and rivers integrated even these out-of-the-way places into the flow of external trade" (Dunaway 1996: 227).

While I have been describing the negative aspects of absentee land ownership, the external focus of infrastructural development, and the lack of reinvestment in Appalachian Kentucky over the past several centuries, I do not mean to paint a portrait of local heroes and exploitative villains elsewhere. As Collins (2002: 153) notes, "neither deterritorialization nor localization are unambiguously good or bad for workers." Oppressive labor conditions and market monopolies can be organized locally as well as transnationally. In rural Kentucky, some judge-executives (holding the highest political office, an elected position in each county), far from being impartial, sent out letters to workers (the citizens they governed) in the 1980s to warn them against joining labor unions or organizing for better working conditions in the textile, machining, and new automobile-related factories. Non-unionized labor forces are one of the resources a county can advertise to multinational corporations to attract them to build a factory in the county's industrial park (a long-tried development strategy in nearly every county). Because having even a very small factory would add to the tax base that provides the salary and benefits to elected officials (sometimes among the few middle-class jobs available), there has been strong incentive for local governments to ensure that workforces are low-wage and compliant rather than advocating for secure, better-paying jobs. The state-led strategy of industrial recruitment has emphasized attracting extractive industries, and as Ron Eller, writing on development in Appalachia, has said:

> Extractive industries tend to produce social and economic inequality, environmental destruction, and short-term growth rather than sustainable incomes and lifestyles. Wherever extractive industries have dominated around the world, they have produced inequality; they often confine an area to single-industry dependence and inhibit diversification. Extractive economies and the extractive elites who thrive on them are inconsistent with long-term thinking. (Eller 2013: 266)

There are local elites who may benefit at least in the short-term from industrial strategies that have little accountability to the residents of the area through the sale of land or other means of production. For example, the originator of the broad-form deed, the now-outlawed form of property deed in Kentucky that separated the ownership of the surface of the land from the mineral rights below (thus enabling coal companies to declare their right to strip a landowner's home or business off the surface of the land in order to get to the coal they owned beneath it), was an Appalachian Kentucky resident.

What is happening in Appalachian Kentucky is not a sudden deindustrialization, although there has been a convergence in the late twentieth and early twenty-first centuries of the loss of garment-sector jobs and the dwindling of jobs in the transnational tobacco and coal industries. There has been a long series of waves of extractive activity for global capitalist markets on the landscape. Appalachian Kentucky is itself not a uniform region, but a collection of fifty-four counties with different histories of extractive industries that have been included through a political process as being served by the Appalachian Regional Commission. Deindustrialization elsewhere has been tied to Appalachia, as when the auto industry moved to Kentucky, Tennessee, and South Carolina for low-wage, nonunionized labor and many workers from Detroit moved south (just as Appalachians moved north for those jobs as the U.S. auto industry was first built).

As Nietschmann (1974) noted on the Atlantic coast of Nicaragua, boom and bust cycles can bring infusions of cash and leave residents to return to subsistence strategies if natural and cultural resources allow that, but when the boom involves extracting the subsistence resource itself, that's what constitutes a massive transformation in what is possible for the region. In the case of Appalachian Kentucky, the latest extractive strategy of mountaintop removal coal mining in coal-producing counties has meant the loss of the *landscape itself*—the ultimate means of production. Those mountains themselves, blasted away, are lost to any potential future uses and are mourned by the many displaced from them, although the post-mined landscape is considered for industrial parks, beekeeping, solar farms, and other uses within the larger region. Long-term costs of mountain top removal mining beyond the immediate loss of natural and social contexts include some reclamation practices that actually discourage forest growth, lack of adherence to mining and reclamation federal guidelines, permanent pollution of headwaters, and ongoing flooding problems. These challenges to the development of sustainable livelihoods in the region, and examples of how residents have worked to address them, are well documented by the authors collected in Morrone and Buckley (2011). There are wide-ranging views and projects related to land use in Appalachia. Postindustrial development in Appalachian Kentucky requires a diverse discussion, because it is a diverse region.

Although Nicholas County has been intensively tied to tobacco rather than coal production due to its geology, there are residents whose livelihoods have nonetheless been linked to the vagaries of the coal sector. The mixed livelihood strategies in the county have included some residents commuting for many years to a small factory in a small community in the next county, Bourbon County, which manufactures machinery for mining. When Joy Mining announced in 2013 it was closing operations in that plant, with secondary industries being affected by plummeting primary production in the coal industry, Nicholas Countians lost employment and benefits. The main sources of health benefits for residents of the hilly county blanketed with small farms have been jobs in factories to which residents commute (sometimes with drives of several hours each way) or in the major local employers, the hospital or the elementary, middle, or high school.

Deindustrialization can happen in a variety of ways. The closing of a factory is a dramatic loss, noted in the press and marking community memory. Changes in the tobacco and coal industries have been more gradual, with some landmark legal decisions but workers saying they would continue until, as one told me, they "hit the wall." I would like to introduce the term "everyday disaster" here, to mean the kind of disaster (natural or economic) that is not sudden and undeniably visible but instead is incremental and diffuse. Everyday disasters can be just as responsible for displacement, for example, as natural disasters, but their displacement may not be as newsworthy as a hurricane, earthquake, or war. Mountaintop removal mining, while providing short-term employment welcomed by some residents, has represented an everyday disaster when it comes to the long-term resource base on which sustainable livelihoods might be possible, including stable and viable soils, forests, and water supplies (cf. Burns 2007). Mountaintop removal has been difficult to bring to national and international attention both because of gag agreements signed as part of settlements with those displaced, and because of its gradualness as an everyday disaster. Not all residents define mountaintop removal as an economic disaster, because it is also promoted as a way to create flat sites for economic development, but the corporate shift from production in the Appalachian coalfields to the Wyoming coalfields over the last several decades has been an indicator of deindustrialization in the region.

Economic disaster rhetoric has been pervasive in Appalachian Kentucky as *various* transnational industries (garment, coal, and tobacco) have been restructured globally. In 1995, for example, a headline in the *Lexington Herald-Leader* read "Tobacco Area 'Disaster' Plan Recommended: Lawmakers Urging Broader Economies for Some Counties" (Wolfe 1995: B1/4). The state representative for Nicholas and Robertson counties, Pete Worthington, was quoted in that article saying, "If you took tobacco out of there tomorrow, you cannot educate the kids in Robertson County. You just won't have enough dollars." In 1998, an article in the *New York Times* about the effects of the changing tobacco industry on Kentucky quoted one rural resident, Mr. Walden, as saying, "We may be headed for nowhere. I think the price supports for tobacco may be finished in a year or two, and if that happens, these little towns around here will just dry up and blow away" (Apple 1998). Returning to Nadel-Klein's point about global commodity production's influence on the landscape, those "little towns" were in all likelihood there in the first place because of the tobacco industry. So what can residents do when they feel abandoned by global capitalist networks? Some have conceptualized it in terms of a battle for survival. An article about Nicholas County tobacco farmers in the *Lexington Herald-Leader* in

1994 was headlined "Farmers Condemn Constant Assault on their Liveli-hoods" (Stroud 1994). A farmer in that article said, "You take tobacco away from Kentucky and you might as well just close it up and let her go."

The responsibility for the decline of tobacco industrial production (and it is definitely a global industry) has not been straightforwardly attributed to the carcinogenic attributes of tobacco products, but more vaguely attrib-uted to government by many farmers (see Benson 2012; Griffith 2009; Kingsolver 2007). The U.S. Environmental Protection Agency was similarly blamed in 2013 for the decline in coal jobs in eastern Kentucky. Senator Mitch McConnell (Republican—Kentucky), for example, wrote a letter to the *Lexington Herald-Leader* to say that his proposed Coal Jobs Protec-tion Act would "beat back the Environmental Protection Agency's war on coal," and that the EPA's regulatory framework for both permitting mines and requiring scrubbing retrofits on older coal-fired power plants that were not affordable would, in the words of a mining executive he quoted, cause residents "to have to move somewhere else, like during the Depression" (McConnell 2013: A13). Multinational coal corporations are themselves shifting production west and offshore, but assigning responsibility for the layoffs from coal-related jobs in Kentucky to EPA regulation is a discourse of convenience, like the anti-regulatory stance of the tobacco industry. The measure of well-being for the citizens in that discourse is providing employ-ment to buy food and healthcare rather than the air and water quality and mine safety that are less visible until they fail. In practice, all of these con-cerns can be heard in coal-producing communities, just as concerns about the health effects of tobacco can be heard among tobacco farmers.

A HISTORY OF THE FUTURE IN NICHOLAS COUNTY

In the mid-1980s, I began doing ethnographic research in my home county on how residents made sense of all that gets glossed as capitalist global-ization and its perceived effects on livelihoods and identities. For over twenty-five years, I have been talking with Nicholas Countians about their views of the future with the impending loss of tobacco as the major cash crop and changes in other transnational industries that contributed to mixed livelihoods. Those changes have included the recruitment by Ken-tucky of the first Toyota assembly plant in the United States, to which Nich-olas County workers have commuted, and the withdrawal of the garment sector from the region, which included Jockey relocating all the underwear production jobs from Nicholas County to the Caribbean. Stories told to me about imagined futures for the county over the past twenty-five years are recorded in *Tobacco Town Futures: Global Encounters in Rural Kentucky* (Kingsolver 2011). Methods in that research included participant observa-tion in activities from clogging (a form of Appalachian dance with African American influences) to tobacco setting, a participatory bicentennial oral history project on the past and future of agriculture in the county, and years of ethnographic interviewing. The postscript of the book consists of essays written by middle school students in Nicholas County about its future. (The book's royalties go to the local school system.) Jamie Berry wrote (in Kingsolver 2011: 162), "I think the biggest problem with our economy is that the farmers only grow tobacco, and many people spend more money on gas than is necessary, just to get to work. If the farmers diversify and grow more crops, and if we can encourage new businesses to move here, I think the economy of Nicholas County will get better, and be successful." Ashlee Garcia, another of the students, pointed out the importance of social capital in the community, including its youth (in Kingsolver 2011: 164–5): "Nicholas County may not be the perfect place to work, but it is a great place to live. . . . The future of our county depends on our residents, and our economy. If our residents do not try to help make the future of our county better, then it won't change. The adults aren't the only ones who can change the future; the young adults and children can even help, because the young adults and children are the future. . . . The economy makes a huge impact on who helps and how much they help, because the economy scares most people."

I have found that everyone has theories about global capitalism(s), not just academics, and that areas represented as deskilled, deterritorialized, or deindustrialized have residents with clear notions of agency as well as structural constraint. It is never just one neat story of community, or of a single commodity; there are constant strands of global/local engagement. Sometimes they bundle in stories of disruption or disaster, but mostly they are "both/and" stories: of globalization having both positive and negative effects, for example. As Arif Dirlik (1996: 22) has phrased it, the local should not be seen as an antidote to the global, but "as a site of both promise and predicament." I agree with Wilson and Dissanayake (1996: 7–8) that the global and local are not an either/or but a "both/and" in considerations of what is desirable and feasible as Nicholas County and other rural Kentucky communities look toward the future in the face of ongoing global industrial reconfiguration.

National investments, through the Appalachian Regional Commission, and state investments, through chamber of commerce-based economic development consulting and funds, in Appalachian Kentucky have largely been geared toward bringing international (absentee) investments in primary extractive and assembly jobs to the region and getting the products and the profits out. Job attraction and retention is the major development discourse in the region across class positions, and the sources of those jobs are usually conceptualized as from outside the region, so laying the ground for them—literally, by declaring some part of the county an industrial park—and hoping and praying and politicking for occupancy is a very common strategy. Pem Davidson Buck (2001) has envisioned this as a plumbing system in which the capital flow is outward, with some captured on the way by local and state elites. NGOs and some state agricultural agencies, also with local elite and some popular support, have focused alternatively on diversifying production strategies that would retain more capital and decision-making power locally, but these have often been focused on small-scale artisanal production and have not included regional marketing strategies.

Many agricultural producers in the region have been "burned" by plans in the past to shift away from tobacco as a cash crop toward growing peppers or cucumbers or tomatoes, without the marketing having been first worked out. One of the problems with living in a zone dominated by absentee land ownership and extractive industries, as noted elsewhere in this volume, is a lack of infrastructure for vertical integration. In order to really shift from being a tobacco town to a tomato town, there would have to be local processing plants to retain any semblance of control over pricing, or sale at all, because the centuries-known advantage of getting Appalachian Kentucky tobacco to global markets is the fact that it keeps a long time. Produce rots quickly, so if a farmer is depending on a transnational buyer coming through with collection containers and they don't show up or decide the peppers are the wrong color (which has happened), there can be a complete loss on the investment of labor and other resources. The tobacco warehouse system depended, also, on buyers from international companies, but if the offer was too low, the tobacco could be stored in the warehouse with the hope that prices would be better later. Now that the Depression-era tobacco production and marketing system has been dismantled, some farmers continue to grow tobacco, but as with produce, they are on their own in contracting with a national or international buyer, and if the buyer does not like the looks of the crop for some reason, the individual farmer is expected to absorb all the risks and losses incurred (which is a return to the system in place before the anti-monopoly legislation of a century ago).

Regional producer cooperatives and light industrial processing plants have been proposed at various points by those seen as both insiders and outsiders in the region over the past half century (see Kingsolver 2011: 60–65), but that way of imagining the future relies on working across county lines, which has been consistently opposed or resisted by rural Kentucky residents, in part perhaps due to the ways in which the small counties have been played against each other in the competition to attract low-paying industrial jobs. Although the Area Development Districts are often named for bioregions or watersheds, the Area Development Districts are considered by the majority I have heard talk of them to be conduits of regional and federal funding, like block grants, rather than inclusive forums for bioregional or watershed planning, just as the Appalachian Regional Commission is not really considered a forum for inclusive planning to promote the well-being of the second most biodiverse region in the hemisphere (next to Amazonia). I have found that those most likely to envision a future for the region across county lines and in permacultural and bioregional terms are young residents of the region, often college-educated, who have decided to stay in the region and create diverse livelihood options through building their own regional networks.

ECONOMIC DIVERSITY REDUX IN APPALACHIAN KENTUCKY

Ashlee Garcia, writing as an eighth-grader in Nicholas County (above), said, "The economy scares most people." That is the economy in which the production of single commodities is dominant and the control of, and profits from, those global industries are imagined to be very distant. J. K. Gibson-Graham (Gibson and Graham) have called on us to refocus away from that dominant view of economies toward the economic diversity which they advocate for the future (Gibson-Graham 2006: 54), and which I would argue has been going on in rural Kentucky all along. In Nicholas County, for example, because it was rarely possible to make a full living off cash-cropping tobacco on small farms, there has long been a mix of economic strategies encompassing everything from one based on looms, grain mills, tanneries, and distilleries at the county's inception in 1799 to one based on commuting to factory and service jobs, informal sector cash work (as in the large informal economy based on the acquisition and sale of prescription medications like Oxycontin), public sector employment (to keep the town and schools going), and new efforts in post-tobacco agricul-tural (re)diversification and tourism. The kin-based and non-cash barter economic strategies Rhoda Halperin (1990) has written about as "making ends meet 'the Kentucky way'" have not stopped, nor have gardening, fishing, and hunting as part of the livelihood mix in many families. Relying on the economic census information (on which the ARC's "economically distressed" classification of counties is based) is not a completely reliable portrait of the community's economy, because individuals mix formal and informal employment, not everyone responds to the census, and there are other structural problems, of course, with the design of the census catego-ries themselves. Women who are farmers, for example, have been under-reported in the U.S. Census of Agriculture, because until 2002 only one member of a household could be listed as the farmer and if multiple mem-bers of the household were farming, usually the man would be reported as the farmer.

When I came back to live in Kentucky in 2011 to direct the Appalachian Center and the Appalachian Studies Program at the University of Kentucky, after having followed events in my home county for decades from the other states in which I lived (through subscribing to the local newspaper and making many visits home), I realized that my own ethnographic work had been as clouded by tunnel vision as many economic development strate-gies, because it was defined by the county lines. There are young people in Appalachian Kentucky who are thinking regionally, beyond county and state lines, about sustainable livelihood strategies for the long haul. A group of 18–30-year-olds called STAY (Stay Together Appalachian Youth), for example, organizes summer youth leadership institutes and looks for ways to create the infrastructure to make a living within their home communities rather than moving away. They are lobbying for broadband access, running community radio stations, providing support for the large numbers of young people in prisons and rehab programs (the crisis unmentioned in the dominant political discourse of their elders), and organizing volunteers to reforest post-mined lands according to permacultural logic instead of traditional forestry logic.

State-based forestry programs promote the culling of "trash trees," or species of trees that are not identified as having high market value. Ecologically, this can be a problem. For example, the woody adelgid (an insect) is killing hemlocks in the Appalachian forests, which shade streams. If the hemlocks die out, the streams will become warmer, changing the environment in turn for several species of fish and amphibians (Christopher Barton, pers.com., 2012). The beech tree would be the natural successor to the dying hemlocks, but those following industrial forestry "best practices" would have culled the beeches. Just as with the transportation infrastructures that are continually a step behind because they were the state of the art for getting a different global commodity to market, it is impossible to anticipate well with a single-species or single-commodity strategy. There are some young people, like those in STAY, who are thinking about social and natural capital and not just monetary capital, and the need to think collectively about economic, natural, and social diversity. Instead of just thinking of one strategy for planting on post-mined lands, like planting switchgrass as a carbon-neutral biofuel that can be burned with coal in aging power plants (a popular greenwashing strategy for mountaintop removal sites), they are discussing planting a range of tree and plant species. American chestnuts are being planted on post-mined lands as an edible species, and bee forage is being encouraged to build the beekeeping industry as an option for post-mined landscapes.

Advocating a return to a nineteenth-century diverse local economy that was hardly cut off from global capitalism would resonate with Local Color literature (Ledford 1999) just fine, but that romantic picture does not feature the enslaved labor contributing to that local production (one in six Nicholas Countians was an enslaved African in 1800) nor the ecological problems caused by various strategies. My grandmother, raised in Nicholas County a century ago, told stories passed down to her about the hillsides being covered in sheep that ate the grass clear down to the stone.

Grazing, in more moderation than that, is a strategy that works on steep hillsides that cannot be plowed. As I studied tobacco production in Nicholas County, I found that although tobacco was symbolically important and the annual tobacco checks when the crop was sold in January structured community debt and repayment cycles, the cattle foraging in the woods and grazing in the fields and on cut hay were quietly subsidizing tobacco production, for those who could afford to maintain cattle. Cattle are cash on the hoof, and can be sold for a quick infusion of cash, as when farm workers needed to be paid (as kin and neighbor-based non-cash labor networks broke down due to the erratic demands of factory overtime and other off-farm work making it difficult to organize work parties).

The Community Farm Alliance, started with Willie Nelson's Farm Aid concerts in the 1980s, lobbied hard during the period of the Master Settlement Agreement (which brought money from tobacco companies from smoking-related lawsuits to tobacco-producing states) for Kentucky to invest in agricultural diversification with those funds that were tagged to go back into farming (some went into healthcare, given the health-related lawsuits leading to the settlement with the major tobacco corporations). In 2001, the Community Farm Alliance issued a "greenprint" for using the tobacco settlement funds, "promoting local control of the state's ag economy through farm-to-consumer marketing networks; creation of produce and livestock processing centers; and consultants and financing to help farmers develop new products and markets" (Estep 2001: B1). The Agricultural Development Board was established to disburse funds to encourage agricultural diversification, and because tobacco farmers were able to get money to invest in diversifying, the agricultural landscape of rural Kentucky is much more diverse a decade later. Much of the money was used to improve barns, fences, pastures, and ponds for cattle production, but there are now also vineyards; llamas, goats, and sheep (and the occasional emu or ostrich); aquaculture berry farms and orchards; and more large-scale vegetable production and farm stands.

COMMODIFYING RURALITY

One strategy that post-coal and post-tobacco communities alike are pursuing for economic development is tourism. Sometimes the abandoned industrial infrastructure itself is reconceptualized as a resource for tourism; examples are coal camp buildings used for arts centers and B&Bs, or tobacco barns painted with 8'x8' quilt squares to create a scenic driving tour. There are doll museums and train museums and coal museums. In Nicholas County, as tobacco waned, having been an out-of-the-way place (literally, because residents of the county seat had voted long ago to keep a nearby state road from going through the town) began to look like one of its strongest assets for development: as an historical tourism destination. In 1997, Kentucky's Governor Patton visited Nicholas County and said, "You've got a beautiful courthouse and how you've worked to preserve it" (Stone 1997: A1). The courthouse square, little changed architecturally since the 1800s, was put on the national registry of historic places (through considerable effort by some residents), a tourism committee was started, and the county jail—long since unfit for housing anyone who might be taken into custody—was restored, along with the train depot and a grocery store that had gone out of business, and made into a tourism center. There are, however, no overnight accommodations in the county, so the tourism experience would have to be a day excursion and a regional approach to linking such local tourism attractions (farm tourism, mine tourism, heritage tourism, etc.) would be very helpful. Abandoned buildings are being put to different purposes across the region, sometimes creating arts centers or retraining centers. Part of the long-empty underwear factory in Nicholas County now houses the first post-secondary education center in the county: a branch of a branch of a community college in the region. Investing in education is considered another way to prepare for a future beyond single-commodity industries.

Because Nicholas County occupies an edge niche on the landscape—at the outer edge of the Bluegrass and in the foothills of Appalachia—it can be imagined quite differently. There are urban residents of Lexington or Cincinnati who buy land in Nicholas County to have access to rural experience (which might be imagined as anything from poetic pastoralism to less regulation for firearm use) and coal company managers from Appalachia who buy land in Nicholas County to have access to the outer bluegrass to imagine themselves as part of the horse farming elite. Increasingly, woodlands in Nicholas County—because land is relatively inexpensive—are being invested in as carbon offsets or as environmental remediation property for construction in urban areas. The commodification of rurality is a strong and conscious part of the economic diversification strategy of Appalachian Kentuckians in the twenty-first century. The imagined disconnection from global markets comprises its market value. Mixed strategies of recruiting tourists and new industrial employers, plugging holes in leaky local economies (cf. Shuman 2007) through such techniques as buy-local phone apps, and using the Internet to find telecommuting jobs or international consumers for artisanal cheeses or organic tobacco are lively efforts among especially those with some capital and regional networks and, not to be assumed, Internet access. Young people are demonstrating the most hopeful efforts to work across the acknowledged frictions (Tsing 2005) of class (e.g., foodies by choice and foragers by necessity), political, species, and rural/urban distinctions to envision more regional, diverse, and inclusive economic futures.

In conclusion, early and intense engagement with global capitalist investment shaped the infrastructure of Appalachian Kentucky, including the placement of towns on the landscape. That infrastructure for industrialization was primarily developed for the purpose of extraction of resources and commodities for the global market, so communities were linked to routes out of the region more readily than to one another. This limited possibilities for regional economic development—a coherent, vertically integrated local food system for example—but that uneven development and deindustrialization has itself has been commodified in the most recent economic development strategies, including historical, agricultural, and ecotourism.

REFERENCES

Apple, R.W., Sr. "For tobacco growers, a changing life." *The New York Times* (1998, Sept. 14).

Benson, Peter. *Tobacco Capitalism: Growers, Migrant Workers, and the Changing Face of a Global Industry*. Princeton: Princeton University Press, 2012.

Billings, Dwight and Kathleen Blee. *The Road to Poverty: The Making of Wealth and Hardship in Appalachia*. Cambridge: Cambridge University Press, 2000.

Buck, Pem Davidson. *Worked to the Bone: Race, Class, Power and Privilege in Kentucky*. New York: Monthly Review Press, 2001.

Burns, Shirley Stewart, *Bringing Down the Mountains: The Impact of Mountaintop Removal on Southern West Virginia Communities*. Morgantown: West Virginia University Press, 2007.

Campbell, Tracy. "The Limits of Agrarian Action: The 1908 Kentucky Tobacco Strike." *Agricultural History* 66 (1992): 76–97.

Clark, Thomas D. *Agrarian Kentucky*. Lexington: University of Kentucky Press, 1977.

Collins, Jane. "Deterritorialization and Workplace Culture." *American Ethnologist* 29 no 1 (2002): 151–71.

Dirlik, Arif. "The Global in the Local." In *Global/Local: Cultural Production and the Transnational Imaginary*, edited by R. Wilson and W. Dissanayake, 21–45. Durham: Duke University Press, 1996.

Dunaway, Wilma A. "Speculators and Settler Capitalists: Unthinking the Mythology about Appalachian Landholding, 1790–1860." In *Appalachia in the Making: The Mountain South in the Nineteenth Century*, edited by Mary Beth Pudup, Dwight B. Billings and Altina L. Waller, 50–75. Chapel Hill: University of North Carolina Press, 1995.

———. *The First American Frontier: Transition to Capitalism in Southern Appalachia, 1700–1860*. Chapel Hill: University of North Carolina Press, 1996.

Eller, Ronald. *Uneven Ground: Appalachia since 1945*. Second edition. Lexington: University of Kentucky Press, 2013.

Estep, Bill. "Farm Alliance Pleads for Local Control: 'Greenprint' Offers Plan for Tobacco-Settlement Money." *Lexington Herald-Leader*, July 29, 2001, B1/3.

Fabian, Johannes. *Time and the Other: How Anthropology Makes Its Object*. New York: Columbia University Press, 2002.

Ferguson, James. *Expectations of Modernity: Myths and Meanings of Urban Life on the Zambian Copperbelt*. Berkeley: University of California Press, 1999.

Gibson-Graham, J.K. *A Postcapitalist Politics*. Minneapolis: University of Minnesota Press, 2006.

Goodman, Jordan. *Tobacco in History: The Cultures of Dependence*. Routledge: London, 1993.

Griffith, David. "The Moral Economy of Tobacco." *American Anthropologist* 111 no 4 (2009): 432–42.

Halperin, Rhoda. *The Livelihood of Kin: Making Ends Meet 'The Kentucky Way.'* Austin: University of Texas Press, 1990.

Kingsolver, Ann E. "Farmers and Farmworkers: Two Centuries of Strategic Alterity in Kentucky's Tobacco Fields." *Critique of Anthropology* 27 no 1 (2007): 87–102.

———. *Tobacco Town Futures: Global Encounters in Rural Kentucky*. Long Grove, IL: Waveland Press, 2011.

Ledford, Katherine. "A Landscape and a People Set Apart: Narratives of Exploration and Travel in Early Appalachia." In *Back Talk from Appalachia: Confronting Stereotypes*, edited by Dwight B. Billings, Gurney Norman and Katherine Ledford, 47–66. Lexington: University of Kentucky Press, 1999.

Lewis, Ronald L. "Industrialization." In *High Mountains Rising: Appalachia in Time and Place*, edited by Richard A. Straw and H. Tyler Blethen, 59–73. Urbana: University of Illinois Press, 2004.

McConnell, Mitch. "Kentucky Fights against Anti-Coal Vendetta: Editorial Wrong to Dismiss My Plan to Create Jobs." *Lexington Herald-Leader*, May 20, 2013, A13.

Morrone, Michele, and Geoffrey L. Buckley, eds. *Mountains of Injustice: Social and Environmental Justice in Appalachia*. Athens: Ohio University Press, 2011.

Nadel-Klein, Jane. "Reweaving the Fringe: Localism, Tradition, and Representation in British Ethnography." *American Ethnologist* 18 no 3 (1991): 500–17.

Nietschmann, Bernard. "When the Turtle Collapses, the World Ends." *Natural History* 83 no 6 (1974): 34–43.

Shuman, Michael. *The Small-Mart Revolution: How Local Businesses are Beating the Global Competition*. San Francisco: Berrett-Koehler Publishers, 2007.

Stone, Leigh. "Governor Talks Tobacco, Industry, at Carlisle Meeting." *The Carlisle Mercury*, September 25, 1997, 1/7.

Stroud, Joseph S. "Farmers Condemn Constant Assaults on Their Livelihood." *Lexington Herald-Leader*, September 14, 1994, A1/A7.

Tsing, Anna Lowenhaupt. *Friction: An Ethnography of Global Connection*. Princeton: Princeton University Press, 2005.

Wilson, Rob and Wimal Dissanayake. "Introduction: Tracking the Global/Local." In *Global/Local: Cultural Production and the Transnational Imaginary*, edited by Rob Wilson and Wimal Dissanayake, 1–20. Durham: Duke University Press, 1996.

Wolfe, Charles. "Tobacco Area 'Disaster' Plan Recommended: Lawmakers Urging Broader Economies for Some Counties." *Lexington Herald-Leader*, October 17, 1995, B1/4.

4 The Afterlife of Northern Development
Ghost Towns in the Russian Far North[1]

Elena Khlinovskaya Rockhill

INTRODUCTION

The Russian Arctic is vast. It constitutes nearly one-third of the global Arctic territory, and almost one-fifth of the Russian Federation territory, stretching 10,000 km from west to east and covering some 3.1 million sq km. It is rich in mineral resources: ninety-five percent of the Russian natural gas and seventy-five percent of the Russian oil deposits are located in the Arctic, along with other non-metallic and metallic resources. Resource extraction was one of the main reasons for the northern development; a Soviet policy of the 1930s aimed at exploring and "opening up" the scarcely inhabited areas to use their natural resources for increasing agricultural and industrial production (CCUSSR 1928). This policy entailed massive population movements to the northern regions and the creation of permanent settlements and infrastructure.

The Magadan region in the Russian Far East is one of such territories. It is one of Russia's most important gold and silver mining territories, holding eleven percent of the known alluvial gold, fifteen percent of hard rock gold, and nearly fifty percent of the silver deposits in the Russian Federation.[2] The discovery of these, and many other, mineral resources brought about economic, social, and structural development of the region. In the 1920s–1950s the region was rapidly populated by the mixture of a forced labor (political, administrative, and criminal prisoners) and free labor force, and starting in the late 1950s, the government further developed a comprehensive system of benefits to attract free labor. These benefits included contract-based work, high monthly salaries, paid vacations, and earlier pensions. This generous package attracted considerable numbers of people, and by 1989, populations reached over half a million people,[3] who were living in some 136 communities, most of which were urban.[4] Many people left the region after their contract was over, but many others stayed on for years, spending most of their adult life in the North before retiring to the western part of the former Soviet Union.

Hypermobility, then, is not a mechanism of capitalism only, as flows of people and resources came to define many socialist development projects, such as Baikal-Amur railroad; the *tselina* project, that is, sending thousands of young people to remote regions to develop and prepare soils for agricultural use; the Youth project of building construction (*komsomol'skaya stroika*); and the northern development project, all examples of the socialist modernization project (on socialist high modernism, see Scott 1998). As Daniel Bell has argued, "Along the axis of production and technology, both the Soviet Union and the United States are industrial societies and thus somewhat congruent" (1973: 5), and "today both systems, Western capitalist and Soviet socialist, face the consequences of the scientific and technological changes which are revolutionizing social structure" (41). Modernization and industrialization cut across political differences.

But this is where similarities end. Firstly, Bell's social forecast envisioned the "coming of post-industrial society," which would follow the industrial phase in what seems like a linear development. What defines a postindustrial society? According to Bell, these are: creation of a service economy; the preeminence of the professional and technical class; the primacy of theoretical knowledge; the planning of technology; and the rise of new intellectual technology (1973: 14–32). Yet as we shall see, in the post-Soviet context these characteristics do not describe contemporary life in the Magadan region. Although no doubt an industrial society in the past and currently undergoing deindustrialization, postindustrial society is stuff of the remote future. Instead of linear sequential development we can observe a rather different depiction, similar to that of Ferguson's Copperbelt history of rural-urban mobility in Zambia: "In a world made up not of neat Platonic types but messy spreads of variation, changing realities must be conceptualized not as ladders or trees defined by sequences and phases, but as dense 'bushes' of multitudinous coexisting variations, continually modified in complex and nonlinear ways" (1999: 42).

Secondly, neither a reduction of costs nor the increase of potential benefits underpinning the capitalist rationale for hypermobility was characteristic of these socialist projects. The North was then in a Soviet planned economy and is now in the Russian capitalist economy, a costly project, given the degree of isolation, great distances from mainland Russia, climate, costs of social benefits and infrastructure maintenance, and the lack in local production with heavy reliance on imported materials. The cost of northern development became an issue immediately after the collapse of the socialist economy in the beginning of the 1990s (Hill and Gaddy 2003). The withdrawal of the state in post-Soviet time had literally pulled the plug: the North was considered by the then government of Egor Gaidar to be overpopulated and too expensive to maintain. As a result, many enterprises were closed—only between 1990 and 2004 some seventy-seven communities were closed (Tseitler 2009)—and the new Russian state set up a program of relocation of people from those communities to the western part of Russia. By 2012, some fifty-seven percent of the population had moved out. The region fell into disrepair. We can use the concept of disconnection here—but what kind, and from what? Certainly *economic*, as the previous state-developed system of northern subsidies and of attracting a labor force had been discontinued. The failing transportation system diminished mobility, which formerly was regular, affordable, and assured. *Ideological* disconnection from the idea of unity of the remote North with the rest of the Soviet Union coincided with the economic collapse. Parallel to the overarching idea of unity ran the local feeling of geographical distance and isolation. Since the 1930s, the region felt so isolated that local inhabitants referred to other places as the *materik*, or mainland, feeling themselves to be living on an island. But if in the Soviet time the feeling of isolation was a reflection of a great distance from the "mainland," in post-Soviet time it was a reflection of the feeling of abandonment by the rest of the country in general and by the state in particular. *Politically*, the Magadan region became a part of the Far Eastern Federal District, with separation of the governmental levels and taxation into federal, regional, and municipal.

How did it come to this? Have the natural resources all been used up? Doesn't Russia need to keep this region populated to maintain its northeastern sovereign border? How can we interpret these dramatic post-Soviet changes? This chapter analyzes a transformative process of disconnection and reconnection, both marked by partiality. As we shall see, the outcomes of disconnection from the market in the capitalist economy postulated by this volume could be applied to disconnection from the state internal market in the socialist economy.

LIFE IN THE SOVIET NORTH: CONNECTIONS

The Magadan region, or Kolyma as it is known in geographical and historical terms, is a remote territory located eight time zones east of Moscow. The region, which borders Chukotka, the Sakha Republic, and Khabarovsk Krai, and comprises a territory of 462,464 km^2, has a regional population of 157 thousand persons; 95.9 thousand of them live in the city of Magadan (All-Russian Census 2010). Magadan town is the administrative hub for the region, with the seaport and the main airport connecting the region with other parts of the world. Magadan is connected with most regional communities by a network of roads built in the 1930s–1950s. The main road is called Kolyma Road, or Kolyma *trassa*. There is no railroad connection either within or without the region.

The modern history of Kolyma, its rapid development and population, starts in the late 1920s with the discovery of a precious commodity, gold. Later, other metallic and nonmetallic mineral resources were discovered, including silver, tin, zinc, lead, copper, wolfram, uranium, and coal, necessary for Stalin's industrialization and modernization plan for the Soviet Union in the 1930s. Until then, the region was scarcely populated by descendants of the first Cossaks, who moved here in the seventeenth century, clergy, and a small number of native people. Just to illustrate how rapidly this region became populated with the onset of industrialization, in 1855 the population consisted of 4,662 persons, 4,118 of whom were native (mostly nomadic Even and Sakha). In 1931, the Soviet government set up the *Dal'stroi*, or the State Trust for Road and Industrial Construction, charging it with comprehensive development of this region to produce gold. By 1938, 113,430 persons worked for *Dal'stroi*, while in 1950, this number increased to 258,100 (for a more detailed account, please see Khlinovskaya Rockhill 2010). Up until 1954, the Magadan region's inhabitants were comprised of the forced labor and free labor. In 1954, a year after Stalin's death, when many prisoners were released from labor camps, the population of the Magadan region dropped to 207,700, but then, attracted by hefty economic and social benefits, the population sustained a steady growth, reaching 391,687 persons in 1989. After that, it was downhill again. In 2008, the regional population was comprised of 165,820 persons, while in 2012, it further dropped to 152,358 persons. Hence the regional population came and left in waves as well as in steady trickles both ways, depending on personal circumstances but also on the state rationale and need for a labor force.

Next, I would like to draw on a few points that would help us make sense of the current situation. Firstly, in Soviet times the Russian Far East in general and the Magadan region in particular had been *connected* to the rest of the country in a number of ways. Politically the region was a part of the Soviet state and governed by the state, republican,[5] and regional administrations. Hence, given that traditionally this territory was not populated by non-native newcomers, the development of this region was governed by the state, and not local, interests. The need for gold justified economic investments, the movement of large masses of people to the Magadan region, and the development of infrastructures there, with the state engaging in exercises of biopower in a Foucauldian sense. Hence the government had to develop transportation infrastructure, provide housing for employees and their families, educational facilities for their children, building construction and mechanical repairs factories, and healthcare and cultural infrastructures. The region was accessible by air only (for passengers), by the sea for freight, and by bush aviation and roads within the region. Despite great distances, transportation was reliable, regular, and affordable, thus connecting the region from within and without. The region was also supplied with all sorts of merchandise from all over the Soviet Union. This program was called "northern supplies" (*severniy zavoz*), which were shipped to the region via the Magadan seaport (as well as through airfreight and partially through railways to Vladivostok and from there, to Magadan by sea) and then distributed to the regional communities via the network of roads. The point here is that the region and its inhabitants, although geographically remote and feeling somewhat isolated, were nevertheless connected to the rest of the country in a framework akin to exchange: gold production was a return on the state investment into the region and its labor force. The inhabitants not only felt themselves a *part* of the country but also a very *important part* of the country: they lived in the harsh northern environment and supplied the country with gold, which was then used as a currency for the state's internal and external needs.

Secondly, the Magadan region was a place of *temporary* residence. For those who came to work in the Kolyma as free labor, the government developed a system of benefits, whereby hired employees were given relocation assistance; a "northern coefficient" was added to their base salary as well as increment increases every six months; they would retire five years earlier than everybody else; and once in two years, their vacation was paid. Most people worked in the North on a term contract, but these benefits were attractive enough to extend their contracts further and further until a temporary arrangement turned into a permanent one. Many people thus lived most of their adult lives there, raising families, acquiring personal and professional networks, and working in their chosen fields for years. Yet even in these cases, there was a tacit understanding that upon retirement, they would move away from the region, as the North was not for "old and tired but for young and ambitious ones" (in the words of one former Magadan resident living in Moscow now). The population, then, was a transient one despite the fact that many people lived there for 30–40 years. This produced a very special social environment whereby at their mature age, when most people in the "*materik*" would settle down, northerners had to confront these expectations of departure but also their feelings of belonging to the North. The feeling of attachment to land, to memories of life in the North, to children and other relatives still living there, was and is very powerful. Living in such ambivalence for years, it took many years to decide to leave or to stay. Some died in Magadan still deciding.

Thirdly, the Soviet economy did not use such concepts as boom and bust. The comprehensive development of the region, including its economic development, was based on the idea of unilinear progressive teleological evolutionism, an endless move forward, and expansion. The region was seen as the "golden gate" of Kolyma, producing gold for the common good of the country and society (economic value), and as its northeast frontier, defending the northeastern borders of the former Soviet Union (political value). Hence even though the population was seen as transient, coming to work there for a number of years but then retiring and moving outside the region, the region itself was presented as a permanent, expanding, and indispensable part of the Soviet Union. State funds were invested not only into geological exploration and the mining industry, the main industry of the northeast, but also into the development of fisheries, the energy sector, transportation, and social infrastructure, such as housing, education, healthcare, and culture. The social order and the tangible presence of the region were felt as immutable.

Taken together, these points—the strong political, economic, and psychological connections of the region with the rest of the country, the temporary nature of northern residence, the permanence of the place, and the evolutionist progressive concept of development—created a particular social and cultural milieu peculiar to northern living. As I have shown earlier, many Kolyma inhabitants lived in two places at once, vacillating for years between a more comfortable life in the *materik* where they left their former homes, friends, and relatives, and a life in Magadan where they had family and jobs, developed their networks, and found pleasant sides of northern living. But ultimately, the decision was their individual, not the state's, decision. Another peculiarity of living in the North was the development of northern identities and narrative-models of northern living. Thus many northern inhabitants saw themselves as young, dynamic, enterprising, well-off, and of good character, as the northern environment required people to help each other, thus creating a sense of community and belonging (Bolotova and Stammler 2010, Stammler and Khlinovskaya Rockhill 2011). Finally, the life course of individuals was seen as circular: with the North being only a stage in one's life and upon retirement, the life cycle returned individuals back to the *materik*. On the contrary, the life course of the region was imagined as linear, open-ended, and permanent. The state was there to stay.[6]

POST-SOVIET CHANGES: DISCONNECTION

The collapse of the Soviet Union in 1991 spelled disaster for the northern program. During his visit to the Magadan region, then head of the Council of Ministers Egor Gaidar concluded that the existing infrastructure aimed at creating permanent settlements cannot be sustained, let alone expanded, and that enterprises should be manned using shift labor. These suggestions for restructuring, along with other profound political and socioeconomic changes in the rest of the country, triggered an avalanche of out-migration. Numerous connections tying the North with the rest of the country had been rapidly dissolving.

The separation of the state into federal, regional, and municipal levels divided the public purse into separate budgets, leaving local administrations to find funds for the upkeep of municipal infrastructures. But with the tax incomes severely restricted, a result of the closures of many state enterprises that used to be *gradoobrazuyushchee predpriyatiye*,[7] the infrastructures of many towns could not be sustained. In communities labeled as "without a viable future" (*besperspektivniye poselki*), enterprises, factories, agricultural farms, schools, kindergartens, and eateries have been closed. Closures brought about loss of jobs and livelihood and relocation of entire town populations either outside the Magadan region, or into larger regional towns, as in the case of Berelekh or Bolshevik, satellite communities of the city of Susuman; or Spornoye, that had been closed down causing many people to move to Yagodnoye or Magadan. "No viable future" was of course from the point of view of the state, as these settlements have been built and populated according to the needs of the state for development areas that served the interests of the state at that time. Whether northern development for mineral resources, or building of the trans-Siberian railroad, people were mobilized to move wherever the country needed them.

The state-funded program of "northern supplies" had ceased; the void was filled by private people who started small businesses supplying Magadan with foodstuffs. Likewise, local state farms had collapsed and local people started growing food locally. It was not until the 2000s that the federal government developed programs to support local agricultural business. Aviation, the only gateway to Kolyma for passengers, became private and changed hands often, some appearing and disappearing just as fast. Consequently, regional airports closed down, the intra-regional aviation network was no more. The only airport that was left was the Magadan city airport; its formerly busy runways often have only one or two airplanes. The night flights have stopped. The transportation system had changed dramatically as well. Public transportation had ceased. Consequently, many infrastructure elements, such as bus stations, cafeterias, hotels, and mechanical repair shops along Kolyma roads became ruins. The list goes on. There was not an aspect of the life of a city, town, or any community that has not been affected. Relocation of residents out of dead and dying settlements was the answer to this human crisis. But if moving to the North was in the interests of both the state and the individual, the decision to leave and its timing was effectively moved into the court of state interests, not necessarily the individual decision of the residents, it would seem. Yet as we shall see, the resilience of the local population takes many forms.

If maintaining the North was an expensive project, moving people out was not cheap either. At the end of the 1990s, the federal government engaged with World Bank (see Nuykina 2010, World Bank 2000) to develop the pilot relocation program, and later on developed and funded its own relocation program, according to which certain categories of people (i.e., non-productive groups of people such as pensioners and handicapped) could receive financial assistance for relocating outside the region. One such category was people from closing down communities. Yanskiy, a small coastal town some eighty kilometers from Magadan, built around a state fish-processing factory, had been closed down. The factory was bought by a private person, and then changed hands again. Although the factory was barely surviving, everything else in the town was shut down: the shops, the school and kindergarten, a medical unit, the local administration. Many people from Yanskiy left using the relocation program, moving either outside Kolyma or into the regional communities on offer. Moving to Magadan is a preferred choice for those who would like to remain in Kolyma but get out of a dying settlement, but Magadan is not a destination stipulated by the local administrations. When no suitable choice was found, some residents simply stayed in closed down Yanskiy. These are mostly pensioners. Ekaterina, a 56-year-old retired resident of Yanskiy, shares:

> Where would I go? My children managed to relocate to Magadan, although it was not a choice on the list of local cities to which we could relocate. They told us, you can move to Arman' or Ola[8] but what's the difference? They are not thriving either. . . . Why bother?

When I asked why she and her husband are not moving to where they came from over thirty years ago, she replied:

> What is left there? We do not belong there anymore. There are no jobs, people are either leaving, or they commute to a next large town for work. There are difficulties with water. At least here we know everybody, our kids are here, there is sea where we fish and forest where we collect mushrooms and berries. I don't know. . . . We are still thinking about it but frankly, I would rather relocate to Magadan to join my children and grandchildren.

She even brought her 87-year-old mother to Yanskiy from the *materik*, as nobody else could look after the old woman and Ekaterina, like many other residents of Kolyma, can no longer afford tickets to fly to her former home. Life in Yanskiy is far removed from the previously held views on the northern life as progressive and comfortable, at least in the future. The "future" reverted them back to the subsistence level, the opposite of "civilization" envisioned for the North. They live in the same private wooden house they occupied in Soviet times, but there is no electricity (it had been cut off) and they do what most people do when living in an abandoned community with cut-off utilities, they use a wire to hook up to the main electrical line to steal electricity. In addition to their pensions, keeping a vegetable plot, a greenhouse, and farm birds (chickens and geese) became of paramount importance as often in winter the only road to Magadan and to a neighboring community of Tauisk become impassable with snow, precluding any shopping for food. When her mother became ill one winter and the ambulance finally made it many hours after the call (they have cell phones which work when they climb the roof of their house to catch a signal), they had to construct a sticks-sledge to drag the 87-year-old about 100 meters to the main road, as the ambulance could not drive to their house through the snow. Here in just one example we see the consequences of multiple disconnection for a single family. Not all of them are negative though. After all, their children were able to move to Magadan and find jobs there, a rare opportunity for a regional resident. The abandoned houses of Yanskiy are either occupied by the previous residents or used as *dachas* (summer houses) by former residents who moved elsewhere in the region, or by other people. Yet the previously state-built and maintained commercial properties, unless reused by private citizens, very quickly disintegrate due to the severe climate.

Ruins are an ever-present feature of any community in the 2000s. The withdrawal of the state, closures, and outmigration left communities scarcely, if at all, populated and looking quite peculiar. There are towns with only a fraction of the previous population and some basic infrastructure and some jobs, such as Seimchan, a formerly thriving agricultural community of 9,963 in 1989, and standing at 2,617 in 2013. There are closed towns that nevertheless have some permanent residents, such as Ust'-Srednekan, which has been marked as being "without a viable future" in 2006, with some twenty-seven persons still living there in 2010, down from 185 in 2005. There are towns with a number of people having *propiska* (housing registration), but which are in fact completely depopulated as the residents have moved to other cities. If they moved to a nearby town, such as from Sporniy to Yagodnoye, some still use the abandoned plots in Sporniy as *dacha* for growing vegetables, thus not severing the ties completely. This pattern is especially well established in places where abandoned villages are still connected with basic infrastructure, such as roads or electricity wires, and with access to biological resources (fish, mushrooms, berries), such as Yanskiy or Kadykchan.

Kadykchan, a town of formerly about six thousand people, was founded during World War II as a settlement for the workers of the coal mine; this coal was used at the neighboring Arkagala Hydro-electric station. Both the mine and the town were built by forced labor. After the explosion in 1996, the mine was closed, people were relocated, electricity and water were turned off, and the town was completely abandoned, although most buildings are still standing. However, one person chose to remain there. Ivan still lives in Kadykchan in a wooden shack auxiliary to a diesel truck and equipment repair facility. He uses electricity poached from the main power line running throughout the area; he shops in a nearby town of Arkagala, some fifteen kilometers away, walking and carrying groceries in his backpack. Nearby woods provide berries and mushrooms, game and fish. For warmth and cooking he uses a wood stove. Although for some this lifestyle may look like an idyllic life in the wilderness, it is important to point out that this is not how he imagined his retirement to be. He would rather live the way he intended, in a nice warm flat with electricity, running hot and cold water, and accessible food supplies, and although he made his choice to endure these difficulties, he in fact was compelled to do so, as neither his old life in Soviet Kadykchan, nor the choice given to him by the state (move to the *materik*) were viable options for him. He says:

> I thought I will remain here when I retire. Good pension, good town, clean water, clean air, nature just outside the town, people I know, why should I go anywhere else? But then there was this explosion, and after that the town boiler[9] froze up and everyone was given state financial assistance towards buying flats and hastily evacuated. My wife and

I used that money and our own funds to buy a flat in central Russia. So we moved there but I could only manage two years, as it is too hot there, I can't stand it. We didn't know anyone there. So my wife stayed there and I returned.

So he remains where he spent over thirty years of his life and still calls home, which is no more than architectural and social ruins now. Although he lives alone, he is often visited by his friends, truck drivers who happen to drive by delivering goods to the remaining regional communities. When I asked how he (and others, I suspect) makes his living, he said that sometimes he hunts, goes fishing, and collects berries. They also collect metal objects, initially found in abundance in the abandoned communities: wires, household objects, cars' and trucks' spare parts. A truckload of these objects will be brought to Magadan to sell to the recycling factory, all illegal, as the abandoned goods are still considered to be state property and technically considered to be stolen. Bribes to the policemen at the police station responsible for checking the cars and trucks often solve the problem. Understandably, he and his friends answered my questions regarding their participation in the infamous business of poaching gold elusively. Yes, he, said, some people mine gold (in 2010 during my fieldwork, gold mining by individuals was still illegal), but this is not easy even for healthy young men, let alone an older person.

Gold mining is the way many people make their living either legally, such as big business owned by private local individuals or multinational corporations, or by smaller companies called *artels*, or by *starateli*, individuals who mine gold illegally. The mentioning of the illegal gold trade immediately brings into a conversation the so-called *Ingushzoloto* (Ingushgold). Ingush people are an ethnic group from northern Caucasus. Many of them were sent to Magadan as exiles because of their nationality, and to labor camps as prisoners during Stalinist repressions. Although many Ingush left the region in the 1950s after the death of Stalin, some stayed behind. The lure of gold brought many more Ingush people to Magadan. "Ingushgold" is a local colloquialism patterned linguistically after the way many official organizations are named, such as *Susumanzoloto* (Susumangold), a former state gold mining organization located in the city of Susuman, now a private business that provides most of the jobs to the remaining 5,560 residents of Susuman (formerly a city of 18,000 in 1991). *Ingushzoloto* refers to the organized criminal ring of people of Ingush nationality who make their living by buying illegally mined gold and then send this gold to the *materik*. One of the most widely discussed pieces of news in the mid-2000s was a car stuffed with gold that was detained by police. That car belonged to people of Ingush nationality who tried to smuggle the gold to the Northern Caucasus. Nobody knows for sure what would they do with this gold, but the local lore says that the money obtained by selling this gold was used to fund the war against the Russian state by the local Northern Caucasus troops.

Ingush people are not the only people that buy gold illegally, of course. Recently in 2013, a man was arrested possessing .5 kg of gold estimated to be worth 800K rubles (approximately $26.5K). These arrests happen all the time. I realized during my visits to many Kolyma settlements that gold mining by all means (i.e., including the old panning method), and by mostly men starting in their early teens, is pervasive and widely spread, constituting both the legal economy and a shadow economy in the Kolyma. Illegally mined gold could be either sold to Ingush people or to the head of an *artel'*, who then includes this gold into their monthly output as being mined legally by them. The state estimates that there are some ten tons of gold being mined, bought, and sold illegally Russia-wide, and the Magadan region is still one of the main producers of gold. In any case, this is a hard and dangerous occupation, for there were many cases of murder of many a *staratel'* (individual gold miners), but one that feeds families of gold miners, who are otherwise left to their own devices for survival as a result of post-Soviet northern restructuring.

Going along the road that connects regional communities was like going through a succession of ghost towns in various states of collapse. The ghost towns were not only ghosts of the towns but also of the memories of previous lives there. Our taxi driver, a former bus driver with thirty years of experience driving on the *trassa*, who was now a part of a small company of taxi drivers, was commenting as we went along:

> This used to be Myakit. There was a police station here. They checked our documents. There was a good cafeteria here and a mandatory resting station with a healthcare facility. You see in the old days, no driver was allowed to be on the road unless you slept for minimum eight hours and had a health check before they let you go. And now . . . nobody cares. You do what you want. If you die of a heart attack, it's your problem.

Myakit was established in 1933 near a mine; both were built using forced labor. Besides gold mining, Myakit also housed the Road Construction administration. The town was shut down in 1994 as a *neperspectivniy poselok*, and residents were assisted in relocating either outside of the region or in towns within the region. Many people tried to stay behind and the local administration decided to erase the town completely; they used bulldozers to do that. Yet a few wooden shacks are still standing. After I noticed a few men between buildings, we decided to stop and visit them. We found nine strong young men, and Dmitry, a man in his early 60s, who were having a meal at the table put in the middle of a tiny square surrounded by these wooden shacks. One of the questions I asked was: "What are you doing here? The place seems completely deserted." Dmitry said:

> This is my home. I was born here. When they bulldozed the town, we were given some money and even though I was able to buy a flat on

the *materik*, I sold it and bought a good flat in Magadan. I am retired. I come here in the summer. We fish, collect mushrooms and berries.

When we left, a friend of mine travelling with us chuckled: "They collect berries, yeah. . . . Did you see thick gold chains on their chests? A generator? A small bulldozer in the back yard? These are [illegal] gold miners. We are at the middle of the gold mining season."

Dmitry used a well-known scheme of meeting his own needs while outwardly complying with the authorities. Using the relocation program's financial assistance to buy flats on the *materik*, Kolyma patriots then re-sell those flats and buy a good flat in Magadan (Magadan property cost less than similar property on the *materik*), effectively counteracting the state's efforts to relieve the North of the "surplus" population. So if anything, these people's lot had improved considerably. They supplement their pension income with income from their gold trade and access to biological resources, while in winter they live in their new flats in Magadan.

There are those who are either less fortunate or less enterprising, living off the summer subsistence but not having jobs or pension. Yabloneviy used to be a small settlement situated along the *trassa*, formerly as a mechanical repair shop built to service road construction. After the closure, residents had to relocate. Amidst a few rapidly dilapidating houses we found two that were still occupied. One resident was a suicidal former businessman who lost his business due to the sharp increase in taxes after a new local tax policy came into effect, and the other house was occupied by three people, a woman and two men in their 40s, who relocated to Palatka, a neighboring settlement, still breathing partially because one of the wealthiest owners of gold mining operations has his headquarters there. These three individuals, as compared to the Myakit group, really do support themselves with fishing and collection of berries and mushrooms, no gold mining. In their barely standing house, we found cranberries drying on a wood stove, small fish drying on a line across the room, and used teabags drying above the wood stove, ready to be reused. All three used to have jobs in Yabloneviy, but with the demise of the town, they moved to Palatka but could not find jobs. One left the region and tried to settle in Khabarovsk, the center of the neighboring Khabarovsk region, and then in Moscow, but to no avail: "I just could not find myself there. Everything is so foreign, I did not know anybody. People are so different—angry, greedy. Life there is all about money, they will kill for it. I came back here. We are thinking about finding jobs in a gold mine. They hire for a season."

Gold mining companies, whether smaller ones mining alluvial gold (*artel'*), or larger ones mining hard rock gold, do offer employment, using a mixture of seasonal and shift labor. Smaller operations hire most of their workers for a season, from about February–March to October when permanent snow cover settles. Larger companies that mine hard rock gold often work year-round, and while some people are hired locally, others are hired from so-called "near-abroad," i.e., former Soviet republics, specifically Ukraine. Men live without their families for a good six months but consider themselves lucky as they make more money there, hundreds of kilometers away, than in their own country. Big operations pay decent money. One has to watch out for smaller *artels*, which not only do not pay as much (their production is not as massive and they do not have resources to invest in serious machinery and basic infrastructure), but there were also cases when *artel'* administration retained part of workers' salaries. One way or another, seasonal and shift work do not lead to the development of any permanent settlements and building any infrastructure other than that directly related to the gold mining operation. In small *artels*, workers live in dormitories created in the numerous abandoned buildings, they have a simple kitchen, *banya* (bath house), and outhouse. Many see this approach as an environmental hazard: if people do not see their place of work as their place of residence, something they belong to, why would they bother taking care of it? Temporariness breeds an attitude of consumerism rather than preservation: one consumes one's environment but does not invest in it.

RE-CONNECTION

The changes I described in the previous section underscore the broken connections: a system once created and maintained by the state lost its rationale and partial disconnection was the way the government solved the problem of the North. However, despite the often traumatic consequences for the communities and individuals alike, what is slowly emerging instead brings about new opportunities for people and the region. We have seen that the void left by the withdrawal of the state had been filled by private initiatives, which means that people created jobs for themselves and offered services to others. While doing so, different connections were fashioned, not only with the rest of country but also outside it, on different levels, from individual to regional. Commerce and trade are alive and well. The difference between Soviet and post-Soviet times is that instead of being connected with the state, the region is restructuring, being governed now not only by the state but also by market rationality, and the global market at that.

For example, I met a 74-year-old woman in the local market selling sunflower oil and tomatoes. She grows tomatoes in her greenhouse in Magadan, but for sunflower oil she goes to visit her daughter and her family in the Krasnodar region in the south of Russia, where she buys home-made oil, ships it by train to Vladivostok, arranges a place on a ship for the oil to be shipped to Magadan, and then sells it in the market (as a pensioner she negotiated the reduced pay for the market stall with the owner of the market). Many of the local stalls sell frozen meats from Denmark and Argentina. They buy from wholesale businesses, which either buy from wholesale operations outside the region (i.e., Moscow) or abroad and ship their merchandise to

Moscow and then to Magadan via Vladivostok. Coveted Japanese cars are bought either directly from Japan, or in Vladivostok where importing Japanese cars is a big business, and shipped to Magadan. Some bioresources (fish, seafood), caught by Magadan private fishing vessels owned by over one hundred companies, are being sold not only in Russia, but exported to China, Korea, and Japan.

On the municipal and regional levels, Magadan positions itself not only as a part of the Far Eastern Federal *Okrug* of the Russian Federation but also as a member of the Asia Pacific Economic Cooperation (APEC). Indeed, the future of the Magadan region, surviving twenty years of post-perestroika changes, now rests on its *potential*. Emerging from the industrial development phase, its postindustrial future is still firmly connected to natural resource extraction and therefore its economy is resource-based. As far as gold and silver production is concerned, although most easily accessible alluvial gold had been mined, there are underground gold deposits that remain available. For example, the "Alexander Matrosov mine," built in 1944, is now producing 1.0–1.2 tons of gold annually. However, a new production is estimated at 225 tons of gold and 64 tons of silver. Besides natural resource extraction, the increasing importance and visibility of the Arctic regions on the global level could potentially make the Magadan region play an important role in the Russian economy. Yet, as the strategic program of socioeconomic development of the Magadan region has stated, such potential can be realized only if the regional and federal government solve the problem of the weak transportation network, for it is not enough to extract mineral resources, they have to be transported and processed. Thus the long-term project of building a railroad from Yakutsk to Magadan is planned to commence in 2016. Another major problem to be solved is the energy-producing infrastructure. Coal extracted in mines of the Magadan region is apparently of low quality, so many enterprises depend on coal imported into the region. The only major hydroelectric station (HES), built in the 1970s, Kolyma Hydroelectric Station, supplies ninety-five percent of the electricity to the regional communities, including Magadan. Another HES, Ust'Srednekan, which has been in the process of being built for the past twenty-two years, is thought to supply electricity to the "Alexander Matrosov mine." Neither Ust'Srednekan HES, nor the mine, had started its work yet. For the past twenty years it has all been in the plans, materializing slowly.

But twenty years, a fleeting moment in time for the regional development, is a long stretch of time in the life of an individual. To live amidst ruins, to hear the stories of better times in the life of Magadan, to hope for a better and more comfortable life, or at least a life not as basic as the one that many people lead this moment, is to imagine oneself living in the dump. A better life is only promised here, but is readily available elsewhere outside the region if one is adventurous and unattached. As one Susuman young woman working in one of two remaining cafeterias put it: "Everyone here wants to leave. It is just not everyone is in the position to do it."

CONCLUSION

Let's now bring a few strands together. This case study supports the ideas of non-linearity and partiality. Hence, although Bell does not give us any temporal frames for his "coming of post-industrial society," when we define the Soviet Kolyma as a part of industrial society, and observe post-Soviet deindustrialization, this does not mean that the Magadan region is anywhere near a postindustrial stage. The regional economy continues to be resource-based, and this, according to Bell, puts it squarely outside the postindustrial concept. No linearity here.

I suggest that this case study could be described by partial connections. The Russian Arctic offers an example of what happens when specific multiple connections established during the Soviet political, social, and economic frameworks are undergoing transformation. We observe that many of these connections are being simultaneously broken and reworked. Disconnection and abandonment do not seem to be a complete break, because partial connections are still maintained. Indeed, as we have seen, many previously established connections have been broken, i.e., the transportation system, northern benefits, and the northern supplies program. On the other hand, it is not possible to claim that the region was completely disconnected and then reconnected to something else, as many of the same connections are still maintained: the region is still a part of the Russian Federation although a new political structure has been instituted (i.e., the separation of the state into three levels, federal, regional, and municipal), airplanes are still connecting the region with the western part of the RF and taxis and trucks still take passengers from Magadan to regional communities; only the form of ownership and the range of services has changed. The same resources are still the basis of reconnection. Hence the transformative process is marked by *partial* disconnection—not from the capitalist market—but from the state, and partial reconnection from an internal state-regulated market to the global market, owing to the precious commodities produced in this region: gold, silver, and potentially, oil. This is also a case of restructuring, as Bell would have it, but not in accordance with postindustrial society (linear view) but rather the market economy: changes in the ownership (state to mixed state and private) and rationalization of economic investment based on market rationale.

Yet although it may seem that the state has withdrawn and the region's precious metal producers have expanded beyond the state-regulated market, the region and its future are firmly tied to the Russian state and its political and economic support. On a different level, the partial withdrawal of the state stimulated the burgeoning of private initiative to the point when only state support, without private businesses, will not be able to hold the region up. They depend on each other for the region to survive, especially in the near future, when the Arctic is assuming an important role in the global community as the next area for resource development. This is Ferguson's "bushes" of multitudinous co-existing variation.

Interestingly, however, the social consequences of disconnection are very similar to those described by other contributors in this volume, and in places as far away as Africa. What Ferguson described with regards to the options for workers of the Copperbelt in Zambia after the fall in production of copper sounds very familiar to the problems experienced by Magadan inhabitants: workers had an option of either staying or going home, but encountered difficulties in reintegrating into their home villages, planning for their "village" retirements, losing many relatives during the years of absence, finding that life in hometowns is no longer their "own," i.e., what they are used to for over twenty years living in an urban area, among others (1999:123–164).

The consequences of disconnection from the market outlined in this volume apply to the disconnection from the state but only partially. As we have seen, (1) abandonment and economic collapse do follow the disconnection; (2) reconnection to a new market does take place (but using the same commodities as before); and (3) persistence of a (remaining) population livelihood continues as a combined effort between the state and private initiatives of local people and private business; the latter proved to be even more dynamic than before the collapse. But the postindustrial future is not what the region is going to experience any time soon.

ACKNOWLEDGMENTS

I am grateful for financial support from the Canadian Social Sciences and Humanities Research Council, which funded the three-year project "Administrative Resettlement and Community Futures in Northeast Russia," part of the MOVE project within the ESF EUROCORS Programme BOREAS. My thanks go to the editors of the book and particularly to Prof. Ismael Vaccaro.

NOTES

1. The chapter is based on ten months of fieldwork during 2007–2009 in the Kolyma Region. All names have been changed.
2. Administration of the Magadan region, 04.07.2013. URL http://magadan.bezformata.ru/listnews/lyudi-perestanut-pokidat-kolimu/12619693/
3. 391,687 persons in 1989, or 555,621 if taken together with Chukotka, which was part of the Magadan region at that time.
4. 328,293 urban versus 63,394 rural inhabitants.
5. Russian Soviet Federative Socialist Republic.
6. Which was probably a reflection of the general perception of the state as an eternal state, as Yurchak had convincingly demonstrated: the feeling of Soviet life in general was as having a fixed and immutable nature, although the feeling of the state as a fixed single entity did not preclude the existence of internal shifts and mutations, and "the more the system seemed immutable, the more it was different from what it claimed it was" (2006: 295).

7. The term denotes an enterprise that became the basis for establishment of a community.
8. Arman' is a neighboring larger community, still breathing; Ola is much further away and still surviving as well.
9. All Soviet towns and cities were, and still are, heated by a central boiler that sends hot water via underground pipes into apartment buildings.
10. http://www.newsru.com/russia/16nov2012/gold.html

REFERENCES

Bell, Daniel. *The Coming of Post-Industrial Society. A Venture in Social Forecasting.* New York: Basic Books, 1973.

Bolotova, Alia, and Florian Stammler. "How the North became Home: Attachment to Place among Industrial Migrants in the Murmansk Region of Russia." In *Migration in the Circumpolar North: Issue and Contexts,* edited by Lee Huskey and Chris Southcott, 193–220. Edmonton: CCI press, 2010.

CCUSSR. 1928. Central Executive Committee USSR. Postanovleniye ot 15 dekabrya 1928 goda "Ob utverzhdenii obshchikh nachal zemlepol'zovaniya i zemleustroistva" [Resolution by the Central executive committee of the Soviet Union on general principles of land use and land allocation, 15 December 1928].

Ferguson, James. *Expectations of Modernity. Myths and Meanings of Urban Life on the Zambian Copperbelt.* Berkeley: University of California Press, 1999.

Heleniak, Timothy, Tobias Holzlehner and Elena Khlinovskaya Rockhill. "Depopulation of Russia's Most Remote Northern Regions." *Osteuropa* 61 (February–March 2011): 371–87.

Hill, Fiona and Clifford Gaddy. *The Siberian Curse: How Communist Planners Left Russia Out in the Cold.* Washington, DC: Brookings Institution Press, 2003.

Khlinovskaya Rockhill, Elena. "Living in Two Places: Permanent Transiency in the Magadan Region." *Alaska Journal of Anthropology* 8 no 2 (2010).

Nuykina, Elena. "Resettlement from the Russian North: an analysis of state-induced relocation policy and its performance on the example of Murmansk region and Yamalo-Nenets Autonomus Okrug." Arctic Centre Reports, Rovaniemi: Arctic Centre, University of Lapland, 2010.

Scott, James. *Seeing Like a State: How Certain Schemes to Improve the Human Condition Have Failed.* New Haven: Yale University Press, 1998.

Stammler, Florian and Elena Khlinovskaya Rockhill. "From 'the Earth' to the North: Understanding Industrialising and De-industrialising the Russian North through Resettlement Analysis." *Osteuropa* 61 (February–March 2011): 347–71.

World Bank. "Russian Federation—Northern Restructuring Pilot Project. Report No. PID8680." September 11, 2000. Accessed February 1, 2007, http://www.worldbank.org.

Yurchak, Alexei. *Everything Was Forever, Until It Was No More: The Last Soviet Generation.* Princeton: Princeton University Press, 2006.

Statisticheskiy Ezhegodnik [Annual Statistical Data]. "Magadan Region. The Territorial Branch of the Federal Statistic Service." MagadanStat, Magadan, 2008.

Tseitler, Maria. *Migratsionniye Processy v Magadanskoy Oblasti.: Istoriya i Sovremennost'* [Migratory processes in the Magadan oblast': History and Contemporary Period]. Territorial'niy Organ Federl'noi Sluzhby Gosudarstvennoy Statistiki po Magadanskoi Oblasti, Magadan, 2009.

5   Cycles of Industrial Change in Maine

James M. Acheson and Ann W. Acheson

INDUSTRIAL CHANGE AND DEINDUSTRIALIZATION

Deindustrialization has been defined as a dramatic decline in the share of employment in manufacturing (Rowthorn and Ramaswamy 1997: 1), a phenomenon producing a good many ramifying effects. The literature on deindustrialization is depressing to read. "Industry" is generally equated with manufacturing. This focus on the decline of manufacturing leads to descriptions of closed factories, long unemployment lines, ghost towns, workers in the prime of life reduced to food stamps, deteriorating schools and declining municipal services, foreclosed homes, rising demand for medical services due to stress, widening income gaps, increases in crime and drug addiction, and greatly reduced opportunities for a whole generation of young people (Bluestone and Harrison 1982; Newman 1994: 123–25). There is little question that people from communities where numbers of industrial plants have closed have suffered greatly for a long time (See Uchitelle 2006 for a very good description of the long-term problems faced by people laid off from manufacturing jobs).

Most recent studies of deindustrialization focus on events taking place since World War II. However, if we take a longer time frame and broaden the perspective beyond manufacturing and factories, another view of industrial change emerges. In this chapter, we focus on Maine's industries over a 350-year period, beginning in the seventeenth century and ending with a discussion of some of the new industries at present and what the future may hold. We also describe, in much less detail, the demographic and cultural changes that have occurred. We conclude by discussing Maine's industrial history in the light of theories of deindustrialization.

As we shall see, Maine industry has undergone a long series of transformations, with older industries being supplanted by newer ones, and these, in turn replaced by others. The effects of this process have varied. Special consideration must be paid to scale and location to understand the impact of industrial transformation on the local level. Though Maine as a whole has not undergone deindustrialization, some communities—especially those in the most rural areas—have suffered greatly.

MAINE GEOGRAPHY AND DEMOGRAPHY

Maine is highly heterogeneous. The geographic, economic, and social characteristics of the state vary enormously as one moves from the border of New Hampshire to the rim counties on the Canadian border (see Figure 5.1). The southern coastal area (York and Cumberland counties) is an extension of the urbanized, industrialized, densely populated eastern seaboard region of

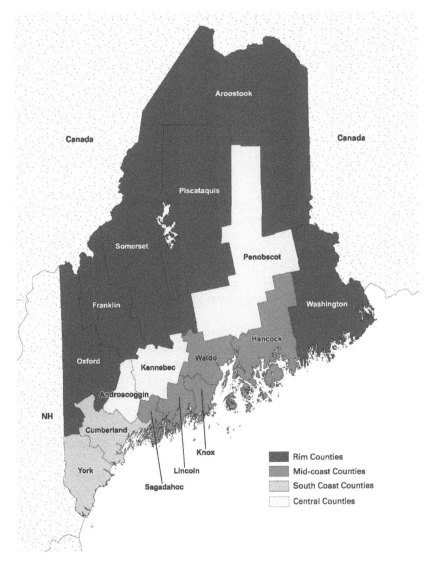

Figure 5.1   Map of Maine (map created by Beth Goodnight, Goodnight Design)

New England. The population has higher average incomes, is younger, and has a higher education level (A. Acheson 2006 and 2010). Portland is the largest city in Maine, and the Portland metropolitan area, with a population of 500,000, has forty percent of the state's population (U.S. Census 2010). The southern coastal area has a large number of small firms and also is home to a few large manufacturing firms. Alternate economic opportunities are good and unemployment is relatively low. Fishing and resource-based industries play a minor role in the economy of the region today.

The rim counties bordering Canada on the west, north, and east (Oxford, Franklin, Somerset, Piscataquis, Aroostook, and Washington), by way of contrast, are rural, sparsely populated, and have little manufacturing. Here the population is poorer, older, less educated, and less skilled than in the southern and central regions of the state. This has long been a depressed region. Economic opportunities are very poor and unemployment is chronically high (A. Acheson 2006 and 2010). Resource-based industries, such as fishing, boat building, blueberry harvesting, and the forest products industry are the backbone of the economy. The tourist industry is relatively undeveloped, with the exception of several large ski areas in the west and the area around Moosehead Lake in Picataquis County.

The mid-coast (Sagadahoc, Lincoln, Knox, Waldo, and Hancock) and central (Androscoggin, Kennebec, and Penobscot) counties stand between these two extremes in both location and economic and demographic characteristics, such as age structure, education levels, and income. Along the mid-coast, fishing and tourism are major industries. The economy of cities in the central region (Lewiston, Augusta, Waterville, and Bangor) used to be based on manufacturing, but there is no longer large-scale manufacturing in this region, with the exception of three remaining paper mills. Service-based industries predominate in the central region, along with some small-scale manufacturing.

INDUSTRIAL CHANGE IN MAINE

Fishing

The history of fishing in Maine and New England is one of serial depletion, where stocks were huge in the early period and gradually declined to very low levels. In the seventeenth century, shipbuilding, lumbering, and fishing were the primary industries. Before the American Revolution, fishing was generally conducted from relatively small boats fishing in inshore waters. After the Revolution, New England fishing expanded rapidly and large numbers of boats began to fish in Canadian waters, going as far as the Gulf of Saint Lawrence, Labrador, and the Grand Banks of Newfoundland (Lear 1998). Cod fishing was a mainstay of the economy. Catches were phenomenally large. Cod were salted, dried, and sold as far away as Europe and the West Indies. By the late seventeenth century, fishing had become Maine's largest industry. Maine towns in this era did well in the fishing business (Green 1906).

The Civil War brought even more prosperity to the fishing industry, as markets expanded to feed the troops. After the war, fishing began to diversify. Factories were established in Bristol and nearby Boothbay to process menhaden (Green 1906: 371); canneries were established in Eastport (Washington County) and other towns to can lobster meat (McFarland 1911: 166); and, most important, the number of herring canneries expanded rapidly (McFarland 1911: 244). Catches of cod and mackerel reached their peak around 1860 (O'Leary 1996: 80ff). By 1885, the fishing industry started a period of definite decline, as stocks of cod, menhaden, and mackerel decreased and competition from fisheries in Canada and the U.S. west coast increased (McFarland 1911: 288).

In the early decades of the twentieth century, several innovations greatly increased the ability to harvest and process fish: motors, otter trawls, and refrigeration and freezing technology. These innovations accelerated the exploitation of fish stocks (Sinclair and Murawski 1997). Depletion of stocks speeded up even more in the early 1960s, when offshore waters of the northwest Atlantic and Gulf of Maine were invaded by a large fleet of foreign trawlers and factory ships that quickly decimated stocks of cod and other species (Playfair 2003). The groundfishery, once the mainstay of the New England economy, is a shadow of its former self in spite of federal management efforts since 1976 (Acheson and Gardiner 2011).

If groundfish were the only failing fishery, the situation might not be so dire. But virtually all stocks in the Gulf of Maine are in decline or decimated, including clams, tuna, herring, and scallops. Some of these fisheries have been completely wiped out. There were seventeen herring plants in operation in the 1950s producing canned sardines, processing 149 million pounds at their peak in 1950 (Ackerman 1941: 34). By 2013, the last plant closed. The redfish industry, which supported a fleet of large trawlers and a freezer plant in Rockland beginning in the 1930s, was closed completely in 1984.

The only bright spot in the fishing scene is lobster, where catches have gone up since World War II. Between 1947 and 1989, lobster catches averaged 20 million pounds. After 1989, Maine lobster catches have always exceeded 30 million pounds each year. The lobster catch total of 126 million pounds in 2012 is a record high level (Maine DMR n.d.).

Agriculture

Agriculture expanded greatly in the seventeenth and eighteenth centuries. It quickly became the primary source of livelihood for the majority of the Maine population. Farms were small subsistence operations growing a variety of crops; farmers maintained enough horses and oxen to provide power, and other animals such as pigs, sheep, poultry, and cows for food and sale. These farms began to decline by the 1840s as people began to leave for the West, where high quality land was cheap, and for the manufacturing centers of southern New England. That exodus has continued to the present day (Carroll 1973: 6; Coolidge 1963: 81–83; Russell 1976: 391–393).

Maine agriculture reached its zenith late in the nineteenth century. Although the marginal farms had gone out of business and the agricultural population declined, most of the high quality farms were occupied. As a result, from the middle of the nineteenth century to 1890, more land was cleared and agricultural production continued to rise (Russell 1976: 393). In southern and central areas the amount of cleared land reached its apex in 1880 (Irland 1998: 3).

The twentieth century saw a decline in both the number of farms and agricultural production. Large numbers of people left farming after World War I, when low prices for agricultural goods produced an agricultural depression. By the 1920s, general farming was on its way to becoming a thing of the past. After 1920, the amount of Maine land devoted to agriculture plummeted sharply and the abandoned farmland began to grow back into forests.

The agricultural enterprises that survived after 1950 were larger and more specialized. Apple, dairy, and chicken farms dominated agriculture in central Maine, and Aroostook County in northern Maine became one of the largest potato growing areas in the nation (Day 1963: 76–90, 135–137). The decline in agriculture is reflected in the decline in the population in rural towns as a whole. The population of virtually all towns in rural Maine was higher in 1850, when agriculture was a key industry, than it was in 1950 (Coolidge 1963: 83–84).

Timber Industry

Southern Coastal and Central Maine
The forests of the southernmost part of Maine (and eastern Massachusetts) began to be exploited in the 1630s and 1640s (Coolidge 1963: 31). A great deal of lumber and barrel staves were produced to trade for manufactured goods from Europe and for rum, molasses, and sugar from the West Indies (Carroll 1973: 70–93). Many of the finest trees were cut for ship construction, which was a major industry at that time (Rowe n.d.: 33–44). By the American Revolution, many of the best stands of trees along tidewater rivers in southern Maine had been cut over.

After 1800, large numbers of settlers moved into what are now the southern coastal and central counties. The population grew very quickly (Allis 1976) and agriculture expanded. With agriculture came substantial deforestation. Farmers not only cleared fields for crops, but also cut logs to sell to local sawmills as a cash crop and to heat their houses. Timber harvesting continued to move further north and east.

Northern Maine

Maine's rim counties and the northern part of Penobscot County contain the largest contiguous forest area in the United States east of the Mississippi. The landscape is dominated by spruce-fir forests and very large lakes. With the exception of the potato growing region of northeastern Aroostook County and the blueberry barrens of Washington County, the land has never been cleared for agriculture.

After the Revolution, land in this region was auctioned off in very large lots by Massachusetts to pay its war debts (Allis 1976). Those who bought this land were interested only in the timber. In the early decades of the nineteenth century, these "lumbermen" focused on cutting the large stands of gigantic virgin pine, which grew commonly to 120 feet high (Coolidge 1963: 47; Milliken 1983). The logs were floated down the rivers to saw mills, where they were cut into boards, loaded on ships, and sold in North American and European ports. By the early 1840s, the banks of the Penobscot River in Bangor were lined with a large number of sawmills and wharfs for large ocean-going boats, and more lumber was shipped from Bangor than any port in the world (Wood 1961: 204).

The peak production of pine was achieved in 1848, and lumbermen then turned to cutting increasing amounts of spruce and hemlock. By 1900, the stands of virgin forests were almost gone (Coolidge 1963: 88–89) and there were substantial reductions in the amount of saw timber produced. As early as the 1850s, lumbermen began to leave Maine for places such as Michigan that promised better harvests (Millikin 1983: 34).

Paper Industry

In the 1860s, the first paper mills were built in Maine, and more were built in the decades that followed. This industry was to have phenomenal growth in the twentieth century. By the middle of the twentieth century, paper-making became the largest and most powerful industry in the state. Paper firms eventually owned 9.6 million acres, or forty-six percent, of all of the forested land (Nadeau-Drillen and Ippoliti 2006: 1, 5). There were sixteen large paper mills, which employed fully one-quarter of the entire manufacturing workforce in the state (Osborne 1974: 1). The influence of the paper company lobby on the legislature was so great that William Osborne (1974), an associate of Ralph Nader, called Maine "The Paper Plantation."

The 1990s were a period of downsizing and consolidation for the industry. Many companies left the state, and their assets were bought by other companies. A large number of plants were closed, and those that remained were substantially downsized (Acheson 2000). At the same time, paper companies sold virtually all of their forest land to other companies. The decline of the paper industry has led to a good deal of unemployment and underemployment, as formerly well-paid paper mill workers have had to seek lower-paying jobs or move to other areas to find work.

Ice Industry

The Maine ice industry began in the 1820s and expanded greatly after the Civil War. Ice was cut with large saws in mid-winter, stored in sawdust in huge storage sheds built along the Kennebec and Penobscot rivers, and then transported by ship in the summer to large numbers of ports in the southern United States and to tropical parts of the world ranging from Brazil to Calcutta (Rowe n.d.: 258–259). At one point in the 1870s and 1880s, there were 244 ice plants operating. In 1890, 3,000,000 tons were harvested and the industry employed 25,000 men and 1,000 horses (Rowe n.d.: 260). The advent of artificial ice and electric refrigeration brought a precipitous end to the large-scale production of ice in the early years of the twentieth century.

Granite Industry

Another industry that boomed after the Civil War was granite quarrying, which was a leading industry for decades along the coast. Blocks of granite were used for building structures, while small chips and rubble were used for paving stones and fill (Rowe n.d.: 262–263). The first load of granite was produced on Vinalhaven Island (Hancock County) in 1829, and in succeeding decades many more quarries were built. These were located primarily along the coast, major coastal rivers, and on coastal islands to facilitate transportation by barge and boat, and where outcrops of granite lay close to the surface. A post-Civil War building boom resulted in a great expansion of the industry. Maine granite was used in a large number of state capitol buildings, courthouses, city halls, libraries, and churches. The peak occurred around 1890, when Maine produced more granite than any other state. Many operations were quite modest, but some large firms were in the business as well. The granite industry shrunk greatly in the twentieth century, as concrete and artificial stone gained widespread acceptance as building materials. Most of the quarries have been closed. A few still produced granite until recently.

   While both the granite and ice industries did not last long, they were very important in Maine coastal communities in the late nineteenth century.

Shipbuilding and Shipping

Shipbuilding in what is now Maine spans over 400 years. The first ship was built in 1607 at the mouth of the Kennebec by the Plymouth Company, and by the 1690s a number of shipyards were in operation on the Piscataqua River along the border with New Hampshire (Rowe n.d.: 51; 56–59). After the American Revolution, shipbuilding expanded rapidly all along the coast (Rowe n.d: 147–165). Shipbuilding employed large numbers of people, not just in the yards themselves but also in ancillary industries (e.g., rope works, pump factories, saw mills, etc.). The peak of the maritime industry in Maine was in 1860. At that time there were "11,375 mariners in Maine," comprising almost one fifth of the working population (Rowe n.d.: 286). Maine ships transported cargoes all over the world.

The first steel ships were built by the Sewall family of Bath (Sagadahoc County, mid-coast) in 1894, and the use of steel for construction of large vessels continued from that time. The most notable firm constructing steel ships is Bath Iron Works, which has constructed warships for the U.S. Navy throughout the twentieth century. At present, it is the fourth largest employer in Maine, with over 4,500 workers (MDOL n.d.: Employers).

Wood continues to be used to construct pleasure boats and yachts. The pleasure boat industry has seen substantial expansion since 1980, while construction of fishing boats has declined with the decline in that industry. Since the 1970s, many small boatyards have shifted to producing boats with Fiberglas hulls, and recently some yards have begun experimenting with composite materials. Boat building is a niche industry, but one that has seen some growth in the last decade.

Coastal steamers continued to operate until the 1930s, transporting both freight and passengers. The rise of automobile and truck transport after that time spelled the end of coastal shipping and passenger transport. Although Maine's once-vibrant coastal shipping industry is no more, the state still has a few ports that are important in interstate and international shipping. Portland is the largest tonnage seaport in New England and is a major east coast seaport.

Manufacturing: Textiles and Shoes

Textile and shoe manufacturing became major industries in the nineteenth and twentieth centuries. These industries were the economic backbone of most of the urban centers in southern and central Maine for decades during that period.

The manufacture of cotton textiles began after 1750. Mills were located in the southern and central part of the state, along rivers where hydropower was available. In 1820, there were twenty cotton mills, concentrated in the cities of central Maine. By the end of the nineteenth century, textile manufacturing "exceeded all other businesses in capital investment and in product value" (Hebert 1951: 422). The twentieth century saw many cotton and woolen mills move to southern states, with a precipitous decline from 1950 onward.

The "shoe shops" [factories] were smaller and more scattered. The first small scale tanneries began in 1809. By 1869, there were 200 tanneries employing 1,020 workers (Hebert 1951: 438), and by 1949, there were 98 shoe factories employing 18,307. In 1960, Maine "produced more shoes than any other state" (Colgan 2006: 6). However, in the latter part of the twentieth century, the number of shoe factories declined as firms moved to places with low cost labor (i.e., Mexico and Asia). By 2013, only one remained.

During the nineteenth century, much of the labor for textile mills and shoe factories was supplied by people who abandoned agriculture for industrial work, and by immigrants. Many workers came from Quebec. Large enclaves of this Franco-American population continued through the twentieth century in cities such as Biddeford, Westbrook, Lewiston, Augusta, and Old Town.

Tourism

Tourism is one of the few industries that has exhibited steady growth from the nineteenth century to the present. As of 2000, it was reported to be the state's "largest source of employment" (Vail and Kavanaugh 2000: 1). Maine tourism has two different facets that need to be considered separately: (1) summer residents who generally own cottages, and (2) short-term visitors who come for a few days and stay in hotels, guest houses, or campgrounds.

Maine tourism began in the mid-nineteenth century. For example, before the turn of the twentieth century, three cottage colonies had been built in Bristol (Lincoln County), along with two summer hotels (Acheson 1978: 29), and the same pattern of growth was true of neighboring towns such as Boothbay Harbor (Clifford 1961: 21). In 1918 in Bar Harbor (Hancock County), one of the state's early and most wealthy summer "colonies," non-resident properties represented sixty-one percent of the town's real estate valuation, according to the 1918 town report. In the town of Bristol in 1895, 13.4 percent of real estate was owned by nonresidents; in 1970, nonresident taxpayers (3,567) outnumbered residents (1,721) (Acheson 1978: 29).

Currently, Maine has the highest proportion of seasonally occupied dwellings in the U.S., 16.4 percent in 2010 compared with the national average of 3.5 percent (U.S. Census 2010). Two "rim" counties where major ski areas are located (Franklin and Oxford) and three coastal counties (Hancock, Lincoln, and Washington) have the highest proportion of seasonal dwellings; in Franklin County, one-third of all dwellings are seasonal (U.S. Census 2010). Seasonal residences and dwellers contribute importantly to the tax base in many towns, and the business generated locally sustains communities that often have few other economic options due to the decline of other industries.

Short-term tourism is another phenomenon. It is a very diverse industry, including hotels and motels, restaurants, stores, art galleries, ski areas, tour boats, and many others. Although traditionally associated with summer visitors, Maine has increasingly become a four-season destination, with the "summer" season starting earlier and extending into fall "leaf peeping." Winter sports activities, especially skiing and snowmobiling, are very important in the economy of communities in Maine's northern and western counties. Vail (2004) notes that tourism revenues in Maine have grown fivefold since the early 1970s, making tourism the second largest sector in the state's economy.

PAST, PRESENT, AND FUTURE OF MAINE'S INDUSTRIAL LANDSCAPE

Broadly speaking, Maine industry has moved through three periods of industrial change. The first began in the seventeenth century and lasted until after the Civil War. The largest industries were fishing, shipbuilding, and lumbering. These industries were located in small towns along the coast and the lower parts of large rivers that emptied to the sea. They were labor intensive and depended on raw materials from the immediate area and access to easy shipping.

The second period, lasting from the post-Civil War era to the late 1970s, was marked by large-scale manufacturing. Cotton and woolen mills and shoe factories were located primarily in the cities of southern and central Maine. These industries used raw materials transported from other parts of the country, which were processed in very large plants with large work forces. The large, technically sophisticated mills of the paper industry were located along the rivers and made paper from pulp cut from local forests.

Maine came to its peak of international importance very early in its history. From an economic perspective, the pinnacle of the state's importance was in the mid-1800s, late in period one. After 1900, when ship construction, shipping, fisheries, and the lumber trade were past their prime, and the granite and ice industries were declining as well, Maine became a quiet backwater where little was happening of national or international significance. The period between World War I and World War II was particularly bad. Maine agriculture suffered from a serious depression, and textile-manufacturing plants began to move to the southern states. Only the expansion of tourism and a thriving pulp and paper industry helped to bolster employment.

The third period, beginning about 1980, has seen acceleration in the decline in manufacturing. Shoe and textile production have become things of the past. The pulp and paper industry has seen downsizing in the number of mills and employees since the 1980s. Technological advances have meant that the same amount of product can be produced with fewer employees. The Maine Department of Labor notes that sixty years ago manufacturing in Maine accounted for forty-three percent of nonfarm employment, but by 2011 it accounted for just 8.5 percent of jobs (MDOL 2012: 1).

Since about 1980, and accelerating in the last two decades, new kinds of businesses have greatly changed the industrial landscape, especially in the southern and mid-coast regions. Some of the firms in this group are part of the service sector, while others depend on sophisticated manufacturing technology and highly skilled workers. For example, in manufacturing, there is the Pratt and Whitney plant in Sanford (York County) making jet engines; the General Dynamics plant in Saco (York County) producing automatic weapons for the military; IDEXX Labs, an international biotech firm in

Westbrook (Cumberland County) specializing in research and veterinary products; Fairchild Semiconductor in South Portland; the Dragon Corporation Plant in Thomaston (Knox County) making cement; and Guilford of Maine (Piscataquis County) producing high performance textiles.

The service sector accounts for the largest share of Maine's jobs. According to data from the Maine Department of Labor (MDOL n.d.: Employers), among the state's ten largest employers in the third quarter of 2012, three were in retail; four in the medical sector (the state's four largest hospitals); two in insurance/financial services; and one in manufacturing. None of these are small, and together they provide employment for thousands of Maine workers. The tourism industry has grown from modest beginnings after the Civil War to become the largest employment sector in Maine in this third period. Although tourism does not have a large single employer (other than LL Bean), it continues as a major component in Maine's service sector, providing many seasonal and some non-seasonal jobs in smaller businesses and in self-employment.

MAINE'S INDUSTRIAL FUTURE

We are still in period three, and it is difficult to see what will happen to the state's current industrial "mix." In the southern part of the state, many of the high tech firms seem to be thriving, along with tourism. The picture for the rim counties of northern Maine is far less certain. The forest products industry, long the mainstay of the economy, is in decline. So far no new industries employing large numbers of people have moved into the region.

If history is any guide, at least some of Maine's manufacturing firms will be replaced by other, newer firms, which produce goods made by technically sophisticated techniques or services. We may see the development of new kinds of industries, growth of existing newer industries such as biotechnology, banking, and medical services, and perhaps the revival of some older ones. A promising new sector is energy production, taking advantage of two of Maine's abundant "resources:" winds and tides. There are a number of land-based wind farms already built, and more in the construction, permitting, and planning stages. Experimental offshore floating wind turbines are planned for 2013–14, with larger-scale industrial development to follow if these prove successful (Acheson 2012; Stone 2013). An experimental tidal turbine is in operation in Washington County. Both tidal and wind power, if they can be economically generated, could be transformative in Maine's economy and communities, both for the direct and indirect employment provided and because Maine's very high energy costs have historically been a drag on development in the state.

One of the state's oldest industries, agriculture, is showing signs of a renaissance. Maine is close to large urban markets in Boston and New York and has abundant water supplies. Increasing water scarcity in other parts of the country, rising transportation costs, and the growth of niche markets for organic foods may present opportunities for modest expansion in agriculture and food processing. Maine is bucking the national trend in having an increase in the number of farms, now more than 8,000, compared with 7,000 only a decade ago (Piotti 2011), as well as an increase in farm acreage.

DEMOGRAPHIC AND CULTURAL CHANGE

After a slight population boom in the 1970s during the "back to the land" movement, Maine has seen only very slight growth in recent decades. It currently is the oldest state in the country in median age (U.S. Census 2010), due in part to out-migration of people of childbearing age and the aging of the remaining population, and in part to in-migration of older retirees. At the county level, net migration has been very uneven. In 2000–2009, the state's average net migration was 3.04 percent. All but one of the state's coastal counties saw net migration in the range of 3.4–6.4 percent, but two rim counties (Aroostook and Washington) had net losses, with average net migration of –.8 percent and –2.7 percent, respectively (U.S. Census. n.d.: Population).

Given the growth of industry in urban areas and the decline of rural industries, it is not surprising that the state's urban and suburban areas have gained population, while many smaller communities, especially those farther from metropolitan areas, are shrinking. Some rural Maine towns with no local industry survive because people who work in nearby cities have moved there to take advantage of the less expensive land and housing available. Suburban sprawl started becoming a real problem beginning as early as the 1960s, especially in the southern part of the state and in areas adjacent to metropolitan service centers. Richert wrote in 1997 that over the last thirty years, "the fastest growing towns in Maine have been 'new suburbs' 10 to 25 miles distant from metropolitan areas" (1997: 44).

The culture of Maine coastal towns, long dominated by members of established families, has also been changing, as increasing numbers of people "from away" have moved in, accelerating the process of gentrification which began in the 1970s (Acheson 1988). Although wealthy retirees have driven up the price of shore land and the cost of housing, they have had a beneficial effect both for the towns' tax base and for local employment. Socially, the fabric of these coastal communities is changing, as newcomers have had an increasing impact in politics, community life, and local organizations. In coastal cities such as Portland, Belfast, and Rockland, fish processing plants, boat repair facilities, bars, and fishermen's hangouts have given way to gift shops, boutiques, art galleries, and upscale restaurants (Hall-Arber et al. 2001).

SCALE AND LOCATION

How Maine looks vis-à-vis industrialization depends greatly on the scale at which it is viewed. If one looks at the state as a whole, the situation is quite positive. In 2012, Maine's unemployment rate was 7.3 percent, under the national average of 8.1 percent (MDOL n.d.: Unemployment). While this is no cause for celebration, other states have suffered far worse. However, within the state there continues to be a wide range in unemployment rates, from a low of 5.8 percent in Cumberland County to a high of 10.7 percent in Washington County in 2012 (MDOL n.d.: Unemployment).

Economic prospects in Maine very considerably from one region to another. Job opportunities in the industrialized urbanized southern part of the state are far better, and they are much worse in the rim counties bordering Canada. The reason for this difference is linked to the character of the industrial transformation that has taken place. In the southern, mid-coast, and central regions, there has long been a diversity of industries. As one industry faded, new ones came on the scene, offering alternative opportunities to the people living there.

Fishing of one type or another and shipbuilding were mainstays of the coastal economy since the early Colonial era. These were augmented in the latter part of the nineteenth century by the ice and granite industries. When those declined in the late nineteenth and early twentieth centuries, much of the slack was picked up by the tourist industry and increasing employment opportunities in shoes, textiles, poultry processing, other manufacturing, and banking and insurance. That was not true in the northern and far eastern counties, whose fortunes have depended almost completely on agriculture and the forest products industry. Here, the "classic" picture of deindustrialization applies. Towns are mired in poverty; unemployment is high; there are few opportunities for young people; and out-migration continues at a rapid pace.

The effect of declining industries depends greatly on economic alternatives and location, as illustrated in the following cases:

Case Example: Paper Mill Closures. Since the early 1990s, a number of paper mills have closed or greatly downsized, but the effect has been markedly different in different locations. In the northern Maine town of Millinocket (Penobscot County), a very large paper mill closed for good in 2008. It had employed almost 5,000 workers in the 1960s. Another one closed in the neighboring town of East Millinocket, but then reopened with many fewer workers. These were the largest employers in the entire region, and their demise has had a devastating effect. There has been a good deal of out-migration; housing prices have declined precipitously; unemployment is over thirty percent; and tax receipts have gone down to the point where the town of Millinocket has had to make massive cuts in services (Sambides 2011). Although a few people commute very far from the area to find work, the distances involved and the rising cost of fuel do not make this a viable long-term alternative. By way of contrast, the closure of the paper mill in Westbrook (Cumberland County), in booming southern Maine, was easy to absorb given the large number of alternative employment opportunities available in the nearby area. The unemployment rate in Cumberland County in 2012 was only 5.8 percent (MDOL n.d.: Unemployment).

The closure of shoe factories in Auburn and Dexter had the same kind of differential impact. The displaced workers of Auburn, in central Maine, could find alternative employment more easily than their counterparts in Dexter, a northern Maine community with literally no other employment possibilities.

Case Example: Rockland (mid-coast). First settled around 1769, Rockland has been dominated by a series of single industries beginning with lime production (for mortar and plaster) in the late eighteenth century, which continued until the 1930s; shipping and shipbuilding became important outgrowths of the lime industry, ending in the 1920s with the adoption of steel boat construction (Fagan 2003: 1). Commercial fishing was the next major industry. Rockland at one time in the 1950s was one of New England's largest fishing ports, home to a fleet of long-distance trawlers, several processing plants, and a good deal of marine infrastructure (Hall-Arber et al. 2003: 357, 359–60). With the virtual collapse of groundfishing, Rockland entered a brief period of economic depression in the 1980s and early 1990s, but quickly pulled out with the expansion of yet another industry, tourism. With the processing plants and marine infrastructure largely gone, the downtown and waterfront have undergone gentrification and today are home to the well-known Farnsworth Art Museum, gift shops, and upscale restaurants. Credit card giant MBNA also played an important role in Rockland's waterfront transformation when it established a major call center there in 2000. The company left Rockland in 2005, consolidating services (and employees) in other nearby mid-coast locations, and its facilities are now used for other purposes (Fleury n.d.).

DISCUSSION

According to Rowthorn and Ramaswamy (1997), there are two explanations for deindustrialization. One is *trade*. Where labor costs are high, firms cannot compete with goods made in foreign countries. As a result, countries such as the U.S. have found themselves flooded with goods made in places such as China and Thailand. Uncompetitive firms either move to cheaper labor markets or close, and their employees become unemployed. The second cause is *technological change*. Manufacturing is "technologically progressive," i.e., able to adopt new innovations quickly (Rowthorn and Ramaswamy 1997: 9) so that more goods can be produced by fewer workers. Rowthorn and Ramaswamy conclude that most deindustrialization is due largely to technical change: "North-South trade has probably had only a limited role in deindustrialization" (1997: 8). Nevertheless, there is a good deal of evidence supporting trade arguments.

Both trade and technological change have resulted in the reduction of manufacturing employment. In the short term, this means that employment in service industries is growing much faster than employment in manufacturing. Manufacturing industries are "technologically progressive," so that it is easier to raise productivity by investing in new technology and to lay off workers. Service industries are less technologically progressive, so that raising output means hiring more labor. As a result, the proportion of the workforce employed in manufacturing in the U.S. declined from twenty-eight percent in 1970 to about eighteen percent in 1994 (Rowthorn and Ramaswamy 1997: 2), and that shrinkage has continued to the present. This process of shrinking manufacturing and rising service industry employment is taking place in many other countries with advanced economies as well. From this perspective, what we are calling deindustrialization is not a sign of failure, but of success. "Deindustrialization is principally the result of higher productivity in manufacturing than in services" (Rowthorn and Ramaswamy 1997: 1–2).

The decline in the manufacturing industries that dominated the Maine industrial scene in the second period was due largely to decisions of business owners to move elsewhere for cost reasons. Mills making woolen goods, cotton goods, and shoes could not compete in price with goods made in the U.S. south or, later, other countries with cheaper labor and fewer regulations. The decline of paper mills occurring since the mid-1980s is more complicated. At first, they downsized and then some either moved their operations or went bankrupt (Acheson 2000). One motive for paper mill closure is a search for cheaper labor, but a more important factor is increasing competition from technically advanced mills in foreign countries.

Maine is far from unique in the United States. Research on rural America by the Carsey Institute suggests that there are four broad types of rural places (Hamilton et al. 2008). Maine has three of these: (1) *declining, resource dependent areas*, places that previously depended solely on agriculture, timber, mining, or related manufacturing, with patterns of boom and bust; these areas formerly supported a blue-collar middle class, but today are characterized either by resource depletion or the threat posed by globalization to low-skill manufacturing jobs, or both (Hamilton et al. 2008: 6). A good deal of interior Maine that was dependent on the timber and paper industries fits this pattern, as did agricultural areas at an earlier period. (2) *Amenity-rich rural places*, especially in lake, coastal, and mountain areas, which attract second-home-buyers, affluent professionals, and retirees. Property values rise, and the mix of businesses changes, but there are increased employment and economic opportunities (Hamilton et al. 2008: 6). The southern and mid-coast regions of Maine fit this pattern. (3) *Amenity/decline places* are a transitional type, with similarities to both amenity-rich and declining resource-dependent communities (Hamilton et al. 2008: 6). Although traditional resource-dependent industries are weaker, they have not vanished; aging populations reflect out-migration; but the areas have potential for growth based on natural amenities (Hamilton et al. 2008: 6). Eastern coastal Maine and interior areas in the mountain and lake regions fit this pattern.

In summary, in long-term perspective, what we are witnessing in Maine and other areas is a switch from a rural, labor intensive, natural resource-based economy to a service-based economy based on an educated workforce in a more urban environment. Is this best described as deindustrialization? Does the term "postindustrial society" fit? We think not. It is a process better described as cyclical industrial change in which older industries are supplanted by more competitive ones. "Deindustrialization," stressing the decline of manufacturing, does not get at the essence of what has taken place in Maine. Traditional industries have been supplanted by new kinds of manufacturing based on advanced technology and a more skilled workforce, which makes it difficult to argue that a postindustrial society has come about. Cowie and Heathcott summarize the situation well when they say, "Indeed, the industrial age is alive and well, even if the locations have changed, and even if the rules of investment have shifted" (2003: 3–4). The process, however, is cruel to people and communities where older industries have left and no new ones have arisen to replace them or where there are no other alternative employment opportunities in the region.

REFERENCES

Acheson, Ann. *Poverty in Maine: 2006*. Orono: Margaret Chase Smith Policy Center, University of Maine, 2006.
———. *Poverty in Maine: 2010*. Orono: Margaret Chase Smith Policy Center, University of Maine, 2010.
Acheson, James M. *Interim Report, Bristol Maine*. Project: University of Rhode Island, University of Maine Study of Social and Cultural Aspects of Fishery Management in New England Under Extended Jurisdiction, National Science Foundation Grant No. 77–06018, 1978.
———. *The Lobster Gangs of Maine*. Hanover, NH: University Press of New England, 1988.
———. "Clearcutting Maine: Implications for the Theory of Common Property Resources." *Human Ecology* 28 no 2 (2000): 145–69.
———. "Attitudes toward Offshore Wind Power in the Midcoast Region of Maine." *Maine Policy Review* 21 no 2 (2012): 42–55.
Acheson, James M. and Roy Gardner. "Modeling Disaster: The Failure of Management of the New England Groundfishery." *North American Journal of Fishery Management* 312 (2011): 1005–18.
Ackerman, Edward A. *New England's Fishing Industry*. Chicago: University of Chicago Press, 1941.
Allis, Frederick. "The Maine Frontier." In *The History of Maine*, edited by Ronald Banks, 141–53. Dubuque, IA: Kendall/Hunt Publishers, 1976.

Bluestone, Barry and Bennet Harrison. *The Deindustrialization of America: Plant Closings, Community Abandonment, and the Dismantling of Basic Industry.* New York: Basic Books, 1982.

Carroll, Charles. *The Timber Economy of Puritan New England.* Providence, RI: Brown University Press, 1973.

Clifford, Harold B. *The Boothbay Region: 1900 to 1960.* Freeport, ME: Cumberland Press, 1961.

Colgan, Charles. "The Maine Economy: Yesterday, Today and Tomorrow." Technical report, Brookings Institution Metropolitan Policy Program, 2006.

Coolidge, Philip. *History of the Maine Woods.* Bangor: Furbush Roberts Printing Co, 1963.

Cowie, Jefferson and Joseph Heathcott. "The Meanings of Industrialization." In *Beyond the Ruins: The Meaning of Deindustrialization,* edited by Jefferson Cowie and Joseph Heathcott, 1–15. Ithaca: Cornell University Press, 2003.

Day, Clarence. *Farming in Maine.* Orono: University of Maine Press, 1963.

Fagan, William F. *From Lime Kiln to Art Galleries: A Historical Anthropogeography of the Maine Coast City of Rockland.* Ph.D. Dissertation. Baton Rouge: Louisiana State University, 2003.

Fleury. "Rediscover Rockland—Where Art and Food Meet," n.d. Accessed July 16, 2013, http://www.downeast.com/node/10755.

Green, Francis B. *History of Boothbay, Southport and Boothbay Harbor, Maine 1623–1905.* Portland, ME: Loring, Short and Harmon, 1906.

Hagen, John, Lloyd Irland, and Andrew Whitman. *Changing Timberland Ownership in the Northern Forests and Implications for Biodiversity.* Brunswick, ME: Manomet Center for Conservation Sciences, 2005.

Hall-Arber, Madeleine, Christopher Dyer, John Poggie, James McNally and Renee Gagne. *New England's Fishing Communities.* Cambridge, MA: MIT Sea Grant, 2001.

Hamilton, Lawrence C., Leslie R. Hamilton, Cynthia M. Duncan and Chris R. Coloscousis. *Place Matters: Challenges and Opportunities in Four Rural Americas.* Carsey Institute, Reports on Rural America, Vol. 1, No.4. Durham: University of New Hampshire, 2008.

Hebert, Richard A. *Modern Maine.* New York: Lewis Historical Publishing, 1951.

Irland, Lloyd. *Maine's Forested Area, 1600–1995: Review of Available Estimates.* Miscellaneous Publication 736. Orono: University of Maine Press, 1998.

Lear, W.H. "History of Fishing in the Northwest Atlantic: The 500 Year Perspective." *Journal of Northwest Atlantic Fishery Science* 23 (1998): 41–73.

Maine Department of Labor [MDOL]. n.d. "Manufacturing Jobs: Trends, Issues, and Outlook." Research Brief, Center for Workforce Research and Information, Maine Department of Labor, Augusta. Accessed April 12, 2013, http://www.maine.gov/labor/cwri/publications/pdf/ManufacturingJobsTrendsIssuesandOutlook.pdf.

———. n.d. "Top 10 Private Employers in Maine by Average Monthly Employment (3rd quarter 2012)." Maine Department of Labor, Center for Workforce, Research and Information. Accessed April 12, 2013, http://www.maine.gov/labor/cwri/publications/pdf/MaineTop50Employers.pdf.

———. n.d. "Unemployment and Labor Force." Maine Department of Labor, Center for Workforce, Research and Information. Accessed July 16, 2013, http://www.maine.gov/labor/cwri/laus.html.

Maine Department of Marine Resources. n.d. "Historical Maine Lobster Landings." Accessed April 15, 2013, http://www.maine.gov/dmr/commercialfishing/documents/lobster.table_000.pdf.

McFarland, Raymond. *A History of the New England Fisheries.* New York: University of Pennsylvania Press, 1911.

Milliken, Roger. "Forest for the Trees: A History of the Baskahegan Company." Unpublished Manuscript. Special Collections, Fogler Library. Orono: University of Maine, 1983.

Nadeau-Drillin, Karen and Jill Ippoliti. *Maine Forestland Ownership: Trends and Issues.* Augusta: Office of Policy and Legal Analysis, 2006.

Newman, Katherine. "Deindustrialization Poverty and Downward Mobility: Towards an Anthropology of Economic Disorder." In *Diagnosing America: Anthropology and Public Engagement,* edited by Shepard Foreman, 121–48. Ann Arbor: University of Michigan Press, 1994.

O'Leary, Wayne. *Maine Sea Fisheries: The Rise and Fall of a Native Industry.* Boston: Northeastern University Press, 1996.

Osborne, William. *The Paper Plantation: The Nader Report on the Pulp and Paper Industry in Maine.* Washington, DC: Center for the Study of Responsive Law, 1974.

Piotti, John. "Farms and the Working Landscape." *Maine Policy Review* 20 no 1 (2011): 56–60.

Playfair, S.R. *Vanishing Species: Saving the Fish, Sacrificing the Fishermen.* Hanover, NH: University Press of New England, 2003.

Richert, Evan. "Why Sprawl Is a Problem: Interview with Evan Richert." *Maine Policy Review* 6 no 2 (1997): 44–49.

Rowe, William H. n.d. *The Maritime History of Maine.* Freeport, ME: Bond Wheelwright Co.

Rowthorn, Robert and Ramana Ramaswamy. 1997. "Deindustrialization—Its Causes and Implications." Economic Issues No. 10. International Monetary Fund. Accessed March 28, 2013, http://www.imf.org/external/pubs/ft/issues10/issue10.pdf.

Russell, Howard S. *A Long Deep Furrow: Three Centuries of Farming in New England.* Hanover, NH: University Press of New England, 1976.

Sambides, Nick. "Millinocket Keeps Going Despite Cash-flow Problems." *Bangor Daily News* 11 July, 2013, B2.

Sinclair, Alan and Stephen Murawski. "Why Have Groundfish Stocks Declined?" In *Northwest Atlantic Groundfish: Perspectives on a Fishery Collapse,* edited by John Boreman, Brian Nakeshima, James Wilson and Robert Kendall, 71–93. Bethesda, MD: American Fisheries Society, 1997.

Stone, Mathew. "Despite 'Low Probability' of Success, Offshore Wind Project Could Be Maine's 'Bonanza,' PUC Chairman Says." *Bangor Daily News,* 13 February 2013.

Uchitelle, Louis. *The Disposable Americans: Layoffs Add their Consequences.* New York: Alfred Knopf, 2006.

U.S. Census n.d. "Historical Census of Housing Tables." Accessed April 12, 2013, http://www.census.gov/hhes/www/housing/census/historic/vacation.htmlhttp://www.census.gov/hhes/www/housing/census/historic/vacation.html.

U.S. Census. n.d. "Population Estimates Program." Accessed April 12, 2013, http://www.census.gov/popest.

U.S. Census. n.d. "Summary Files SF-1, American Fact Finder, 2010." Accessed April 12, 2013, http://factfinder.census.gov/faces/nav/jsf/pages/index.xhtml.

Vail, David. "Tourism in Maine's Expanding Service Economy." In *Changing Maine 1960–2010,* edited by Richard Barringer, 429–49. Portland: Edmund Muskie School of Public Service, University of Southern Maine, 2004.

Vail, David and Wade Kavanaugh. *Tourism and Livable Wages in Maine.* Augusta: Maine Center for Economic Policy, 2000.

Wood, Richard G. *A History of Lumbering in Maine, 1820–1861.* Orono: University of Maine Press, 1961.

6 Dwelling in a Pollution Landscape

Vanesa Castán Broto

INTRODUCTION

Georges Seurat completed his monumental picture "Bathers at Asnières" (1884) before his great breakthrough, the invention of pointillism (Figure 6.1). Yet, who could argue that this is not a masterpiece! The picture draws you in immediately but simultaneously relaxes you with its pastel colors. Not only does "Bathers at Asnières" present a beautiful view of the River Seine as it flows through the Parisian suburbs of the late nineteenth century, but it also provides rich insights about working class life at that time and place.

In the picture, we see a group of working class men enjoying a rare moment of leisure on the banks of the river Seine. The central figure of the painting is the somber figure of a young man of large stature, sitting on his own clothes, eyes presumably lost in his thoughts. In front of him, a boy with a red hat actively enjoys the water. Behind him, there is a row of lazy figures lying on the grass, wearing working class attire. Viewers do not see their anonymous faces but can enjoy the expressivity of their body language. In the background, behind a dividing line of small boats and poplars, the silhouettes of industrial buildings and the smoke coming out of their chimneys dominate the scene in the same way a dark shadow over the window may change the mood of a relaxed scene. The detail of the landscape and its effect on the observer's mood has a similar impact to that of the Dutch Masterpieces of the seventeenth century, in which background details shape the overall intent of the painting (think, for example, of Cuyp's "River Landscape with Riders"). Here, however, these details have an altogether different significance.

In this painting, Seurat magisterially portrays a pollution landscape—a landscape in which human experiences are mediated by the very transformation of that landscape in a new and unique way. Landscapes themselves are the products of socio-nature interactions: they are neither visual representations for the exclusive enjoyment of human eyes, nor are they the mere result of ecological processes. But pollution landscapes emerge in a period in which the dynamics of socio-nature interactions and their impacts

Figure 6.1   Georges Seurat, "Bathers at Asnières" (courtesy of the National Gallery in London)

on landscape have changed in dramatic ways. At Asnières, Seurat's bathers are enjoying their time. The painting is, on one hand, an ode to the achievements of the working class within the process of industrialization, a proto-image of workers as potential consumers who enjoy their leisure time. On the other hand, the painting also provides a certain insight about the environmental costs of economic achievement. It stands in stark contrast with the romantic representations of landscapes that preceded the impressionist and post-impressionist periods. For horizon, we have a line of factories. For clouds, dark smoke. And for water, a darkened mirror. Looking at the painting, I wonder whether Georges Seurat expected viewers to imagine the smells and the heaviness of the hot air within the picture. What did the water in the Seine taste like?

In this painting, Seurat both celebrates the achievements of the industrial revolution and explains how it unfolds over the landscape. In doing so, Seurat's painting captures the social relationships within a pollution landscape and their dwelling experiences. Dwelling refers to the intimate relationship that develops between a landscape and the people who inhabit that landscape during their life course (Ingold 2000; Thomas 1993). Dwelling implies a lack of distance between people and things; in places of dwelling humans engage with the landscape through daily practices rather than by detached visual contemplation (Ingold 2000; Macnaghten and Urry 1998; Thomas 1993). Those relationships and the landscapes they generate are in constant evolution, but certain characteristics may solidify, structuring the lives of those who live in that landscape. Pollution is one of them. Environmental pollution is a key issue that, once it emerges in a landscape, its inhabitants find it very difficult to explain it away. As "pollution landscapes," these are not simply landscapes containing pollution, but rather, these are landscapes in which the pollution is an active component producing a collective experience of nature and place (Castán Broto et al. 2007). What Seurat's painting captures is not simply that pollution may influence the experience of the landscape—and how workers spend their leisure time—but rather, that there is an intimate relationship between the features of a pollution landscape and the ways people living in that landscape think about themselves and act accordingly.

Industrialization was legitimated on the back of dreams of modernity and progress, with a landscape of "smokestacks that dramatically appeared on the horizon" (following Ferguson 1999) that symbolized the rise of the middle classes. However, especially with the application of structural adjustment policies in distant corners of the world since the 1970s, many of these areas whose landscapes changed under the dreams of industrialization have now undergone a painful process of deindustrialization and economic decline. As Ferguson (1999: 12) explains, "the circumstances of economic decline have affected not only national income figures and infant mortality rates but also urban cultural forms, modes of social interaction, configurations of identity and solidarity, and even the very meanings people are able to give to their own lives and fortunes." Economic decline not only permeates the lives of those living through it, but is also imprinted in the landscape itself. As Seurat's painting aptly portrays, landscape production was qualitatively different under industrialization. There were new elements in the landscape, full of purpose. The extent to which industrial development was perceived as a transgression was related to the future promises that the chimneys provided for those living under their shadows. Postindustrial landscapes, however, are characterized by the lack of purpose in the transgression of industrial systems, as is evident in large wastelands and abandoned brownfields. Such lack of purpose is related to the very same "sense of decline and despair" that Ferguson found in the lives of those who struggled to live in the Zambian Copperbelt in the late 1980s.

What are the future possibilities for those dwelling in a postindustrial pollution landscape? Can they actively promote actions and visions that revalue their locale and enable them to hold the promise of a future life in that pollution landscape? In this chapter, I relate everyday life in a postindustrial pollution landscape to the capacity of its inhabitants to promote and achieve political action. In doing so, I use the concept of dwelling to look at how inhabitants in a pollution landscape portray themselves. This helps to characterize social relationships within a pollution landscape and, in particular, its political consequences in a given planning context. The argument is developed by reassessing a case of coal ash pollution in Bosnia and Herzegovina and with reference to my previous work on this case.

FROM STIGMA TO DWELLING: REINTERPRETING
THE POLLUTION LANDSCAPE

How people frame pollution helps us understand the reactions to a pollution landscape of those who inhabit it. People's understandings and experiences of pollution are mediated by the context in which they emerge (Parkhill et al. 2010). Take for example McGee's (1999) work on local responses to contamination from lead mining in the community of Broken Hill, Australia, between 1992 and 1996. In Broken Hill, she found an apparent lack of response to local pollution. The issue was only recalled when it gained widespread public attention, and, even then, public discussion diminished with time. Gaining recognition is a difficult step for a pollution problem. The classical work on the Love Canal disaster by Edelstein (2004) emphasized that the identification of pollution is not a trivial thing, whether this is because of the amorphous and invisible nature of chemical exposure; the difficulties in diagnosing its presence and consequences; the reassurances (if present) by industry or local authorities about the safety of the area affected; or personal circumstances, such as the pride of ownership of a contaminated land parcel (Capek 1993). However, local knowledge about pollution cannot be underestimated. Irwin identifies several types of local knowledges that may contribute to the construction of an environmental pollution claim from direct observations of spatial transformations, health impacts, or even systematic data collection (Irwin 1995).

In the Broken Hill study, after identifying the local condition and the hazards associated with it, the community took little proactive action against it. Most of the responses were taken privately, and activism was reduced to collaborations in lead exposure management. McGee attributed this to the dependence on the polluter and disagreements between families. She described the proliferation of individual coping strategies as emerging from a form of "frontier individualism" that was closely related to the attribution of stigma to other families. Stigma is not only attributed to those living in a particular place but to the place itself (Castán Broto et al. 2010; Parkhill et al. 2013).

This kind of analysis has been useful to understand how local residents make sense of and explain their lives and roles within a pollution landscape. Yet, by focusing on the perceptions of the place and, in particular, how such perceptions are skewed toward a particular negative understanding of the place (and the social construction of a stigma), such analyses overlook that people actually live in those landscapes and, to do so, they may be compelled to suspend those concerns with which they cannot actually deal (Burningham and Thrush 2004). The question is whether a pollution landscape emphasizes transformation—and thus, the capacity of residents to deal with such transformation—or threat (Parkhill et al. 2013). As McGee (1999) showed in her study, the creation and reproduction of stigma through pollution accounts led to the division of the community and the adoption of individual strategies to cope with the pollution. This co-opted possibilities for community action.

These considerations are particularly important in postindustrial pollution landscapes and declining economies because of the difficulties in finding a responsible party for the pollution and, even when responsibilities are established, to ensure that such a responsible party can find means to compensate affected residents (Castán Broto 2012). Cases like the Love Canal example (Edelstein 2004) show that residents are able to organize themselves toward a common goal to actively denounce a pollution attempt and demand compensation (Aronoff and Gunter 1992; Capek 1992). On the basis of redistribution of goods or direct compensation for environmental consequences, community action can be mobilized around ideas of environmental justice. Of course, compensation is not enough to address the issues claimed by activists. Recognition of the damage done and representation in decision-making processes are often equally important (e.g., Agyeman 2005). Yet, the prospect of compensation that follows recognition is most often a way to galvanize the community into any form of organized action.

So, what happens when that prospect for compensation does not exist, not only because of the difficulties in identifying a single agent behind the health and environmental degradation of a pollution landscape but also because any potential actor toward whom claims are directed lacks the capacity or resources to actually compensate residents and other citizens suffering the pollution? How can community action be brought about in that context?

In this chapter, I argue that in order to move toward organized community action for a sustainable future, discourses of environmental transformation and social change in a pollution landscape need to move away from narratives that emphasize the prevalence of stigma and the attribution of responsibilities for the production of that landscape. Instead, I would like to understand to how local residents dwell in such landscapes, and how dwelling practices relate to their capacity to represent their own concerns and their ability to bring about action that responds to such representations.

The notion of dwelling (from the Latin *habitare*), connects life with the space of living. Heidegger (1971) described dwelling as a fundamental practice of "being-in-the-world," through which humans are able to make ourselves "at home." This relates dwelling not just to utilitarian aspects of having shelter and livelihoods—but also to the practices, experiences, and conceptions in space which mediate the creation of space itself. Ingold (2005: 503) has advocated a dwelling perspective that emphasizes that although "we may imagine ourselves to be living on one side of a boundary between society and nature, and non-humans to be living on the other . . . such imagining is only possible for a being that is already situated in an environment of human and nonhuman others, and committed to the relationships thus entailed." Dwelling is, however, not the same as experiencing or interpreting the world, as it is specifically directed at the material life practices that lead to the making of the landscape. Through dwelling, pollution landscapes are further transformed and incorporated in life practices, so that new forms of owning landscapes emerge—forms that are sensitive to the threats of pollution and yet remain wedded to future communities.

LANDSCAPES OF POSTINDUSTRIAL TRANSFORMATION IN TUZLA

In the late 1960s, siting the new thermal power plant in the growing and prosperous city of Tuzla must have been an obvious choice. It fit the economic strategy of those decades in the former Socialist Republic of Yugoslavia, in which republics were differentiated according to their perceived competitive advantage. In such an economic map, the then Socialist Republic of Bosnia and Herzegovina was to be a site for mineral extraction and heavy industry. Thus, alongside the old historic administrative capitals—Travnic, Sarajevo—emerged the new industrial capitals like Zenica and Tuzla. Coal was the key resource that constituted the basis of industrial production in the Republic.

These choices have shaped the spatial development of Tuzla and its satellite towns (Figure 6.2). The coalmine history starts in the mining satellite towns, such as Banovici, where one of the last mines remains today.

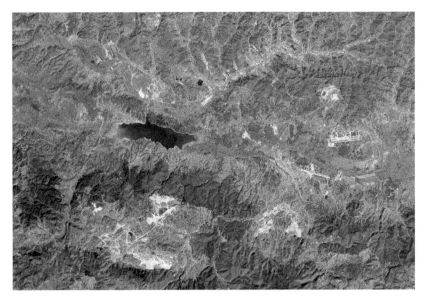

Figure 6.2   Satellite Image of Tuzla and Surrounding Areas (courtesy of NASA's Earth Observatory)

Interpreting the satellite image in Figure 6.2, Smailbegovic and Lindsey (2009) explain:

> Several large mines and their associated debris (tailings) are scattered across the image. Four large open pit mines appear in a clockwise arrangement starting southeast of Tuzla: Dubrave, Djurdjevik, Mrdici, and Banovici, all of which produce brown coal. At the upper left corner of the image is the Kreka strip mine, which produces lignite. East of the inactive Ontario Strip Mine, lavender-colored patches are fly-ash deposits—the residue left over from coal burning at the Tuzla power plant.
>
> The transition from underground mines to more profitable large-scale surface mines has led to soil degradation, dramatic changes to terrain, and water and air pollution. Scientists at the University of Tuzla have estimated that open pit mining has degraded at least 20,000 hectares (about 50,000 acres) of land in the country, with the majority of the damage occurring in the Tuzla Basin. Remediating some of the worst pollution hotspots in the Tuzla Basin is part of a new agreement among cities and local industry to make industrial activities in the area more environmentally sustainable.

The abundance of coal made it easier to make the decision to establish the thermal power plant in the entrance of Tuzla, which overtime grew to become one of the greatest sources of energy in the country. A dam in the nearby town of Lucavak also provided abundant water needed to manage the cooling process, clean the plant, and dispose of large amounts of coal ash. Many other industries established themselves around the plant, attracted by, among other factors, the availability of energy. These were prosperous times for Tuzla. Between the late 1950s and the mid-1980s, the growth of industries was coupled with an exponential growth in working populations. Migrants came every day to the city from every corner in Yugoslavia, adding to the already diverse mix of population. In 1971, Tuzla's population according to the Socialist Federal Republic of Yugoslavia population census was 107,293. The 1991 Yugoslav census reported 24,325 people more, an increase of twenty-three percent over twenty years. The census also reported an increase of people who reported themselves as "Yugoslavs," that is, people who declined to ascribe themselves to a single ethnic minority, from 2.36 percent in 1971 to 16.71 percent in 1991.

In the 1980s, the first signs of economic decline emerged. Economic adjustments affected the city and its industries. The impact of industrialization on the local resources became evident suddenly and local residents organized themselves and staged protests against the rampant pollution. In the villages surrounding the power plant, residents had seen for decades how the disposal of large amounts of coal ash was transforming their landscapes as they knew them. Large amounts of forests had disappeared, first during the excavation of coal and later, under giant dams, which contained a mixture of ashes, coal waste, and water.

These giant ash dams—that today occupy more than 150 hectares—constitute an additional environmental hazard. As ashes sediment, the finest particles of fly ash are suspended in the water, and eventually deposited in the most superficial layers of the ash deposits. In Tuzla, the combination of strong winds with the hot and dry weather during the summer caused storms of black ash, during which the ashes nearly covered everything in a layer of black dust. Residents organized themselves to demand action against this from the power plant, and in the late 1980s the plant implemented the first actions toward covering and re-vegetating the oldest coal ash disposal site in the village of Dreznik. Soil scientists and engineers from the universities of Tuzla and Sarajevo studied the old sites and developed strategies for their long-term regeneration.

In 1991, the Bosnian conflict erupted. The city was in shock, not only because of the dismembering of the socialist regime in Yugoslavia and the raising of nationalism, which led to the Serbian aggression in Bosnia and Herzegovina, but also because of the distinct anti-nationalist politics of the city of Tuzla. Tuzla was the only city in Bosnia where nationalist parties had not won in the municipal elections—and the city remains averse to nationalism to this day. The siege of the city by the nationalist Serbian forces during the war did not stop its residents from going about their lives, trying to live through the most abnormal situations: "On the day of our marriage, as we walked out of the registry office, the shelling started," was the observation of a friend who lived in the city through these years. He spoke about it without a hint of sadness in his story.

The power plant was a key strategic objective and one that the people of Tuzla fought to maintain during the war. The plant was kept open by operatives who risked their lives each morning by walking the short distance between the city and the plant. The road that communicated between the city and the main industrial park around the power plant was exposed to shelling attacks. Not all the industries survived. After the war, many people found themselves jobless. The power plant itself halved its own workforce, with under 1,000 workers in the late 1990s. Moreover, Tuzla, a self-declared non-nationalist haven but situated near the front line, received a high influx of war refugees, who were hosted and hidden by local populations but who, in the late 1990s, found themselves with little prospects for economic prosperity in Tuzla.

When I started my research in Tuzla in 2005, under the premise of understanding residents' concerns about the power plant and their environment to adapt potential solutions for land regeneration to local demands, I found a general climate of desperation and discontent. Residents were fearful, on the one hand, of the damaging consequences of pollution in their landscape. Many had followed training with international NGOs concerned with the environment who had warned them about the detrimental impacts of pollution on the environment but had left them without appropriate tools to operate within a fragmented governance landscape. Claims regarding the need to recognize the environmental damage on the landscape were met with anxiety by industries which were themselves struggling in the new economic climate of globalization. The social responsibility that local companies had previously demonstrated under the system of self-management was now regarded as an obstacle to achieving competitiveness and profits for companies to survive. And for those who didn't "ditch" those aspirations to serve both the economy and the society, they found themselves at the mercy of international investors, who, in one report, bought what once had been prosperous companies for as little as one dollar. International investments also brought new aspirations, symbolized in the new expensive supermarkets (*Merkator*), which joined the former Socialist Republics economically but not socially.

This is the context in which environmental justice demands—articulating the clean environment as "a human right"—have emerged in Tuzla. But simultaneously this is a context in which people have continued going about their lives independently of the claim-making activities in their particular locale. Dwelling in the pollution landscape, local residents have been able to reinvent what that landscape signifies in their lives. The following sections explore some of the aspects of dwelling through a reconsideration of previous analyses of the case (Castán Broto 2012 and 2013; Castán Broto et al. 2007 and 2010).

POSTINDUSTRIAL LIFE IN A POLLUTION LANDSCAPE

Most people interviewed in the communities around the disposal sites in Tuzla were seriously concerned about the health and ecological impacts of environmental pollution. Environmental problems were perceived as an interrelated complex, where sources of pollution and effects are hardly separated. Local residents talked simultaneously of the dust pollution from the disposal sites, air pollution, water contamination from the mining activities, subsidence, and other environmental problems that interact in the pollution landscape.

Most residents argued that pollution was not due to one single industry—the power plant—but rather, pollution was the result of a long history of industrial activity in the area. "The power plant is not the only polluter here," said in different ways workers at the power plant, local residents, and a municipal representative. A local representative of the activist group "eco-green" (*eko-zeleni*) stated that they had identified up to twenty-eight "main polluters," including the companies "2nd of October" (which makes tar/asphalt), HAK (which is a chemical factory that closed during the war and, after reopening, in the mid-2000s received foreign capital), and ANGROSIROVINA (a company that makes agricultural products). The mines are also cited as a source of pollution (particularly regarding problems with underground waters), even though their activity has slowed down greatly in recent years.

While, because of its size, history, and prominence, the power plant could be considered the main polluter, it also has had a key role in the area, both as a source of employment and to support further industrial development. One of the key factors that changed dramatically after the war was that employment became suddenly scarce. In their interviews, people asserted that "you live to work" and that "without companies there is no life." When asked what is the main problem in their communities, interviewees immediately highlight employment, whereas when asked about the future of the communities, they immediately see little future because of lack of employment. Working is also regarded as a means for participation in the economy and the growth of different companies. In this way, unemployment competes with pollution as one of the main problems of the community after the closing of several local industries (the soda plant, the chemical plant HAK, some of the mining pits) and the modernization of others, such as the power plant. Residents also showed their concerns about the employment prospects for the youth and their opportunities for living and recreation in those communities. They see little future prospects other than migrating and leaving impoverished and elderly communities behind.

Residents explain their difficulties in managing household finances; in particular many people have problems paying their water and electric bills. This problem was aggravated in the early 2000s, because bills that were not paid during the chaos in the war were then charged retroactively. For old people, "[the payments of] retirements are very small compared with the price of the medication [and] medical examinations." Those who receive social security payments say that these have been reduced after the war in comparison with the increases in prices: the change of regime and monetary unit has reduced individual incomes.

In this context, people rely on the black market to provide additional sources of income. The black market flourished during the war and interviewees argued that some individuals took advantage of the chaotic situation to become millionaires. Nowadays black market activities supplement the income of unemployed people, and a commonly expressed thought is, "You have to cheat to manage." These activities include selling secondhand clothes from charity organizations; charcoal trading; timber extraction from coppices; sale of home garden products; and poaching. Residents attempt to avoid activities that they consider undignified, such as digging through garbage or going to the "soup kitchen." Yet, many residents explained that they have actually survived thanks to the aid sent by other members of their family living in foreign countries. While some people talked about emigration as the only possibility for the future of the community, more pessimistic interviewees asserted that they knew from their family that the situation in other countries was not much better than that in Bosnia.

There is a constant worry about infrastructure. People complain about the lack of "everything." Overall, the view is that services are available, but they are not affordable. Moreover, the state of the infrastructure is in general poor. The communities are widely spread and fragmented and subsidence problems limit their distribution as well as leave some of the communities isolated. Up to 2009, there were frequent cuts in the electricity and water supplies. Access to services has become more difficult, and interviewees now complain about their difficulties visiting the local doctor based in a clinic a few kilometers away. The garbage collection system is quite poor and too expensive, as a result garbage is dumped everywhere. Even people living close to the disposal sites throw their garbage on them and some claim they have seen trucks illegally bringing garbage from other places.

The sewage system is also very poor, particularly for houses which are considered illegal because they were built or remodeled during the 1990s and did not follow existing legislation. Individuals have solved this issue by putting in place their own septic tanks. These tanks, however, are poorly maintained and frequently overflowed with water, which causes conflicts among the community. For instance, in Dreznik, locals were worried about the consumption from a local well because of its proximity to a septic tank. The presence of community wastewaters interacts with the discharges from the industry, which result in a common perception that "there is wastewater everywhere." Overall, pollution adds to a catalogue of life challenges that emerged after the war, but that have only increased in the decade following it.

Market capitalism has led to a massive shift in understanding how to manage the local economy, which has not been easily translated into the experiences of citizens, particularly those citizens who have found themselves unemployed and with little prospects for joining the new labor market. The war brought about a lost decade, during which there was little renovation of mostly outdated infrastructure and industries fled the area. Lack of employment and lack of infrastructure have been met by a profound shift of cultural, administrative, and political institutions, and local residents continuously face demands to adapt. Such adaptations are developed in everyday strategies, which try to scrap a livelihood out of the landscape transformations. One such strategy has been cultivating the coal ash disposal sites.

APPROPRIATING THE POLLUTION LANDSCAPE THROUGH WASTELAND CULTIVATION

There are different ways in which local residents have appropriated the pollution landscape through their dwelling practices. Perhaps the most salient is the initiative of local residents to cultivate the sites. Local people from Šićki Brod recall as a victory forcing the power plant to cover the disposal site [Plane] in 1987/88 to protect them from the dust. Following this, in

1991 Drežnik was also covered. Once the disposal sites were covered with soil, some local residents looked at them as a new resource:

> Ramiz:[1] Right before the war we asked about . . . that space down there. And we addressed the director of the power plant through our local community with the request . . . to give us some areas to use for cultivation during the war. And the director's decision at the time was to mark out plots of about 800 to 1,000 square meters.

Actual attempts to cultivate the sites emerged during the war, when hardship and the increased population (due to the influx of refugees) led to the use of every bit of land to provide for the immediate needs for food in the besieged city. These initial experiments resulted in excellent harvests. Thus, when the war finished, cultivation continued. Land was allocated to those who had claims to the area because their land had been covered by the ashes. Local residents reported that the distribution of land was made within the local communities, giving priority to some groups, such as the power plant workers. During the war (from 1991 to 1995), those farming the disposal sites had to give a part of the produce to the army. Some people explain that they also had to pay the power plant:

> Hamid: Who wanted [to farm], they paid for it . . . the power plant took that money for them. They gave you a parcel . . . to farm it. And it was like that before . . . 5 or 6 years back [before the 2000s], whoever took that still cultivates it now but nobody is paying anymore.

Thus, after the war, those who were already farming continued doing so without any outside control, although most interviewees point out that the actual number of people cultivating the land has dropped, due to doubts about its security and the departure of refugees. By the mid-2000s, a group of local "coal ash farmers" had organized themselves into a producers' association. Some farmed as an additional activity, having small home gardens or small flocks of goats that roamed around on the sites. But others—especially those promoting the farmers' association—sought to increase the scale of the exploitation.

Cultivating the sites is an opportunistic strategy, one that makes the most from the environmental transformation of the coal ashes. After disposal, the sites opened up large extensions of flat land, which, covered with the right type of soil, may be rich in nutrients, depending on the composition of the ash. Moreover, the ashes are able to absorb water, providing a water reservoir for crops during the dry summer season. When asked about the quality of the agricultural produce in the disposal site of Dreznik, a local resident said:

> Alija: Oooooh! It has showed it in the last ten years, it put to envy our famous [fertile] planes, Samberija and Posavina. You just need enough

Figure 6.3　Ploughing of Sites previously Covered with Soil Uncovers Ashes (photograph by author)

> fertilizer following the regulations of experts. . . . And add that it is very easy to cultivate, the ground is light.

Other interviewees, however, highlighted that the results are erratic, "like a lottery." The yield is highly dependent on the weather conditions. One key limiting factor is the distribution of rain: although the ashes retain more water than conventional soils in the area, during the dry season they also absorb more water and thus, if there is not an existing reservoir, the ash soil may need more water than the conventional one in a drought. Indeed, some interviewees explained that they discontinued cultivation in 1998, three years after the end of the war, because of severe droughts in the area. Hence, the newly formed farmers' association is putting emphasis on creating an irrigation system for the sites.

For those unemployed, cultivating the disposal site means having a lifeline occupation, from cultivating vegetables to keeping sheep. The lack of opportunities and the transformation of the economic landscape have led to emphasis on cultivation:

> Miloš: People have their own experiences. A lot of them said that they won't sow anymore, and again, every year, they sow. Because they don't have any other place to do that.

Worries about the safety of these crops are, however, widespread, and have surely had an effect in the decreasing number of people farming in the sites during the last years and the abandonment of some of the allotments which were sowed before. An interviewee in Bukinje says:

> Mirza: Something can be cultivated there. . . . But what grows there, if we're talking about fruit and vegetables, I wouldn't give it to my cattle to eat, let alone human beings.

To make such strategies of landscape appropriation effective, however, requires the adoption of a particular identity and their consequent ability to invoke a particular kind of knowledge, which can be included within the policy process. Presenting oneself as a powerless individual provides the ground for deferring responsibility for action to other actors. Those who cultivate the sites are aware of the risks that cultivating the sites could potentially pose, particularly through the migration of heavy metals and sulphates to the food chain. Take for example the case of Alija, one of the farmers in the site of Dreznik who is promoting cultivation of the sites. When prompted, he explained that he was not concerned about the pollution, but rather, about the lack of expert advice on that pollution:

> *Alija*   Let me tell you I'm not competent and I shouldn't make any claims about it, but we only hope that what we sow hasn't been forbidden by anyone and that's the reason why we think there is no pollution. But do we have anything in writing? We don't. I guarantee you that we don't have anything in writing. . . . We don't have a report about the well. . . . I don't know if even then anyone analyzed the water, that well. However, people talk over coffee, they say: "Yes someone analyzed the water" but they don't know who or when and there is no report; to this very day there have been no reports but we only talk over coffee: "Someone analyzed it." But, is there a report? No.
> *Translator*   So what is your concern about the water?
> *Alija*   We are concerned that there are no results from experts.
> *sample*   [He continues explaining how cultivation could help them to make a living from the disposal sites and concludes:]
> *Alija*   If only the experts would give us regulations!

This excerpt provides an insight into how Alija copes with pollution as a justification for him cultivating the sites and using the water from wells, which could potentially be creating a health hazard within the community. To legitimize his position, he explains that farmers assume the land is safe because no expert has told them that it is not; this is what "they," "ordinary citizens," fear, but they do not have "anything in writing" to prove that the disposal sites actually do pose a risk to the community.

The underlying assumption is that there is no pollution risk if experts do not explicitly confirm it. This excludes the idea of ignorance and reduces pollution to a hazard, which "experts" can identify and put "in writing."

Asked about his concerns about the wells (those that he "talks [about] over coffee"), Alija answers: "We are concerned that there are no results from experts," that is, he is afraid that the fragile institutional structure of Bosnia and Herzegovina is unable to provide him with the "results" that will guarantee the safety of his livelihood practices.

Hence, for Alija's discourse, the problem resides in the lack of formalized knowledge that he can refer to in case he is prompted with questions about the safety of cultivation and drinking water. He presents this as a simple problem of translation of expert knowledge into results and regulations. He does not claim his right to be represented because he is only an "ordinary citizen" whose opinion should not matter in a fact-led policy process. What we find here is a strategy that leaves him powerless to claim any type of relevant knowledge in relation to the sites, despite the fact that he lives only a few meters away from one of the oldest ones. Yet, deferring his right of representation to experts legitimizes his cultivation practices on the disposal sites: it is a strategy to appropriate the landscape that has been transformed by those others who already left.

Residents who are concerned about the need to regenerate the sites argued that the power plant and other institutions should take responsibility for the regeneration of the coal ash disposal sites, and felt that there are not forums to translate their opinions:

> Ismet: My opinion as a citizen cannot influence [the policy process] at all. If they do it [regeneration of the disposal sites] in accordance with the Law on Environmental Protection, then it's maybe irrelevant what they build there. But if they don't do it [in accordance with the law], as they usually don't, then there's no use in [me] claiming anything.

Ismet assumes that the Law of Environmental Protection contains provisions which, without doubt, guarantee their protection against environmental pollution. This is perceived as a problem of law implementation, and how individuals can ignore or overrule it. His opinion "as a citizen" has no value. In this context, this emerges as a powerful argument to advance local demands: Ismet's claim suggests that where there is a proper system in place, the opinions of local citizens are irrelevant, because "the right thing" will be done. In doing so, the argument of some of those who are building claims against polluters is not different from that of those cultivating the sites. The underlying assumption is that rational arguments are sufficient to establish their case, whether this is about site cultivation or regeneration. If only citizens could "know" about how to react to pollution, they argue, then pollution would not be a problem at all:

> Hamid: We have to know and we have to be educated as citizens. So that you know [that] where there are different industries you shouldn't plant plums and apples because we know it will affect them.

All the arguments explained above help to deny the very materiality of the environmental problem and defer responsibility to abstract external actors—experts, regulators. Pollution, they argue, would not be a problem "if only we had regulations" or "if Law directions were followed" or "if we were educated as citizens about how to behave." Having deferred their responsibilities to those with "better knowledge" to represent them, these interviewees suggest that they are only waiting to be told what they have to do. The very conception of the self which is performed in this identity seems to prevent them from taking real action to overcome the problem. In contrast, this does not prevent them from making claims on the grounds of their own vulnerability.

Thus, while cultivating the land represents an innovative strategy to appropriate the landscape through dwelling practices—through everyday actions which contribute to maintaining and developing livelihoods—this also represents an attempt that turns its back on the collective experience and the history of environmental pollution in the area by refusing to acknowledge the local capacity to identify and reflect upon pollution risks. Cultivating this wasteland may come at a high cost for the community, not only because of the potential detrimental impacts on the health of some local residents but, moreover, because the perception of the risks on the sites and the distribution of land titles of a "newly formed" land are both processes that tend to divide the community. These ideas have also been fostered from the plant and by scientists (within an international team in which I participated) that regard cultivation as emerging from the local ingenuity to face a difficult situation. Yet, for all their enthusiasm in wasteland re-cultivation, this team was not able to rule out the possibility of food chain contamination from the disposal sites, for example, from arsenic compounds, sulfates, and heavy metals such as nickel. Land appropriation in a pollution landscape is thus, a contradictory process; one that emerges associated with opportunities for local livelihoods but that does not dispel the possibility of environmental hazards looming in the background.

DWELLING WITH POLLUTION

Land cultivation, as a strategy of landscape appropriation, is, however, practiced by a minority of residents in the communities around the disposal sites. Although there has not been a census since 1991, local residents and officials report that more than 8,000 live in the immediate proximity of the disposal sites (and only a few dozen cultivate them). Thus, despite is visibility and claims to ingenuity, this is still an activity practiced by less than one percent of the affected population.

On the other hand, there is a considerable percentage of the population which is concerned not just with the potential harmful effects of cultivation—which ultimately are considered as staying within the families taking that risk—but on the overall effects that the pollution in the area may be having generally in their lives. Paradoxically, while some residents took the new availability of land as an opportunity, for many others pollution meant putting under risk their small home gardens on which they relied for times of hardship. There was a widespread claim about the ways pollution had taken away some of their crops, especially plums (*šljiva*), a beloved fruit for many Bosnians who make liquor from it. When explaining how pollution affects their lives, residents are able to show the deep expertise that has grown through their experience of the pollution landscape:

> Ramiz: And all those vegetables which got leaves as they grew, those vegetables have slag [from the ashes] on them. So you don't have to be an expert to assess if it's good or not good for the health of the people. It isn't nice to see it, or consume it, and I'm not taking into account now . . . the presence, the toxic presence of those substances in the vegetables that people consumed.

To support their claims, some local activists make constant references to the health of children; the difficulties in dealing with health conditions; the loss of beautiful areas where their identities could be celebrated; or the need for democracy. Even those interviewees who stated the need for expert knowledge demonstrated a sophisticated understanding of the socio-ecological situation. Residents themselves are able to reflect upon why contextual knowledge seems to be vanishing in some of the discourses of landscape appropriation. For instance, a local interviewee justified what he identifies as "lack of knowledge" among the local population:

> Mesa: It's normal that those people sometimes don't listen, or listen and don't understand and so on. But, you cannot say that people don't know. They know a whole lot. However, they don't know how to express it like someone who does it more and who is more active in that part. He [the active individual] knows how to express it, but others can't express it, but they feel the presence of that [the pollution] a lot.

Mesa's argument refers to the lack of ability or practice to express knowledge (in a particular, accepted, way), but this is not equivalent to a lack of knowledge about the environmental issues per se or about the effects those issues have on the environment. For, Mesa observes, there is a difference between gaining knowledge from pollution experiences and articulating it in a way that can be heard and acted upon by other people and institutions. For instance, an interviewee explained her frustration in trying to bring her concerns to her representatives:

> Sofie: I'm a nobody in this. . . . If I [dare to say something], whatever I said, people would laugh at me. That's how it is. I would be laughed at, and the person who I would tell it [her opinion] to, who would be

able to do something about it, would find me hilarious. You know, that's our mentality, because I am not the authority.

Concerned residents have thus organized themselves in different types of supporting organizations to collectively push for certain proposals, such as an environmental NGO (*Eko-zeleni*), a women's organization, a "hunters club," or a cooperative of honey producers. The opinions of these "activists" about what is to be done about environmental pollution within the community varied according to their perceptions of the governance structure. For instance, Muhamed complained about the lack of care of different government institutions for the local community:

> Muhamed: They love us just as Bajro loved his mother,[2] and Bajro killed his mother, that's how much he loved her, [and] that's how much the Prime Minister Hadžipašić loves us, that's how much the Federation loves us, that's how much the Canton, and also the Municipality, love us.

The metaphor works powerfully because of the reification of institutions such as the Municipality, the assignation to institutions of a "nurturing" role, and the description of actions of the municipality with words tainted with emotional meanings (being uncaring, killing somebody). This type of attitude contrasts with other activists' perspectives in the area. For instance, within the same local community, Mahira conferred a completely different identity to the municipality:

> Mahira: We cannot say that the municipality is the one to blame for all this. No, I wouldn't agree with some of our local politicians who want to put all the blame on the municipality. No! We must start from the top legislation, so the laws passed by Bosnia and Herzegovina, the Federation of Bosnia and Herzegovina[3] which controls the companies, which are unfortunately managed by their political people, players, who rarely act upon [publicly agreed-upon] political decisions.

Mahira does not reify the municipality and therefore, does not confer an identity other than the set of identities of the many individuals who "manage it." These individual identities are built upon private interests and can disrupt the policy process. As a consequence, Mahira establishes an alternative relationship with the Municipality and proposes other ways to influence policy decisions:

> Mahira: The other evening, we had a public discussion about electricity, central heating, water supply, and other things. We reached a conclusion which we sent in writing to the Municipality of Tuzla. And then the

Municipality of Tuzla will, according to those public discussions, make decisions. They will make decisions which will then be implemented.

In Tuzla, perceptions of the government institutions have been highly influenced by rapid changes that have occurred as a result of the transition from the regime in former Yugoslavia to the current governance system characterized by a chaotic structure conceived as the only alternative to stop war and genocide. Institutions are tainted by corruption scandals at all levels and confused by the inconsistencies arising from the new regulatory systems coexisting with former Yugoslavia conventions (Vickland and Nieuwenhuijs 2005). Still, within the same context different ideas of institutions are constructed, in which the lack of trust is directed toward either individuals or the institution as a whole. The result is that local people find alternative ways of liaising with their Municipality according to the perception that they have of it.

Recognizing the contextual knowledge that residents hold and the complexity of governing the environment, including a realistic understanding of the capacities of existing institutions, moves residents toward strategies that truly envision a collective future and one which is not necessarily tainted by dystopian visions of further technological appropriation of the pollution landscape. Instead, many activists have been able to make a sober assessment of the actual opportunities that emerge in and around Tuzla, and the ways they can access institutions to bring about better quality of life in a postindustrial economy.

THE MAKING OF ALTERNATIVE FUTURES

Local residents have emphasized that their landscape is not just one which has been technologically transformed, but also one in which, alongside the waste disposal site and the pollution, one can find interesting and original features. Coal extraction has shaped the Tuzla suburbs where production is now concluded. In Šićki Brod, for example, coal extraction has completely refashioned the horizon lines. Today, the old open cast mine has been transformed into a leisure area. The last efforts to extract coal tapped into the water table and the water flowed into the giant crater excavated over decades of coal extraction. This new water body was seen as an attractive feature by local residents, who named it "the prospect" (*Kop*), and it became a new attraction to the area, especially during the summer. The lake Kop is highly valued by local residents, who use it for a multitude of recreational activities, particularly during the summer. Since in 1998, the power plant started to advance plans to construct a new disposal site on that lake, local residents have actively organized action so that the lake has been preserved—so far— as a valuable feature of the local landscape.

The lake in Šićki Brod builds upon similar contradictions, such as the salt lakes in the center of Tuzla, where the old salt mines—excavated over centuries—have now been reinvented as "the Pannonian lakes," the only large salt lakes in a city in Europe.[4] These salt lakes are now an important tourist attraction for the city. The lake Kop does not have such scale, but it is equally important for the prospects of a small suburban community. It represents a recuperation of the mining legacy, which builds upon the postindustrial contradictions of a pollution landscape. Like the Pannonian lakes, for example, the lake Kop is also associated with a subsidence problem that is now threatening the security of a dozen of families whose houses are on the cline overlooking the lake.

Practical attempts to construct opportunities in a pollution landscape are thus crucial in the making of a collective future. Local activists have long associated their demands for a better environment with proposals for the reforestation of the disposal sites, reduction of the prices of electricity, and improvement of the supply and development of a district heating system. As the power plant has established itself as the main electricity producer of the country, its managers now have the opportunity of reflecting upon the power plant's role within the local economy. What some of the power plant managers expressed only in private in 2005—their concerns about how pollution from the plant could be affecting local residents—were expressed in late 2011 as part of the discourse of public utility of the plant, especially promoted by some managers who were trained under the paradigm of self-management in which workers and residents were considered an integral part of the power plant. Adversarial relationships with the municipality, which claimed the need for the power plant to pay an economic compensation to the municipality for the pollution, have clearly softened in the space of only six years. Now the power plant is building the district heating system and local activists' discourses of environmental degradation show themselves more open to negotiation and willing to discuss collective futures.

This does not mean that all the history of environmental pollution can be erased from the landscape, but it points out the importance of a dialogue in which industries recognize the value of local experiences of pollution and act upon those. In my latest interviews with local residents in October 2011, many expressed worries about both their health and their future prospects. There were still claims about the long history of pollution and the chaotic governance structure. And yet, the sense of desperation had somehow ameliorated, even among those who attributed serious illnesses they were suffering to the pollution. Their explanations of how they now lived with pollution celebrated the changes in attitudes and action that started to be visible from within the municipality and the industry. These achievements are, however, not to be attributed to the openness of the power plant or the proactive action of the municipality. In 2005, there was little recognition of the importance of local views on the pollution, other than those who fitted with existing plans to recover the sites for productive use. In 2011, however, local residents had demonstrated that through a combination of dwelling practices and activism they were able to assemble the arguments to point to possible routes for improvement in their communities. Whether their important role in shaping this pollution landscape for a working future is recognized by others is, however, another matter.

ACKNOWLEDGEMENT AND DEDICATION

I was able to spend time thinking through the argument in this paper and writing thanks to an ESRC Future Research Leaders fellowship called "Mapping Urban Energy Landscapes" (Grant number: ES/K001361/1).

For the support they gave me in Tuzla, I wish to thank especially Jasmina Raslan and Gorica Stevanovic. I'd like to dedicate this paper to the young Branka who, with many others, will inherit the city and the responsibility to make it even better.

NOTES

1. All the names are pseudonyms.
2. "*Vole nas ko Bajro mater*" is a popular saying.
3. The country Bosnia and Herzegovina is divided into two entities, "Federation of Bosnia and Herzegovina" and "Srpska Republic." Tuzla belongs to the "Federation of Bosnia and Herzegovina."
4. See http://www.economist.com/blogs/easternapproaches/2012/07/tuzlas-lakes (accessed 8 August 2013).

REFERENCES

Agyeman, Julian. *Sustainable Communities and the Challenge of Environmental Justice*. New York: New York University Press, 2005.

Aronoff, Marilyn, and Valerie Gunter. "Defining Disaster—Local Constructions for Recovery in the Aftermath of Chemical Contamination." *Social Problems* 39 (1992): 345–65.

Burningham, Kate, and Diana Thrush. "Pollution Concerns in Context: A Comparison of Local Perceptions of the Risks Associated with Living Close to a Road and a Chemical Factory." *Journal of Risk Research* 7 (2004): 213–32.

Capek, Stella M. "Environmental Justice, Regulation and the Local Community." *International Journal of Health Services* 22 (1992): 729–46.

Capek, Stella M. "The Environmental Justice Frame—A Conceptual Discussion and an Application." *Social Problems* 40 (1993): 5–24.

Castán Broto, Vanesa. "Exploring the Lay/Expert Divide: The Attribution of Responsibilities for Coal Ash Pollution in Tuzla, Bosnia and Herzegovina." *Local Environment* 17 (2012): 879–95.

Castán Broto, Vanesa. "Employment, Environmental Pollution and Working Class Life in Tuzla, Bosnia and Herzegovina." *Journal of Political Ecology* 20 (2013): 1–13.

Castán Broto, Vanesa, Kate Burningham, Claudia Carter, and Lucia Elghali. "Stigma and Attachment: Performance of Identity in an Environmentally Degraded Place." *Society & Natural Resources* 23 (2010): 952–68.

Castán Broto, Vanesa, Paul Tabbush, Kate Burningham, Lucia Elghali, and David Edwards. "Coal Ash and Risk: Four Social Perspectives in a Pollution Landscape." *Landscape Research* 32 (2007): 481–98.

Edelstein, Michael R. *Contaminated Communities: Coping with Residential Toxic Exposure.* Cambridge: Westview press, 2004.

Ferguson, James. *Expectations of Modernity: Myths and Meanings of Urban Life on the Zambian Copperbelt.* Berkeley: University of California Press, 1999.

Ingold, Tim. "The Temporality of Landscape." In *The Perception of the Environment: Essays in Livelihood, Dwelling and Skill*, edited by Tim Ingold, 189–208. London: Routledge, 2000.

———. "Epilogue: Towards a Politics of Dwelling." *Conservation and Society* 3 (2005): 501–508.

Irwin, Alan. *Citizen Science: A Study of People, Expertise and Sustainable Development.* London: Routledge, 1995.

Macnaghten, Phil, and John Urry. *Contested Natures.* London: Sage, 1998.

McGee, Tara K. "Private Responses and Individual Action: Community Responses to Chronic Environmental Lead Contamination." *Environment and Behavior* 31 (1999): 66–83.

Parkhill, Karen A., Catherine Butler, and Nick F. Pidgeon. "Landscapes of Threat? Exploring Discourses of Stigma around Large Energy Developments." *Landscape Research* 39 no 5 (2014): 566–82.

Parkhill, Karen A., Nick F. Pidgeon, Karen L. Henwood, Peter Simmons, and Dan Venables. "From the Familiar to the Extraordinary: Local Residents' Perceptions of Risk When Living with Nuclear Power in the UK." *Transactions of the Institute of British Geographers* 35 (2010): 39–58.

Smailbegovic, Amer and Rebecca Lindsey. 2009. "Tuzla Valley Coal Mines, Bosnia and Herzegovina." National Aeronautical and Space Agency's Earth Observatory. Accessed April 24, 2015, http://earthobservatory.nasa.gov/IOTD/view.php?id=38337.

Thomas, Julian. "The Politics of Vision and the Archaeologies of Landscape." In *Landscapes: Politics and Perspectives*, edited by Barbara Bender, 19–48. Oxford: Berg Publishers, 1993.

Vickland, Scott and Inez Nieuwenhuijs. "Critical Success Factors for Modernising Public Financial Management Information Systems in Bosnia and Herzegovina." *Public Administration and Development* 25 (2005): 95–103.

7 The Trouble of Connection

E-Waste in China Between State Regulation, Development Regimes, and Global Capitalism[1]

Anna Lora-Wainwright

INTRODUCTION

In June 2013, I made my second visit to several villages in Treasure Town (a pseudonym), a town in South China with a long history of e-waste recycling. Juanjuan, a 19-year-old first-year medical student who grew up in the area, agreed to host me in her family home as she had done on my previous visit in 2012. We slept in a small room built on the corner of her brother's plastic processing workshop. The machinery to melt plastic sat unused, however, surrounded by dozens of large bags of small plastic pieces ready to be sold. In previous years, when business was thriving, he could earn 100 thousand yuan in a month from plastic trading, but business had declined since the economic crisis, the prices were too low, and nobody had been trading in the past few months. Her brother, and many like him, had switched to computerized embroidery to make ends meet.

One evening, Juanjuan and I chatted with her neighbors, Linge and Lindi, two brothers in their early twenties who dismantle CD drives and circuit boards. Juanjuan's cousin (also in his early twenties and trading plastic) marched into the room waving his smartphone and in an urgent tone of voice announced: "Teacher, don't do this research anymore, we're over [they'll close us down]. Look at this report." He proceeded to show us a six-minute video clip aired the previous day on national television (no longer available online) describing the dire environmental health effects of e-waste processing in the region.

I was familiar with the report. It had been aired on national TV (on a different channel) a few days previously, angering many in the city government who accused it of lacking solid scientific evidence.[2] They did not relish the increased pressure by the provincial and central government (which would inevitably follow the report) to crackdown on e-waste trade. The central government had already made several attempts to do so over the past decade, with a limited amount of success. Juanjuan's cousin and her neighbors Lindi and Linge also attacked the report for making overblown claims. "That person must just be allergic to something. I've never heard of this happening," said Linge about the migrant worker who blamed e-waste for scars on his legs. He was confident that the statistic whereby nine out of ten children suffer from lead poisoning can't be true for the whole town. Juanjuan agreed: "It's exaggerated." Her cousin speculated cynically: "Journalists just want to put on a show." But where city officials feared a slur on their reputation, these young men—involved as they are in e-waste trade and processing—saw the report as a direct condemnation of their economic, social, and cultural lives.

Their comments go right to the core of what I will call "the trouble of connection." Firstly, the region is connected to the rest of the world through high-profile media reports which create a poor image for the locality on a global scale and spur largely ineffective efforts on the part of the city and town government to curb e-waste trade and processing. It is because of reports like these, these workers suggested, that their business is going so poorly. A second form of connectedness—to the global market—entailed a different though related type of trouble: vulnerability to market fluctuations, which are an intrinsic part of capitalism. These forms of connection (through media exposure and market flows) underpin the current partial disconnection of local informal (small and unlicensed) recycling from the global e-waste trade. Conversely, good connections (*guanxi* in Chinese) with networks of entrepreneurs and with local officials are instrumental to the success of local recyclers, brokers, and traders.[3]

This chapter starts by situating itself vis-à-vis the concepts of recycling and postindustrialism, the relevant literature on e-waste (globally and in China), the anthropology and geography of waste, political ecology, China's environmental challenges, and the anthropology of disconnection. This is followed by a brief account of research methods and by a substantive discussion of the case study. It charts how the global economic crisis and new e-waste governance regimes designed to tame and disconnect the informal sector (which does most of the recycling work) have affected those working in it, what they think of the transition, and how they cope with it.

POSTINDUSTRIALISM AND CHINA'S ENVIRONMENT: E-WASTE AS HAZARD AND COMMODITY

Postindustrialism may be defined as a period in which industry is no longer at the core of economic life and when the prevalence of manual labor declines. Situated as it is at the intersection between production of goods and provision of services, manufacturing and de-manufacturing, recycling is both industrial and postindustrial. It also troubles the distinction itself in several ways, showing that there is no simple evolutionary progression from industrial to postindustrial but rather an overlapping of both. The postindustrial proliferation of electric and electronic goods since the new information age has produced a vast amount of goods which become obsolete at an incredible speed. Indeed, obsoleteness is encouraged by the production of ever-new models. Recycling then is the result of this abundance of goods, but it is also dictated by a Malthusian sense of resource scarcity, which is both a remnant of industrial history and a postindustrial preoccupation. Waste and product obsolescence have long been part of the capitalist system (see Baran and Sweezy 1966). What is new, rather, is a wider sense that some of these industrial commodities, such as certain metals used in the electronic industry, are now increasingly scarce and have market value when recycled.[4]

Heavily reliant on manual labor in poor conditions and with little use of sophisticated technology (see for instance Ecologist 2010a), e-waste recycling in Treasure Town nevertheless processes raw materials and components for products consumed in postindustrial times. It responds to a call to achieve sustainability, which is typically postindustrial, but its effects are mixed. It is at once a path toward sustainability on a global scale (by re-using resources which would otherwise be wasted) and yet it undermines sustainability at the local scale, by bringing severe environmental degradation upon the localities which host it. Finally, recycling troubles the division between production and consumption which is at the root of the distinction between industrialism and postindustrialism. Recycling essentially re-inserts consumed items previously discarded as waste into the production cycle. Through the labor of (most often informal) workers, components of otherwise defunct TVs, PCs, refrigerators, and other vestiges of modernity are salvaged and resold to become part of "new" commodities. E-waste recycling then—with its reliance on heavy manual labor and its roots in both resource scarcity and speedy technological obsolescence—is part and parcel of (post)industrial capitalism. Similarly, places like Treasure Town embody many of the contradictions and cyclical processes and failures of capitalism.

Several overlapping conceptual frameworks may be adopted to examine waste (for an excellent overview, see Moore 2012). Flows of hazardous waste and the ways in which it is treated offer a prism to understand social relations and values and to raise questions over social justice (see, for instance, Checker 2007, Lerner 2010, Pellow 2007). Waste is often relocated to poorer communities, betraying the uneven power relations which underpin its disposal. Waste recycling has provided a polluting but lucrative source of development in contemporary China. E-waste is the fastest growing form of solid waste (Brigden et al. 2005) and plays an important role in economies of waste conversion. It comprises a range of discarded or waste electrical and electronic equipment (WEEE) such as computers, TVs, VCRs and DVD players, stereos, telephones, and mobile phones as well as white goods such as washing machines or air conditioning units. Recycling of electric and electronic goods requires manual work and is often polluting. Heavy metals leech into the soil and contaminate the air and the water. Several studies have documented the toxic effects of e-waste processing, particularly "roasting" (heating in ovens or over grills) and acid baths used to recover valuable metals from circuit boards (Huo et al. 2007).

These conversions from waste to value intersect with the uneven political economies which made developed countries' waste a resource for those less developed. Industrialized nations export e-waste to developing countries like China, where insufficient environmental regulations, lax compliance, and corruption create "pollution havens" (Alexander and Reno 2012; Minter 2013; cf. Kirby and Lora-Wainwright 2015a).[5] Although China bans imports of electronic waste, this is relatively easily circumvented, especially given the need for raw material and demand for jobs. The UN estimated that "approximately eight million tons of e-waste are smuggled into China every year. For the region, this value could be rounded to ten million tons a year. At a value of around $375 per ton, this market is worth $3.75 billion in East Asia" (Tuoitrenews 2013). Scholarship on e-waste typically maps its flows, chemical qualities and potential harm, management methods, and existing legal and bureaucratic frameworks and policies regulating its trade and disposal (e.g., Hosoda 2007). For these reasons, e-waste trade and processing are often described as examples of environmental injustice (Joines 2012). E-waste is presented as economically useful but hazardous (Tong and Wang 2012).

In some senses, e-waste fits this paradigm well, given the serious harm of heavy metals which leach into the environment through its processing. A political ecology approach (Peet and Watts 1996) might focus on the injustice of such uneven distribution of harm (see Pellow 2007). This approach sheds light on some of the inequalities intrinsic to the success of e-waste recycling in Treasure Town. Indeed, not all who live locally are equally exposed to the environmental harm caused by e-waste de-manufacturing. Workers, many of whom are migrants from other parts of China, are disproportionately affected, as they take on the most dangerous jobs. Conversely, successful bosses and their families often live in nearby towns to avoid the worst effects of pollution. However, political ecology and environmental justice are also partly inadequate for understanding the vicissitudes of e-waste in Treasure Town for several reasons. Firstly, China's rapid development is also generating huge quantities of e-waste, and a recent report estimated that China would see a seven-fold increase in mobile phone waste and four-fold increase in old computer waste by 2020 (Ecologist 2010a). An increasing amount of the waste, therefore, is generated domestically rather than "dumped" on China from elsewhere. Secondly, unlike other types of hazardous waste, e-waste has a strong potential to be recycled, and some of its components are extremely valuable. Too strong an emphasis on the harm of e-waste would therefore obscure its potential benefits and value through conversion. Indeed, as this chapter illustrates, this seemingly irresolvable tension between value and harm is at the very core of how workers and local communities perceive e-waste, and it motivates the mixed reactions by the local government to demands for stricter management and formalization. In light of this, the chapter approaches informal recycling as "scalvaging," a fusion of scavenging and salvaging, to convey the mixed attitude and mixed identity of the materials and goods recycled as both waste and resource (see Kirby and Lora-Wainwright 2015b).

Thirdly, WEEE is not only a technical or ecological problem to be managed, but also deeply rooted in social relations, economic opportunities, and cultural contexts (Gabrys 2011). Simply portraying e-waste as an environmental and health hazard masks its ambivalent condition as both waste and commodity, hazard and opportunity (Lepawsky and Mather 2011). The question of how these and other conceptions of e-waste intersect is an important one for any anthropological study. While social science research in this spirit has been carried out on waste more generally (Alexander and Reno 2012; Kirby 2011; Zimring and Rathje 2012) and particularly on the creation of value (Hawkins and Muecke 2003; Reno 2009), it remains little known how those directly involved with processing and trading e-waste relate to it (for an exception, see Lepawsky and Billah 2010) and to the recent partial disconnection of a previously central, global hub.

Fourthly, representations of victims of industrial pollution as inherently against it fail to grasp the complex ways in which communities attempt to balance concerns with pollution's harm against many other challenges, such as finding work, building a home, and facing healthcare and education costs. This demands a rather different type of political ecology, one attentive to both the effects of national policies and international markets on scalvaging practices but also to the complex undertones of current responses to a changing global and national e-waste scene. This is akin to "micropolitical ecology," which examines how "political, economic, and social interactions influence grassroots visions of industrial development and actions to address it" (Horowitz 2012: 23). This approach encourages researchers "to dissect simplistic, essentialized interpretations of environmental struggles" and to examine local particularities and complexities without romanticizing the grassroots (ibid.: 29).

China's environmental challenges are daunting and by now well known (see Economy 2004, Shapiro 2012, Watts 2010). China has developed legal frameworks (Stern 2013, Van Rooij 2010) and a range of instruments and bureaucracies to deal with pollution (Holdaway 2010, Johnson 2010, Kostka and Mol 2013). Implementation, however, remains a challenge, especially when local environmental protection bureaus (EPBs) lack funding, authority, and independence from other government bureaus, which are more concerned with economic growth (Tilt 2010). Growing scholarship has documented citizens' efforts to tackle pollution (Geall 2013; Liu 2014), though the limits to citizens' agency remain complex and considerable (Lora-Wainwright 2013). Those who depend on polluting firms for their livelihood may be aware of their harm but come to accept it as inevitable, focusing instead on attempting to extract some benefits from it in ways more consonant with the priorities of local industry and local government (Lora-Wainwright et al. 2012). In some cases, local communities' tolerance of pollution may be due to their powerlessness (Auyero and Swistun

2009), but this is not the case for Treasure Town. Here, many who opened family-run e-waste processing businesses have become wealthy, sometimes almost unimaginably so. Their acquiescence to pollution is largely due to the fact that so many in the community are both perpetrators of pollution and its victims. Even workers (including migrants) earn more than they might in other industries or from farming, and therefore tend to minimize the risks involved. This underpins the complex and often conflicting attitudes to e-waste among the local community.

In a seminal analysis of modernity and its decline in Zambia's Copperbelt, James Ferguson (1999) highlights the genealogy and inadequacies of standard narratives of modernity and mobility. He traces the process of disconnection in what had previously been seen as a hopeful, emerging Zambia and the transitory nature of connectedness when previously successful economic models become outmoded. Indeed, the copper wires produced by Zambia literally connected the world, being used in power cables and telephone cables. New technologies of connection, however, are less reliant on copper. This advance in global connectivity then is a cause of Zambia's marginalization; the connection revolution disconnected Zambia (ibid.: 243). Importantly, places like Zambia, which become excluded from modernity, are not outside the global capitalist system by virtue of recent disconnection, decline, and disinvestment, but rather they are "as much a part of the geography of capitalism as the booming zones of enterprise and prosperity" (ibid.: 242). Globalization creates new ways of connecting places but also of bypassing them.

Processes which currently affect Treasure Town are in some ways similar. Elements which had been until recently the basis of Treasure Town's economic success—lax environmental regulation, informal trading networks, and cheap manual labor—have now become stigmatized. But there are also differences. Where in Zambia decline is caused by deindustrialization and disinvestment, in Treasure Town it is not only shifts in the market but also shifting e-waste management regimes, government controls, and national and international investment in formal recycling plants which threaten to disconnect local family-run e-waste recycling workshops from the global flow of e-waste. In addition, such attempts to disconnect informal recycling are by no means effective and result instead in counter-discourses which cast informal recycling in a more favorable light, and in adaptive practices to maintain it. Subsequent sections map the mechanisms, origins, and results of such disconnection, the discursive and policy framings which regulate e-waste trade and processing, and locals' experiences, practices, and competing discourses of livelihood, ecological modernization, and environmental justice.

RESEARCH METHODOLOGY

The sensitive nature of this topic and fieldsite made long-term participant observation unfeasible. The needed permissions to settle in the area would likely never be granted, and given the detrimental effects of foreign media attention on the local economy, locals would at best be unwelcoming toward a foreign resident, at worst openly hostile. My local host and collaborator, Prof. Li Liping (Shantou University), was inimitable in devising alternative strategies to conduct in-depth qualitative research. She introduced me to Juanjuan, a university student whose hometown is close to Treasure Town. Through her exceptional kindness, I was able to stay with her family for brief but extremely intensive visits in September 2012 and June 2013 and meet her relatives and friends who are involved in the e-waste trade and processing. In the course of these visits, I conducted participant observation and ten in-depth interviews. My colleague, Peter Wynn Kirby, and my student, Loretta Lou, also took part in some of the fieldwork. A few families, including Juanjuan's, have become friends and precious key informants who welcomed me into their e-waste workshops and patiently shared their experience with me over several insightful conversations. Language, however, was also an obstacle to full-blown participant observation. Though I speak Mandarin, the local language is radically different, making it impossible to follow conversation among locals which did not involve me directly.

To compensate for these shortfalls and with the help of Prof. Li, I recruited ten students at Shantou University whose hometowns are close to Treasure Town and who speak the local dialect. I trained them in social science research methods over several days, explaining my research focus, discussing the interview outline, and conducting in-depth structured interviews with them so they could learn in practice. After an initial trial period, five of these students carried out forty in-depth interviews in Treasure Town, which they recorded and transcribed in Mandarin in full. As several of the interviewees were familiar with the interviewer, the tone of interviews is usually informal and relaxed, resembling closely the kind of exchange typical of anthropological fieldwork. Given the limited amount of participant observation possible, this seemed the best approximation and the most effective way of obtaining an "insider view" on local experiences. Interviewees included some village-level officials, a family who runs a private quality certification office, managers and workers of small e-waste workshops (including migrant workers), as well as villagers not directly involved with e-waste. Though attempts were made to interview evenly across the gender line, men tended to be more outspoken and willing to be interviewed, therefore women are underrepresented in the sample. Manual workers also proved relatively unwilling to be interviewed, due to their long working hours and to fears of repercussions should their employers come to know they had spoken about the often poor working conditions. Dr. Luo Yajuan assisted me in analyzing interview transcripts and locating relevant media reports, policy documents, and official statements, which provided an invaluable counterpart to interviews and fieldwork.

TREASURE TOWN'S DEVELOPMENT REGIMES, SHIFTING POLICY CONTEXTS, AND GLOBAL CAPITALISM

Treasure Town has a population of roughly 150,000 people, over 100,000 of them migrant workers from the surrounding area as well as other parts of China. More than eighty percent of local families are involved in e-waste businesses. Although reliable statistical data on e-waste imports is virtually non-existent in China due to their murky legal status (Tong and Wang 2012), there are over 5,000 family workshops processing more than 20 million tons of e-waste per year (Chi et al. 2011). Treasure Town's development as a center for disassembly is due to its history and geography. Due to its lowland morphology, the area is prone to flooding, making agriculture an unreliable source of livelihood. The presence of convenient trade routes and a historical experience with trade allowed the development of waste recycling since the 1950s, and after economic reforms this became a vital source of development (Zhang 2009: 982; interviews with local residents, 2013). As growing amounts of e-waste were produced by developing countries and exported to China, locals began to specialize in e-waste processing. Treasure Town developed a global reputation as a center for e-waste dismantling. This attracted migrant workers, who in turn provided the cheap labor force needed to fuel the industry's success.

This is a common pattern in much of South and coastal China, particularly Guangdong province, which since China's economic reforms in the 1980s has become a magnet for young men and women from poorer rural regions in search of work. In global manufacturing hubs like Shenzhen, large factories sit alongside smaller family businesses run by local entrepreneurs who capitalize on their kinship networks. The economy of the region, which forms the foundations of China's economic miracle, thrives by exploiting a vast underclass of migrants as wage laborers who have little job security, are regarded as uncivilized and backward outsiders, and are quickly dismissed when business is slow (Lee 2007; Pun 2005).

In response to the influx of e-waste from abroad, China joined the Basel Convention on the Control of Transboundary Movements of Hazardous Wastes and their Disposal in 1990 and endorsed its amendment in relation to e-waste in 1995. In the same year, the State Environmental Protection Agency (now the Ministry of Environmental Protection) selected 460 enterprises and certified them as importers and processors, raising their number to 509 in 2002 (Tong and Wang 2012). However, increasingly strict controls failed to curb smuggling: e-waste recycling provided the large share of tax revenue to Treasure Town's government and many locals benefited directly from this lucrative trade, though benefits were unevenly spread and concentrated in the hands of powerful local families. Business and entrepreneurial networks articulated via connections or *guanxi*—particularly with local government officials but also with traders, brokers, and suppliers of material—made it possible for the best connected families to maintain their businesses despite economic slowdown and regulatory crackdowns. These conditions gradually turned Treasure Town into the largest e-waste disassembly site in China (Zhang 2009: 982).

As business continued to thrive, the first disturbing images of Treasure Town's e-waste processing emerged on the international media and in 2002, the Basel Action Network (BAN) published a report titled "exporting harm," exposing the issue of exporting hazardous waste from developed to developing countries and focusing on the Treasure Town region (BAN 2002). China responded by tightening import rules and issuing a national strategy of Circular Economy (endorsed again in the most recent Five Year Plan, 2011–15) based on the principle that goods and materials should circulate in closed loops, ensuring efficient reuse (Zhang 2009: 983). It also organized a joint commission to develop regulation on e-waste management based on the principle of Extended Producer Responsibility (EPR), therefore placing the burden of responsibility for recycling onto producers (Tong and Yan 2013). The implementation of these plans and regulations over the next decade, however, was uneven to say the least (ibid., Tong and Wang 2012).

While policies and regulations failed to bring e-waste trade and processing under control, the global economic crisis of 2008 delivered a severe blow to local businesses. All interviewees without exception talked of the negative effects of the crisis. Those trading raw materials were hit most harshly. As capacitor recycler Guo explained, "in 2008 the price of copper declined by sixty percent, goods which were worth 1 million yuan became worth 300 thousand overnight, so they didn't want to sell. If they did, their savings decreased, so those who couldn't resist went bankrupt" (interview, June 2013). Linge also remarked, however, that the entire business is a chain, so if raw material traders are unwilling to trade their goods, other recyclers (like him) are also affected. China's government reacted to the economic crisis with efforts to boost domestic consumption. Ten percent subsidies were offered for exchanging old electronic goods for new ones (old-for-new Home Appliances Replacement Scheme, HARS, *yijiu huanxin*) through certified companies. This diverted a considerable amount of WEEE from informal to formal recyclers and effectively caused a short-term spike in recycling. But when the scheme expired at the end of 2011, recycling businesses faced a shortage of goods (Tong and Yan 2013). Renewed efforts to curb e-waste trade and processing in Treasure Town in 2012 and 2013 deepened the effects of the crisis. The MEP banned metal washing and severely polluting plastic waste and emphasized the need to close or move polluting industries, upgrade recycling facilities, and stop the flow of illegal waste (MEP 2012: 32; People's Daily Online 2012). Guangdong province responded by issuing further demands to the municipal level to reform e-waste dismantling and establish a circular economy park in Treasure Town (China Environment Net 2012; Shantou City Environmental Protection Bureau Net 2013).

The gradual and uneven disconnection of Treasure Town from the e-waste trade has had several overlapping outcomes. First, for those worst affected, the economic crisis and government crackdowns resulted in (some-times) temporary economic collapse. This was particularly the case for those who traded raw materials, engaged in activities which were at the center of crackdowns (like acid baths), those who rented business premises, and those who were heavily indebted. Second, the disconnection of informal WEEE trading and processing was intended to lay the ground for a reconnection to circuits of e-waste via large-scale, formalized recycling plants, which are easier to control and manage and where (the government argued) pollution could be avoided or at least decreased. In other parts of China, such as in Ziya, near Tianjin, "circular economy" parks have already been established, but Treasure Town has proved stubbornly resistant to them.

This partial failure to disconnect and regulate Treasure Town underpins the third outcome: the persistence of the population's livelihood through informal e-waste recycling with the overt or covert cooperation of the local government, particularly for the less polluting parts of e-waste processing, such as dismantling goods into end-products and cutting plastic. This is in large part a result of powerful kinship ties and *guanxi* networks among some businesses and the collusion between businesses and local government offi-cials. Divergent interests and incentives by central state authorities (which promote environmental protection) and local governments (which prioritize economic growth), produce a fertile middle ground for informal recycling to continue. Local entrepreneurs exploit the sporadic implementation of envi-ronmental protection mandates, which is the key to their economic success. This relative lawlessness with regard to environmental protection goes hand in hand with the very lax to non-existent implementation of the one-child family planning policy (which applied in rural China until recently). Many of the families interviewed had five or six children, some as many as eight, as they perceive a large family to be a symbol of status. With this in mind, local families invest much of their earnings to build five- or six-story homes on their ancestral land, even when, wary of pollution, they only live there inter-mittently if at all. These lavish homes are seen as "face projects" (*mianzi gongcheng*): an exercise in making the family's economic success conspicu-ous.[6] Together, these elements (the local government's willingness to turn a blind eye and pride in family size and success) support the resilience of informal recycling.

Fourth, the most polluting (and therefore sensitive) parts of e-waste pro-cessing have been decentered to neighboring towns, which benefit from the same trade routes, social networks, and economic incentives for local govern-ments to turn a blind eye. There, residents and local governments who wit-nessed the wealth accumulated in Treasure Town are keen to join in the trade and processing and without the pressure attached to being a long-standing hotspot. As several research participants commented, metal washing has moved to nearby towns, into the hills. In this way, well-established and wealthy families from Treasure Town have also been able to relocate the most polluting steps in e-waste processing to neighboring towns without actually losing business. These last two outcomes are examples of great local resilience and adaptation to a new regulatory environment and new e-waste management regimes. They testify to the importance of strong kinship networks and powerful alliances with members of the local government. The following section will examine how locals explain, justify, and maintain such resilience, and why they reject formalization.

DISCONNECTION AND LOCAL RESILIENCE

Locals present a range of alternative discourses around the current transition and the condemnation of their activities as backward and polluting. First, many pointed out during informal conversations and interviews that Treasure Town used to be relatively poor, and it was indeed poverty and poor farming conditions which drew locals to recycling.

> The government has the biggest responsibility for the environment, because when we first started, not a single person in the older generation knew that plastic would pollute, you cannot blame them. People did it to survive. If you had told them from the start how big the impact on the environment was they would not have dared to do it and the problems we have now would not exist. Now everyone is doing this business, all of a sudden you tell them to stop, it's impossible. . . . The biggest responsibility is on the economy, for the sake of development we sacrificed the environment, and what's more we don't have skills, we can only work at the low-end. (Li, man in his twenties operating a plastic processing workshop, 2013)

Li puts the blame on the government and on economic pressures rather than on locals, portraying scalvaging of e-waste as a necessity, driven by their lack of other skills which would have enabled them to do less polluting work. He highlights that the government did nothing to stop them until a time when they were already dependent on e-waste for their livelihood, and by then it was too late. For similar reasons, Juanjuan's father (who had engaged in plastic processing but recently stopped because of low profits) was skeptical of any government plans to clean up recycling, "because the market will choose cheaper goods, and those who do it with low technology hiding away and not joining the centralized government-run plants will offer cheaper products." The informal sector, by definition, is refusing to be disconnected; it pushes the boundaries of attempts to innovate by finding different ways or places in which to survive. In this portrayal, the informal sector is responding to economic incentives, but it is those incentives, rather than scalvagers, which should be blamed for pollution. In this way, locals at least partially subvert accusations that they only care to be rich and frame their original activities as efforts at ensuring subsistence.

Further moral (and economic) justification for scalvaging is drawn from China's history under reform. The architect of China's economic reforms, Deng Xiaoping, famously encouraged some to "get rich first," moving away from egalitarian communism and encouraging small private enterprises. As Juanjuan's father commented, "Aren't people here doing just that?" Indeed, family-run recycling businesses fit very well with China's early reform development regime, which promoted rural industrialization and township and village enterprises (TVEs). TVEs are widely regarded as a crucial engine of China's development under reform (Oi 1996). In coastal areas with good trade routes, waste processing became a source of development and the Chinese government allowed it largely through non-intervention. Migrants further fuelled the success of these enterprises, by providing a steady flow of cheap laborers (Lee 2007; Pun 2005).

A third alternative discourse opposes the definition of informal recycling as the main problem (as is the case in current regulations) and reframes it instead as a way to minimize waste. Linge, who recycles circuit boards, defended his line of work: "if you don't process these circuit boards it's wasteful (*langfei*), if you didn't recycle you would lose so much money every year." Similarly, he argued, locals dug up plastic and circuit boards previously buried or thrown in the river to extract additional material they now knew to be valuable, such as Pd (palladium). Some apparently became rich after buying land for real estate development and discovering buried discarded boards. In this way, locals present their activities as aimed at earning a living, but also rescuing value from goods and materials which would otherwise be wasted. In the same vein, they are keen to highlight that their work is not the only source of pollution. Lindi, for instance, stressed that diapers, which have recently become ubiquitous, create serious pollution in their village, as they are dumped by the road and dragged around by dogs. Nearby towns, particularly those specializing in textile production and dyeing, also pollute the local river. By highlighting other sources of pollution, locals refused to be cast as the only culprit.

Fourth, where the state's discourse of ecological modernization promotes technological advances and large plants, locals voiced skepticism about the effectiveness of green technology required by the government and the supposedly cleaner nature of larger plants. Two recent government requirements were building higher chimneys for ovens and installing eco-ovens and tail gas treatments. But as one recycler put it: "seventy to one hundred percent of people don't want to install the filter . . . it is not effective, using it is even worse than being without it, the processing speed cannot keep up with the speed of burning, so the filter does not release waste gas, it pushes it down. The equipment is not good enough" (interviews 2013). Similarly, Linge suggested the filter was actually harmful to those using it: "if you don't install it, you'll smoke people on the road; if you do, you'll smoke yourself [the smoke will come out into the processing room]." Locals also opposed the local government's monopoly on selling eco-ovens and filters.

Linge explained: "if you haven't gone through the government to buy and install the eco-oven, they will fine you for not having the right equipment, even if you install the exact same one." This had happened to his previous boss, who paid sixteen thousand yuan to replace an identical eco-oven that had only cost three thousand yuan. The fact that the government would charge so much more than the market price and fine those who had installed the exact same machine without buying it from the government was taken as clear evidence that the local government wanted to make money, not to clean up. Locals voiced similar objections to large formal recycling plants. Their experience with large plants locally (both e-waste processing plants but also other industries) suggested that they are not necessarily cleaner. Juanjuan's father pointed out: "large plants secretly emit polluted air and water (*toupai*) too. It's very easy: if you pay, you can pollute."

This phenomenon is symptomatic of the gap between local and central government I mentioned above. In turn, locals question whether the local government itself actually wanted to decrease pollution. When I asked capacitor recycler, Guo, how he thought the government could balance a focus on economic development with environmental protection, he replied "local officials most of all think of themselves." Lindi offered a very clear account of what he saw as the rationale behind the town's Environmental Protection Bureau's work: "EPB officials say they want you to stop, they imprison people and fine them, but actually they hope you can keep polluting so they'll keep earning money from fines. They won't report you, they'll charge you a 'protection fee' (*baohu fei*), and put the money in their own pocket. . . . They will say 'next time don't do it' but actually they hope you continue so they can get more money" (interview 2013).

The same skepticism was targeted at the local government's clean up initiatives. Immediately after the latest damning report was aired on CCTV in June 2013, I noticed a digger extracting sludge from the local stream (which had long since turned black and stagnant) for several days. Juanjuan's father interpreted it as a "face project"—making visible but superficial efforts to tackle pollution with the aim of cleaning up the locality's reputation rather than pollution itself. He added that this was common practice. "When higher government officials come to inspect, the local government clean up the roadside, they make it pretty (*piaopiaoliangliang*), they plant some flowers, they only show them the clean parts. But nothing changes, it's all a con (*pian ren de*)." Similarly, he alleged that plans for circular economy parks are only excuses for the local government to earn money from land sales, and that they would not enforce any environmental protection regulations. When I showed him a pamphlet from the Ziya circular economy park, near Tianjin, he sniggered and shook his head, laughing bitterly at the language: "they said the same things here, I can't stand it (*kanbuguan*), it is not going to happen." His reaction to a pamphlet about a recycling plant in Japan I had visited the previous month was markedly different. "I believe it could work there." His jarring reactions to similar projects in China and in Japan highlight that he is not opposed in principle to circular economy parks, but rather believes that local government (and local people) would be unwilling or unable to make them succeed.

In these statements, locals' chronic lack of trust in the local government is transparent. Here, the usual narrative, which blames locals for only wanting money, is directed at the local government. The skepticism over the local government's motives underlies locals' refusal to comply with regulations. Conversely, those who are engaged with e-waste trade and processing rely on such blurred boundaries between legality and illegality and on the complicity of local officials to sustain their businesses.[7] Such complicity is not incidental but rather rooted in the development model promoted since China's economic reforms. Fiscal decentralization since the early 1990s allowed a great deal of local discretion in capitalist development to local (county and township) governments. The gap between regulations mandated by the central state and the capacity and willingness of local government to implement them is a well-known feature of contemporary China (see, for instance, Kostka and Mol 2013). Local entrepreneurs exploit and fuel this gap. This has often resulted in collusion between powerful entrepreneurs and the local government, which turns a blind eye to environmental abuses in exchange for tax revenue, fines, or even bribes. This phenomenon has attracted central state condemnation (through state media reports and inspections by representatives of the higher levels of government) on the one hand, and nurtured attempts by local governments and entrepreneurs to subvert or circumvent regulations on the other. The critical discourse by local capitalists toward the local government is by no means unitary and impinges on their relative position within these relationships. Those like Linge, Lindi, Guo, and Juanjuan's father, who do not benefit substantially from such arrangements and to the contrary suffer environmental consequences, are fiercely critical of these practices.

CONCLUDING THOUGHTS

For China's central government, Treasure Town's success is based on an earlier economic model, which is out of step with the current calls for "ecological civilization," "circular economy," and "scientific development." UNEP likewise stated that e-waste cannot be left "to the vagaries of the informal sector" and that large-scale collection and recycling facilities need to be established (Ecologist 2010b). The discourse of formalization construes informal workers as the villain, as part of an outmoded and primitive development regime. Like copperbelt workers in Zambia, Treasure Town's scalvagers, who had previously fitted so well with China's development model, are now made into outcasts; no longer vehicles of development but obstacles to it. This narrative of modernization is, as all modernist narratives are, teleological and evolutionary. From the national standpoint, the transition is straightforward enough. Informal, manual recycling of e-waste should be wiped out in favor of mechanized and formalized processing (Xue et al. 2013; Yang et al. 2008), fitting with the strong international image China is keen to project. Victims of their own success, scalvagers in Treasure Town are doomed by their previous connectedness to become disconnected from this next, inevitable stage of development.

This conveniently linear narrative obscures the essential role scalvagers played—and continue to play—as an important engine of development on the national and global scale, even as the sustainability of their locality is clearly undermined. It displaces responsibility for pollution onto them instead of asking deeper questions about the structural incentives which nurtured this economic model, let alone critiquing the unsustainable pace of consumption and obsolescence of electric and electronic goods. It also fails to propose feasible ways to integrate informal workers into new e-waste management regimes and make use of their significant skills. It proposes that they may join formal parks, but the high fees for permits, rent, and equipment are serious disincentives.

Scalvagers contest these hegemonic representations of informal recycling as outdated and backward. They remain unconvinced that the proposed shift would decrease pollution. Their work is at once industrial (working in poor conditions and involving manual labor), and postindustrial (in so far as the proliferation of WEEE is a postindustrial phenomenon and recycling responds to concerns for sustainability). Recycling itself eludes easy categorization into industrial or postindustrial models of production and consumption. Scalvagers refute easy timelines which would cast their way of life into the dustbin of history, without any chance of being recycled. By paying due attention to their counter-discourses and strategies—as a micropolitical ecology demands—we may understand scalvagers' reactions to the recent changes in all their complexity. At stake is not only their livelihood but much of the social, cultural, and moral infrastructure of their lives. Unless their view of, and relationship with, the local government changes radically (whether this be through further collusion with the local government or by managing to circumvent regulation without the local government's complicity), it seems unlikely that disconnection will ever be complete.

NOTES

1. A generous grant from the John Fell OUP Fund supported data collection. I thank Dr. Peter Wynn Kirby for his collaboration on this project, Prof. Li Liping for her invaluable help in coordinating data collection, and several students (including Loretta Lou) for assisting with interviews. I am grateful for a Victor and William Fung Foundation for funding Dr. Luo Yajuan to assist with data analysis. A Leverhulme Trust Research Fellowship (RF-2012–260), the Philip Leverhulme Prize in Geography, and a writing residency at the Rockefeller Foundation Bellagio Center provided the necessary time to collect

data and write this chapter. Comments from Thomas Johnson, the book editors, and one anonymous reviewer helped greatly to improve it.
2. More systematic and larger-scale research on environmental contaminants and public health in the town had not been possible because the government did not grant permissions to do so.
3. *Guanxi* (connections or relationships) are an important culturally rooted concept and set of practices for cultivating reciprocity (see Osburg 2013; Yang 1994).
4. I am grateful to an anonymous reviewer for highlighting this point.
5. These geographies are also becoming more complex than they may have initially been, as developing countries themselves produce and consume an increasing amount of electric and electronic goods, and South-South trade is becoming more common (Lepawsky 2014, Lepawsky and Billah 2010).
6. This pattern is also typical of this region, see Chan, Madsen and Unger (2009).
7. Corruption among local officials, local protectionism, and the challenges of implementing central state policy at the local level, particularly with regard to environmental protection, are central themes in scholarship on China, which I do not have the space to discuss here. See, for instance, Kostka and Mol (2013).

REFERENCES

Alexander, Catherine and Joshua Reno, eds. *Economies of Recycling: The Global Transformation of Materials, Values and Social Relations.* London: Zed Books, 2012.
Auyero, Javier and Debora Swistun. *Flammable.* Oxford: Oxford University Press, 2009.
BAN. *Exporting Harm: The High-Tech Trashing of Asia.* Seattle: Basel Action Network, 2002.
Baran, Paul and Paul Sweezy. *Monopoly Capital: An Essay on the American Economic and Social Order.* New York: Monthly Review Press, 1966.
Brigden, K., I. Labunska, D. Santillo and M. Allsopp. *Recycling of Electronic Waste in China and India: Workplace & Environmental Contamination.* Amsterdam: Greenpeace International, 2005.
Chan, Anita, Richard Madsen and Jonathan Unger. *Chen Village: Revolution to Globalisation. Third edition.* Berkeley: University of California Press, 2009.
Checker, Melissa. *Polluted Promises: Environmental Racism and the Search for Justice in a Southern Town.* New York: New York University Press, 2005.
Chi, Xinwen, Martin Streicher-Porte, Mark Wang and Markus Reuter. "Informal Electronic Waste Recycling: A Sector Review with Special Focus on China." *Waste Management* 31 no 4 (2011): 731–42.
China Environment Net. "Provincial Party Committee Secretary Comments Twice on the Effects of Multidepartmental Strike Action on Guiyu's E-waste Pollution Staged Clean-up," December 5, 2012. Accessed September 9, 2013, http://www.cenews.com.cn/xwzx/zhxw/ybyw/201212/t20121204_733157.html.
Ecologist. "Low-Cost E-Waste Recycling in China Releasing Catalogue of Pollutants." September 3, 2010a. http://www.theecologist.org/News/news_round_up/582564/lowcost_ewaste_recycling_in_china_releasing_catalogue_of_pollutants.html.
———. "UN Warns India and China Over Growing Problem of E-Waste." February 22, 2010b, http://www.theecologist.org/News/news_round_up/420967/un_warns_india_and_china_over_growing_problem_of_ewaste.html.http://www.theecologist.org/News/news_round_up/420967/un_warns_india_and_china_over_growing_problem_of_ewaste.html.

Economy, Elizabeth. *The River Runs Black: The Environmental Challenge to China's Future.* Ithaca: Cornell University Press, 2004.

Ferguson, James. *Expectations of Modernity. Myths and Meanings of Urban Life on the Zambian Copperbelt.* Berkeley: University of California Press, 1999.

Gabrys, Jennifer. *Digital Rubbish. A Natural History of Electronics.* Ann Arbor: University of Michigan Press, 2011.

Geall, Sam, ed. *China and the Environment: The Green Revolution.* London: Zed Books, 2013.

Hawkings, Gay and Stephen Muecke, eds. *Culture and Waste.* New York: Rowman & Littlefield, 2003.

Holdaway, Jennifer, ed. "Special Issue: Environment and Health in China." *Journal of Contemporary China* 19 no 63 (2010): 1–22.

Horowitz, Leah. "Micropolitical Ecology. Power, Profit, Protest: Grassroots Resistance to Industry in the Global North." *Capitalism, Nature, Socialism* 23, no 3 (2012): 21–34.

Hosoda, Eiji. "International Aspects of Recycling of Electrical and Electronic Equipment." *Journal of Material Cycles and Waste Management* 9 no 2 (2007): 140–50.

Huo, Xia et al. "Elevated Blood Lead Levels of Children in Guiyu, an Electronic Waste Recycling Town in China." *Environmental Health Perspectives* 115 no 7 (2007): 1113–7.

Johnson, Thomas. "Environmentalism and NIMBYism in China: Promoting a Rules-Based Approach to Public Participation." *Environmental Politics* 19 no 3 (2010): 430–48.

Joines, Jennifer. "Globalization of E-waste and the Consequences of Development: A Case Study of China." *Journal of Social Justice* 2 (2012): 1–15.

Kirby, Peter W. *Troubled Natures: Waste, Environment, Japan.* Honolulu: University of Hawai'i Press, 2011.

Kirby, Peter W. and Anna Lora-Wainwright. "Peering Through Loopholes, Tracing Conversions: Remapping the Transborder Trade in Electronic Waste." *Area* 47 no 1 (2015a): 4–6.

Kirby, Peter W. and Anna Lora-Wainwright. "Exporting Harm, Scavenging Value: Transnational Circuits of E-waste between Japan, China and Beyond." *Area* 47 no 1 (2015b): 40–47.

Kostka, Genia and Arthur Mol, eds. "Special Issue on Environmental Politics in China." *Journal of Environmental Policy and Planning* 15 no 1 (2013): 1–139.

Lee, Ching Kwan. *Against the Law: Labor Protests in China's Rustbelt and Sunbelt.* Berkeley: California, 2007.

Lepawsky, Josh. "The Changing Geography of Global Trade in Electronic Discards: Time to Rethink the E-waste Problem." *The Geographical Journal* 180 (2014): 1–13.

Lepawsky, Josh and Charles Mather. "From Beginnings and Endings to Boundaries and Edges: Rethinking Circulation and Exchange through Electronic Waste." *Area* 43 no 3 (2011): 242–49.

Lepawsky, Josh and Mostaem Billah. "Making Chains That (un)make Things: Waste–Value Relations and the Bangladeshi Rubbish Electronics Industry." *Geografiska Annaler: Series B, Human Geography* 93 no 2 (2011): 121–39.

Lerner, Steve. *Sacrifice Zones. The Frontlines of Toxic Chemical Exposure in the United States.* Cambridge, MA: MIT Press, 2010.

Leung, Anna, Zong Wei Cai, and Ming Hung Wong. "Environmental Contamination from Electronic Waste Recycling at Guiyu, Southeast China." *Journal of Material Cycles and Waste Management* 8 no 2 (2006): 21–33.

Liu, Jianqiang, ed. *Chinese Research Perspectives on the Environment. Volume 3. Public Action and Government Accountability.* Leiden: Brill, 2014.

Lora-Wainwright, Anna, ed. "Special Section: Dying for Development: Pollution, Illness and the Limits of Citizens' Agency in China." *The China Quarterly* 214 (2013): 243–393.

Lora-Wainwright, Anna, Yiyun Zhang, Yunmei Wu and Benjamin van Rooij. "Learning to Live with Pollution: How Environmental Protesters Redefine Their Interests in a Chinese Village." *The China Journal* 68 (2012): 106–24.

Ministry of Environmental Protection, China (MEP). 2012. "Bulletin on China's Environmental Conditions." Accessed September 9, 2013, http://www.mep.gov.cn/gkml/hbb/qt/201306/W02013060657829202739.pdf.

Minter, Adam. *Junkyard Planet*. New York: Bloomsbury, 2013.

Moore, Sarah A. "Garbage Matters: Concepts in New Geographies of Waste." *Progress in Human Geography* 36 (2012): 780–99.

Oi, Jean. *Rural China Takes Off. Institutional Foundations of Economic Reform*. Berkeley: University of California Press, 1996.

Osburg, John. *Anxious Wealth: Money and Morality among China's New Rich*. Palo Alto: Stanford University Press, 2013.

Peet, Richard and Michael J. Watts, eds. *Liberation Ecologies: Environment, Development, Social Movements*. London: Routledge, 1996.

Pellow, David. *Resisting Global Toxics: Transnational Movements for Environmental Justice*. Cambridge: MIT Press, 2007.

People's Daily Online. 2013. "2012 Report on The Ministry of Environmental Protection's 3 Large Campaigns on Solid Waste Pollution Prevention." Accessed September 9, 2013, http://env.people.com.cn/n/2013/0107/c74877–20121784–4.html.

Pun, Ngai. *Made in China: Women Factory Workers in a Global Workplace*. Durham: Duke University Press, 2005.

Reno, Joshua. "Your Trash Is Someone's Treasure." *Journal of Material Culture* 14 no 1 (2009): 29–46.

Shantou City Environmental Protection Bureau Net. 2013. "Municipal Environmental Protection Bureau's 8 Big Measures to Implement the Spirit of the Provincial Government Meeting on Guiyu Pollution Clean-up Work." Accessed September 9, 2013, http://www.stepb.gov.cn/zwxx/wshbdt/201305/t20130523_6551.html.

Shapiro, Judith. *China's Environmental Challenges*. Cambridge: Polity Press, 2012.

Stern, Rachel. *Environmental Litigation in China: A Study in Political Ambivalence*. Cambridge: Cambridge University Press, 2013.

Tilt, Brian. *The Struggle for Sustainability in Rural China: Environmental Values and Civil Society*. New York: Columbia University Press, 2010.

Tong, Xin and Jici Wang. "The Shadow of the Global Network: E-waste Flows to China." In *Economies of Recycling: The Global Transformation of Materials, Values and Social Relations*, Edited by Catherine Alexander and Joshua Reno, 98–117. London: Zed Books, 2012.

Tong, Xin and Lin Yan. "From Legal Transplants to Sustainable Transition: Extended Producer Responsibility in Chinese Waste Electrical and Electronic Equipment Management." *Journal of Industrial Ecology* 17 no 2 (2013): 199–212.

Tuoitrenews. "UN Report Reveals Major Criminal Activities in East Asia-Pacific." Accessed August 15, 2013, http://tuoitrenews.vn/society/12236/un-report-reveals-major-criminal-activities-in-east-asiapacifichttp://tuoitrenews.vn/society/12236/un-report-reveals-major-criminal-activities-in-east-asiapacific.

van Rooij, Benjamin. "The People vs. Pollution: Understanding Citizen Action against Pollution in China. *Journal of Contemporary China* 19 no 63 (2010): 55–77.

Watts, Jonathan. *When A Billion Chinese Jump: How China Will Save Mankind—Or Destroy It*. New York: Scribner, 2010.

Xue, Mianqiang Xue, Jia Li, and Zhenming Xu. "Management Strategies on the Industrialization Road of State-of-the-Art Technologies for E-waste Recycling: the Case Study of Electrostatic Separation—A Review." *Waste Management Research* 31 no 2 (2013): 130–40.

Yang, Jianqiang, Bin Lu and Cheng Xu. "WEEE Flow and Mitigating Measures in China." *Waste Management* 28 no 9 (2008): 1589–97.

Yang, Mayfair Mei-Hui. *Gifts, Favours and Banquets: The Art of Social Relations in China*. Ithaca: Cornell University Press, 1994.

Zhang, Liping. "From Guiyu to a Nationwide Policy: E-waste Management in China." *Environmental Politics* 18 no 6 (2009): 981–7.

Zimring, Carl and William Rathje, eds. *Encyclopaedia of Consumption and Waste*. Thousand Oaks: Sage, 2012.

8 A Legacy of Sugar and Slaves
Disconnection and Regionalism in Bahia, Brazil

Allan Charles Dawson

INTRODUCTION

Salvador was colonial Brazil's capital until 1763 and served, until the decline of the cane industry, as the principal point of sale and export for the vast plantations of the region known as the Recôncavo, the area of fertile agricultural land which surrounds the Bay of All Saints from which Bahia takes its name. Salvador, in the late eighteenth and nineteenth century, was a city that displayed all of the splendor of an urban center in its prime—sugar was king and Salvador reaped its profits on the backs of slaves who labored in the fields and mills or *engenhos* of the Recôncavo. But with the declining fortunes of sugar cultivation, a large and increasingly restless slave community, and the relocation of Brazil's capital to Rio de Janeiro, the opulence that was Salvador started to fade. By the end of the nineteenth century, Salvador bore all of the hallmarks of a once great Latin American city in decline. Only recently has the city started to recoup a small portion of its economic might through petroleum, auto manufacture, and tourism. Salvador is starting to thrive again, not to the sound of sugar mills but to the hum of tourism, steel, and oil. But what of the Recôncavo? The small towns that ring the Bay of All Saints are still primarily agricultural, cultivating cacao, bamboo, spices, fruits, and significantly smaller stands of cane. These communities, though still economically oriented toward the city of Salvador, are shades of their former glory—towns where poverty is endemic, levels of literacy and education are low, and where the emerging "miracle" of this BRIC country is largely unfelt.

The state of Bahia takes its name from the large Bay of All Saints or *Bahia de Todos os Santos* that has long been a natural harbor for ocean-going vessels making trans-Atlantic voyages. Historically, many European powers, including the British, French, Spanish, and Portuguese, would use the bay as an important anchorage as they headed southward through the tropics in order to round either the Horn or eastwards, toward the Cape of Good Hope and Asia. In 1510, a Portuguese ship was wrecked on the coast of the southernmost tip of land that juts into the bay and separates its calmer waters from the Atlantic. In 1534, a city was founded at this same point by Francisco Pereira Coutinho, who named it *Vila Velha* or "Old Town." Later, in 1549, the first Portuguese Governor General of Brazil and official representative of the Portuguese Crown renamed the city Salvador or the City of the Savior and established it as Brazil's first capital. Salvador became the first Catholic diocese in Brazil and one of the most important cities in the Americas until the port of Rio de Janeiro eclipsed it and the capital of Brazil was moved southward.

Salvador is the third most populous Brazilian city, after São Paulo and Rio de Janeiro, and the most populous city in northeastern Brazil, and a majority of Brazilians perceive Salvador, indeed the entire state of Bahia, as the Blackest and most "African" region of the country and the northeast as perhaps the poorest and most underdeveloped region of the country. Salvador was the capital of Brazil until 1763 and was one of the most important commercial ports in all of South America. Salvador was—and still is—the main port for the productive capacity of the vast interior of Bahia, the Recôncavo, the zone of fertile agricultural land that surrounds the Bay of All Saints from which Bahia takes its name. Salvador, throughout the eighteenth and well into the nineteenth century, was truly a place of opulence and lavish splendor, and even today in the twenty-first century, the legacy of this epoch of plenty is palpable in the design, architecture, and layout of the city of Salvador—even to the point of the city's division into upper and lower halves. In addition to sugar cane, other crops, such as tobacco—which was used to trade for slaves on the coast of West Africa—coffee, cotton, and cacao were also cultivated. Beyond this region, in the thinly populated and arid *sertão* or semi-desert, extensive cattle ranches developed around the São Francisco river in order to provide meat to the urban metropolis of Salvador.

After the crash of the sugar market at the end of the nineteenth century, the abolition of slavery in 1888, and the proclamation of the Brazilian republic in 1889, Bahia became something of a stagnant economic region in turn-of-the-century Brazil. Salvador, and indeed much of the northeast, fell behind the thriving industrial centers of the southeast and lost increasing numbers of workers to the factories of São Paulo and Rio de Janeiro (Kraay 1998). Today, Bahia and the northeast remains one of the poorest regions of the country, with a population concentrated around the large coastal cities with considerably depopulated communities in the agricultural lands that surround them. Most of the population is now employed in the service sector, working in the petroleum or petrochemical industry, or engaged in the booming tourist trade that seeks to capitalize on the state's legacy of slavery and historic connections with the cultures of the West African Coast. The 2010 Brazilian Institute of Geography and Statistics (IBGE 2010) census estimated that there are about 14 million people living in the state of Bahia with approximately 2.7 million living in the city of Salvador and its surrounding environs and suburbs.

ECOLOGY AND ECONOMY

The Bay of All Saints and the surrounding Recôncavo sit at below 200 meters elevation and are lush, green, and rolling. The topography is one of broken escarpments and hills covered in a variety of green ground cover and forest. In between these hills and *tabuleiros* or plateaus are the numerous rivers that water the fields of this rich and verdant zone of cultivation. By the end of the seventeenth century, most of the tropical coastal forest that lined the bay had been cut down and replaced with agriculture. Current estimates for the size of the region circumscribed by the term Recôncavo are that the region encompasses approximately 1,200,000 hectares. Uncertainty about this number arises from a number of factors, including the growth of industry and residential neighborhoods surrounding Salvador and the expansion of the arid *sertão* regions further inland. Water is key to understanding the ecology of the Recôncavo. The principal rivers are the Paraguaçu, the Sergipe, Açu, and Subae, but these are fed and extended by smaller streams and tributaries that flow across the land. Most sugar plantations were founded along the floodplains of these rivers, in the interstices between the river's estuaries and the overlooking bluffs (Schwartz 1985). This location provided access to water, power for the mill, and transportation out of the countryside across the bay into the city of Salvador.

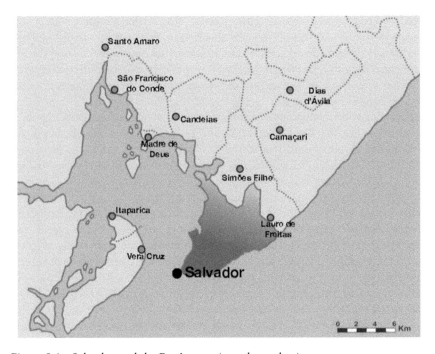

Figure 8.1   Salvador and the Recôncavo (map by author)

Throughout Salvador's history, it has depended upon and has been intimately linked with the lands of the Recôncavo. Most planters or *fazendeiros* maintained homes in Salvador, conducted business and sold their products in the city, and dominated the region's insatiable demand for enslaved Africans to work the fields. However, clear distinctions between city and countryside were maintained. As Schwartz notes in his monumental study, *Sugar Plantations in the Formation of Brazilian Society, 1550–1835*, "Salvador represented urban, cosmopolitan life; the interior was perceptibly different: rustic, removed, but also aristocratic, at least in colonial times. In truth, however, most of the Recôncavo lands were within a day's travel from Salvador" (1985: 78). This separation, though certainly weakened, continues today. Towns such as Santo Amaro, São Felix, and Cachoeira, once a day's travel from Salvador, are now attainable within just a couple of hours by road. Yet this seemingly minor, quick jaunt into the country is made more profound and acute by that same sense that even though the hustle and bustle of twenty-first century Salvador are just "down the road," one has truly entered a more, as Schwartz puts it, rustic and disconnected part of Bahia. To be sure, the trappings of modern Brazil, including Bahia's emphasis on Afro-Brazilian culture and religion as key selling points of the tourist trade, are all present. But it is also clear that this part of the state of Bahia is very much removed and cut off from the industrialized coastal region surrounding Salvador—an irony considering that it was once this very region that fuelled and fed the grandeur that was colonial Salvador.

Now, the succession of different regimes of cultivation and extractive industry and their concomitant requirement for massive amounts of enslaved labor in Brazil and in Bahian Recôncavo in the nineteenth century is well documented (Andrews 2004; Freyre 1956; Furtado 1959). The present chapter then, focuses specifically on the cycles of the sugar industry in Brazil and how the cultivation of the crop impacted the economic and social connections between the countryside of Bahia and the metropolis of Salvador. Moreover, it explores how, after the final decline of sugar cultivation oriented toward the global market in the late nineteenth century, the Recôncavo becomes significantly disconnected from the city of Salvador and, ultimately, from the positive change in fortunes in Salvador in the late twentieth and early twenty-first century. Additionally, this work emphasizes how the same processes that served to sever the economic ties between the Recôncavo and Salvador were also responsible for disconnecting Bahia from the rest of Brazil and relegating the state as a backward and impoverished marginal region.

A LEGACY OF SUGAR AND SLAVES

In order to understand how abolition and the concomitant collapse of the sugar trade in Bahia impacted the dynamic between Salvador and its hinterland environs in the Recôncavo, we must first start with an examination of the configuration of plantation-based sugar cultivation in Bahia in the nineteenth century. By the early 1800s, the state of Bahia accounted for approximately forty percent of all sugar exports from Brazil, and most of this sugar came from the *engenhos* along the coast of the Recôncavo. The history and heritage of Salvador's connection with the Recôncavo is one rooted in the past of slavery and sugar cultivation. This fundamental point should be taken to mean that, regardless of the complicated and multiple layers of interconnectedness that existed between this city and country, the essence of this connection and ultimate disconnection is bound up in labor. For slavery, if it is anything, is a labor discipline (Scott 1994). If production was to continue in the mills and *fazendas* of the Recôncavo, a clear connection with the point of importation for enslaved labor—largely, but not exclusively, the cities of the Bahian littoral—needed to be maintained.

The Recôncavo was a major center of sugar and tobacco production in Brazil and ranked as one of the oldest and most entrenched slaveholding regions in Brazil and throughout the Americas (Barickman 2009, 584). However, the Recôncavo of northeastern Brazil differed from the other cane-cultivating regions of Brazil in a number of important ways. The Recôncavo held onto slavery until the very last days of abolition and depended almost exclusively on slave labor. Slave-owners rarely complimented or augmented their workforce with free labor and this was largely due to the number of in-demand alternative crops—tobacco, cacao, and manioc—that existed for small planters, free peasants, and sharecroppers to cultivate. Consequently, by the middle of the nineteenth century, the fertile region surrounding the Bay of All Saints had a prosperous, rich, and diversified agricultural economy that was oriented toward local demand, toward the grand and opulent city of Salvador, and toward external markets.

Northeastern Brazil was the hemispheric point of origin for many of the innovations and techniques of large-scale cane cultivation in the Americas and, by the mid-nineteenth century, was one of the largest sugar producing regions in the world. However, by the 1870s, the importance of cane in the Brazilian economy was being eclipsed by the southern Brazilian coffee industry and by competition from the Cuban cane and European sugar beet cultivation (Scott 1994: 91). Bahian slaves continued to be held by Recôncavo planters, but their number started to diminish as slaves were sold to the south, fewer slaves were imported from the coast, and significant numbers of slaves started to gain freedom or were transferred to non-cultivating labor (Slenes 1975). Yet despite the decline in sugar prices and the market for cane, many planters refused to part with their slaves, and even in the late 1880s, on the eve of abolition in Brazil, with fears of revolt or marronage still very real in the minds of many *fazendeiros* after the revolt of 1835 (Reis 2003) or the now legendary tales of *quilombos* such as Palmares (Anderson 1996), there were almost 77,000 slaves held in Bahia (Scott 1994: 92).

In addition to a large slave population throughout the northeast, the practice of allowing *moradores* or labor tenants had been entrenched for some time in the Recôncavo (Schwartz 1985). These *moradores* included previously freed slaves, interior communities of mixed descent, and poor, rural white Brazilians. They occupied planter's land and cultivated for themselves in return for the provision of labor to the *engenho*. Slaves freed after abolition continued this practice and started cultivating for their own purposes without permission or leave from the landowner and, importantly, without contributing to the planter's coffers. During this post-emancipation period, in the wake of the collapse of the Empire of Brazil, immigration to the coffee-growing and rapidly industrializing southern states of the country was subsidized, but the formerly productive plantations of the Recôncavo were abandoned by the new government and no support was provided for the supply and organization of labor in this region. Consequently, landowners often turned to hiring thugs or *capangas* in order to press labor into working the cane fields and mills. *Moradores*, slaves, and seasonal labor from the *sertão* could no longer be relied upon and the decline of the Recôncavo brought about by global and regional changes in sugar cultivation continued (Morton 1980).

The movement from a system of widespread dependency on slavery to an emphasis on free labor was sharp and economically profound for the plantations of the Recôncavo—abolition would have a dramatic effect, causing rapid stagnation of the Bahian sugar trade. As Barickman points out, "on the sugar estates of the Recôncavo, abrupt change, not continuity, marked the end of slavery and the immediate aftermath of abolition" (2009: 587). In essence, an available pool of wage laborers and alternatives to slaves were simply not available in the Recôncavo—the planters had simply not relied upon these forms during the heyday of sugar and slaves. Consequently, the transitions and ultimately, the disconnect that weakened the ties between Salvador and its rural cultivating regions around the Bay of All Saints, were not a sudden shift from slavery to available wage labor, but rather, as Scott puts it, a transition "from slavery to hybrid work forms" that included migratory labor, labor tenants, and rural smallholders, "which in turn evolved slowly toward wage labour, with deviations and reversals along the way" (1994: 94; Schwartz 1996). While these changes were taking place, sugar production itself was being transformed. To fight off the turning tide of an industry and a market that was in a slow and inexorable downturn, planters first started reorganizing into large, centralized mills or *engenhos centrais* in the 1870s and 1880s that were subsidized by the Brazilian state—these central operations did not cultivate their own cane but processed the crop of all the planters in an area, large and small, *moradores* included. Farming of cane by smallholders and sharecroppers for processing in the large centralized mills was an important "intermediate" group in Bahia and was referred to as either *fornecedores de cana* [cane furnishers] or the smaller *lavradores de cana* [essentially sharecroppers] (Scott 1994: 94).

This practice, again part of the last gasp of a failing economic model, did not continue much past the 1890s.

Yet why did Bahian planters believe that the wealth and profits brought about by slave-based cane cultivation could continue without interruption when evidence from across the hemisphere indicated not only the declining fortunes of cane production throughout the Americas but also the slow march toward emancipation and freedom that was upending plantation systems that relied entirely on enslaved African labor? Part of the reason for this is that even in the 1870s, Bahian planters in the cane regions of the Recôncavo still held significant numbers of enslaved laborers and depended almost exclusively on this labor and seemed unable to incorporate free laborers into the work forces employed on their estates; instead, they depended "overwhelmingly" on slave labor (Barickman 2009: 632). As Galloway notes, "The Northeast clung tenaciously to slavery . . . given the financial investment which slavery represented for many individuals, its importance in the labour force of the major industry of the region" (1971: 591). Further, Brazilian sugar cultivation at the time of abolition fell significantly behind the innovations and changes seen in other hemispheric sugar economies, thus making the plantations of the Recôncavo unable to compete globally (Leeds 1957).

When abolition arrives in Brazil in May 1888, the labor economy of the Recôncavo finds itself in disarray and the almost complete collapse of the Bahian sugar industry rapidly follows (Graden 2006). Wealthy landowners and planters maintain that they will be forced to turn over their land, without compensation, to those same slaves who once worked it. Barickman cites the statements of one Baron of Moniz Aragão, a slave-owner and planter in the Recôncavo, who described the impact of abolition on the cane-producing town of São Francisco do Conde as "disorganized and in a state of regrettable confusion" and called the demands of newly-freed slaves for access to the land that they once cultivated "nothing less than the communism of property" (2009: 628). He continues to cite Brazilian state officials who depicted the "former opulent centres of sugar production" in the Recôncavo as "reduced to shabbiness" (Barickman 2009: 628).

NINETEENTH AND TWENTIETH-CENTURY DISCONNECTIONS

Despite the precipitous decline of the sugar industry in nineteenth century Bahia, Recôncavo planters continued to precariously cultivate sugar into the 1900s. However, by the turn of the century, other crops had started to supplant the importance of sugar in the Recôncavo. Furthermore, these new crops and their concomitant fortunes helped to maintain Salvador's dwindling splendor for the continuing decades. Increasing consumption of cigars in Europe created new demand for tobacco, and this helped restore tobacco as the principal crop of the Recôncavo (Prado Jr. 1945). Throughout the twentieth century, tobacco proved to be the region's most important crop and has continued to be a renewed source of revenue for Bahia.

Coffee also began to become a more important crop with sugar's decline—though nowhere near as dominant as in the southern states of Minas Gerais, São Paulo, and Paraná where the altitude and more temperate climate provide better growing conditions. However, insufficient numbers of Recôncavo planters transferred their wealth over to coffee after the decline of sugar. Those few who did convert to coffee or tobacco cultivation were able to arrest the decline of the Bahian planter class and Salvador's fortunes for a short period of time. However, by the 1920s, due to increasing temperatures, low productivity, and greater competition from southern Brazil and elsewhere in South America, these remaining landowners either fled Bahia or gave up large-scale cultivation completely (Maia 1991: 196).

Other crops, such as manioc, citrus fruits, and spices began to make up the changing agricultural mix of the Recôncavo, but none of these crops combined were sufficient to bring in the kind of profits and wealth made possible by cane cultivation with enslaved labor. As such, with transformations in the agricultural mix of the Recôncavo, significant changes in the labor market of the region began to occur in the early twentieth century, and this would have a profound impact on the region's economic and social ties with the city of Salvador and with the regional character of the state.

By 1900, the major economic zones of the state of Bahia had been firmly established and these, until very recently, have maintained throughout the past one hundred years. Farthest from the city of Salvador in the arid *sertão*, backcountry ranching and mining made the interior of the Bahian west a frontier zone that was often economically oriented more toward the central and Amazonian regions than it was toward the coastal capital of Salvador. However, an important point of connection between the *sertão* and the Recôncavo can be found in the history of settlement of this frontier zone—one rooted in the marronage of escaped slaves from the plantation. The movement of escaped, freed, and former slaves into the *sertão* is crucial to any exploration of the linkages between this region and the plantation societies of the Bahian Recôncavo. Many slaves along the coast saw the *sertão* as a place of sanctuary and of escape from the brutalities of slavery (Doria 1995 and 1996; French 2006; Lavergne 1980; Price 1999).

Smaller cacao plantations developed along the southern coast of Bahia and also further north, towards the state of Sergipe, where small sugar estates managed to continue well into the twentieth century. But the heart of Bahia continued to be the city of Salvador and the cultivating region of the Recôncavo. Bahian society in the small towns of the Recôncavo was, according to Borges, "informal and simple. Most country households lived apart from their neighbours, with their dogs, their hut and their pig. . . . Their rituals were those of the Catholic holy calendar. . . . There was little or no education in the countryside" (Borges 1992: 19). Moreover, this pattern continued well into the twentieth century. Occasionally, the odd rural family in the Recôncavo might pick up and head out to the *sertão* or to Amazonas, but from the late nineteenth and into early twentieth century, the Recôncavo lost much of its former economic might and there was little change to the sleepy, rural life of the farming communities around the bay.

During this period, the population of the Recôncavo began to slowly drift toward the urbanizing center of Salvador (Castro de Araujo 1999). Whereas in the past, Salvador and its surrounding environs had been the administrative center, home to wealthy Recôncavo planters, and the main port of disembarkation for slaves and export of agricultural produce, Salvador started to become a destination for landless Recôncavo peasants seeking economic opportunities in the city. From a town in 1872 of 130,000, this number would more than double by 1940 as families from the surrounding countryside left cultivation behind for urban existence (Borges 1992: 11). This slow, but inexorable depopulation of the immediate countryside around Salvador turned the once highly productive and lucrative *engenho* towns around the bay from important centers of cultivation and wealth production into increasingly dilapidated and neglected towns with little in the way of industry, infrastructure, or community.

A further disconnection at play in the decline of Bahia's fortunes in the late nineteenth century and into the twentieth century is the dramatic shift that Bahia suffered within the national geometry of power within Brazil. From the mid-nineteenth century through to the decline of the sugar industry and the severing of the potent economic and agricultural relationship between the Recôncavo and Salvador, Bahia also lost national and regional prestige in Brazil. Whereas Salvador and Bahia were once the cradle of Brazilian society and of the contemporary Brazilian state, they now began to represent everything that was seen to be underdeveloped, "backward," and economically stagnant about the northeast. The decline in Bahia's economic fortunes led immediately to a decline in the region's political influence and the ascent of the more powerful southern states of Rio de Janeiro—then the capital of Brazil—and São Paulo. To be sure, much of the social and cultural stigma applied to Bahia by the southern states had much to do with the perceived social "backwardness" of the northeast—or to be less euphemistic about it, the generally accepted belief that Bahia was Blacker and more rooted in the culture of rural, enslaved Africans than the rest of the country. This view of Bahia as uniquely undeveloped—in a Brazil now actively engaged in a nation-building and identity project oriented at forging an industrial power in the tropical, southern hemisphere—was also perpetuated by ideas about the Bahian *sertão* as a lawless and wild place peopled by a "mixture of ignorant folk, *mestiços*, along with the stains of Indians and African slaves" (Calógeras 1930: 3).

An important part of this kind of prejudice toward the once powerful state of Bahia—really, Salvador and its vast estates in the Recôncavo—lay in how the tropical environments were believed to influence the "behaviors" of different societies, especially those of rural and sylvan areas. European scientists in the early twentieth century attempted to apply distorted interpretations of Darwinian models to almost every field of inquiry, including an understanding of societies under colonial rule in the tropics. As such, these "scholars" sought to infantilize peoples living in tropical climes as children suffering from a laziness or "torpor" who were emotionally excitable, in need of the firm hand of "cool-headed" Europeans (Greenfield 1993). Such ideas about the deficiencies of "tropical" peoples were seized by Brazilian elites, such as Calógeras, as an explanation for what they saw as the "backwardness" of the *sertão* and, concomitantly, Bahia.

In response, the remnants of the Bahian elite in Salvador, surrounded by migrant populations from the countryside—many of whom had formerly worked for or had been enslaved by these families—attempted to deny the decline and push back against the derision directed at Bahia. This reaction included the publication of a literary journal entitled *a nova cruzada*. Romo writes, "(The new crusade) acknowledged the state's diminished status but also declared its goal of ensuring that "the title of Athens, the illustrious city of Demosthenes, returns to [the city of] Bahia" (2010: 5). These kinds of comparisons evoked the idea that Salvador, as the original capital of Brazil and still a city of some repute in the Americas, could someday reclaim its former glory and, moreover, that any aspersions cast on its culture or society were more properly directed at the backwards hinterlands of the *sertão* or, at the very least, toward the countryside of the Recôncavo. However, such hopes were dashed in the early twentieth century, as Bahia rapidly became known for symbols associated with Blackness, with enslavement, with Africa and, in terms of the orientation of the rest of Brazil—certainly of southern Brazil, with the past.

Bahia, once the most important area of production in the country, became more associated with folkloric ideas of Brazil's past and, importantly, with its ethnic and racial makeup. By the early 1900s, some in Brazil were referring to Bahia as *a mulata velha*, or, as Romo notes, an "[Old Mammy], reflecting a national conception of Bahia as overwhelmingly non-white and, no less significant, as aging and tradition-bound" (2010: 5). These ideas become entrenched in Freyre's (1933) *casa-grande e senzala*, in Ramos' (1934) writing on the culture and mentality of Afro-Brazilians, in Nina Rodrigues' (1932) ideas about the place of African contributions to Brazilian society, and ultimately in a century of Brazilian literature that continued to eroticize and folklorize the Blackness of Bahia. These authors, through trying to celebrate and engage ideas about the unique aspects of the Brazilian racial experience, served ultimately to depict Bahia as a state frozen in time and removed from the processes of modernization and industrialization that were slowly taking hold in the cities of the south. Salvador was a city to be sure, but it was a city that was too much like its rural, predominantly Black hinterlands, and thus it remained politically and economically on the margins.

Indeed, it is not hyperbole to suggest that the rise and fall of Salvador as one of Brazil's preeminent cities is largely due to its history of slavery, of the wealth created from enslavement, and from the cultural and racial struggles borne of the interface between African, European, and Indigenous cultures in Bahia's plantations and hinterlands. In the colonial era and up until abolition, Salvador defined itself by the profits produced on the backs of slaves in the Recôncavo. Aristocratic *senhores de engenho* managed to stretch this mode of production and all the benefits it provided to the planter class, albeit with considerable difficulty, into the post-abolition world with a diversified approach to the radically altered labor market. However, this rich and lavish existence could not persist and ultimately, Bahia would find itself as a world left behind to the industrialization enjoyed by the cities of southern Brazil.

CONTEMPORARY RECONNECTIONS

Bahia, for much of the twentieth century, lost out to the southern cities and states of Brazil in the race to modernize and industrialize. There is, of course, an irony here. Globally, the modern age, if it was ushered in by any historical or economic force at all, was very much created by the networks of dependency, control, and exploitation forged by slavery and all of the concomitant economic benefits—for the slave-owner—that allowed modern capitalism to flourish. Building upon the work of C. L. R. James (1938) in *The Black Jacobins*, Williams (1961), in the profoundly impactful volume *Capitalism and Slavery*, develops a paradigm shifting model for how African enslavement served to free and develop European capital accumulation and thus helped facilitate European colonial and agricultural expansion into the Americas and the Caribbean. These two volumes have been crucial in pushing forward thinking on the relationship between slavery, capitalism, economic development of American empires, and Atlantic modernity. The plantation, in all its iterations throughout the Americas, was the very fruit of human rationality and at the core of a project to use enterprise as a way to free capital and the human spirit—while at the same time imprisoning and condemning the spirit of millions of other humans. The plantation created modern civilization in the Americas while being the very epitome of brutality and savagery. Bahia, as an extension of the Caribbean birthplace of plantation-generated modernity, was an integral part of the modern Atlantic world.

But this plantation heritage, in terms of industrialization and twentieth-century modernization, did not accrue, in the long term, much benefit to Bahia. To be sure, the region is now rapidly industrializing. Salvador, or more precisely, its suburb of Camaçari, is now one of the major industrial hubs of Brazil, with a petroleum refinery, one of the largest plastics and petrochemical plants in South America, and a major assembly plant of the

Ford Motor Company. But for much of its twentieth century history, Salvador was considered little more than a quaint tourist city typified by the cobblestones of its old quarter and by the historic connections to sugar, slaves, and cultivation in the rich countryside of the Recôncavo. Even today, despite—after more than a hundred years—increased economic and industrial vigor, Salvador is often seen as a metonym for the rustic, rural world of the Recôncavo or as a potent elaborating symbol, not just for a Bahian legacy of plantations and slaves, but of all that is Black, that is African, indeed all that is packaged into the concept of race in Brazil. Many in southern Brazil and throughout the continent see a trip to Bahia as little more than a trip into Brazil's colonial past. This then, is the legacy of the *engenho* and the plantation in Bahia. Plantation agriculture and slavery helped to fuel and empower the expansion of Brazil and ultimately the development of the industrialized southern states, but it was a mode of production that was ultimately untenable much beyond the end of the nineteenth century. Moreover, the legacy of slavery and cultures of Blackness begat by the plantation and celebrated by the contemporary Bahian state that intimately linked the commodity and labor markets of Salvador and the Recôncavo would ultimately prove to be the symbolic shackles that bound, in the identity discourse and narrative of a modernizing Brazilian state, Bahia to the past. The cultural heritage of Bahia's past, typically called patrimony by state agencies and the tourist infrastructure, has been elevated to an essential component of Brazilian racial discourse. That which was once derided by the metropoles of power in the South and by the vestiges of planter society in early twentieth century Bahia—Blackness, Africanity, and the rurality of the Recôncavo: all of them a consequence of slavery—is championed by state agencies and businesses alike seeking to recoup some level of economic success after decades of being shut-out of Brazil's industrial development. Indeed, valorizing a culture that was once seen as backward has not proved sufficient. Now, the Bahian state and the tourist and cultural patrimony infrastructure actively seek to re-Africanize and re-authenticate the legacy of a Black Bahia that is one of the major tent poles of a mythical Brazilian tropical identity by supporting various agents and entrepreneurs of identity as they seek to excavate African purity, religious orthodoxy, and cultural distinctiveness apart from the forms of Blackness and Afro-Brazilian identity found throughout the country. Here, state-based cultural heritage or patrimony agencies, carnival associations, religious congregations, and scholars receive acclaim as they recover the African past from the contamination of syncretism and the oppression of a racist state—often leaving other, less-noted and less-celebrated manifestations of Blackness untouched, unmentioned, neglected, or displaced—both figuratively and physically (Collins 2008; Dawson 2012 and 2014; French, 2006; Parés 2004; Selka 2005).

Now certainly, there are other areas throughout the plantation regions of the Americas that have slipped into folklorized depictions of a bygone era. But the rub here is that Salvador was once the capital of Brazil and one of the most important productive regions in the hemisphere. Few could have anticipated in 1888, certainly not the planters of the Recôncavo aggressively clinging to slavery, that their region and urban home would soon be seen as little more than a charming colonial backwater with little to no political voice in the newly emergent Brazilian Republic. Moreover, tourism that emphasizes and plays up this plantation heritage is now crucial to reintegrating aspects of life in Salvador with the world of the Recôncavo. Towns like Cachoeira, Santo Amaro, and São Felix are now just as important on the itinerary of a visitor seeking to uncover "authentically" African Bahia as visits to religious congregations in Salvador or to the shop-filled streets of Pelourinho, Salvador's historic old quarter. However, the economic impact of the touristic transformation seen in Salvador is largely unfelt in the towns of the Recôncavo. Tourist monies flow briefly into these communities during important Afro-Brazilian religious or musical festivalsm such as the Feast of the Good Death in Cachoeira or at performances of the *Samba de Roda* dance—now proclaimed by UNESCO as a "masterpiece" of oral and intangible heritage. However, beyond these events and cultural attractions, little remains in the Recôncavo of the region's economic clout: education levels are extremely low; poverty and unemployment is endemic throughout much of the countryside; and health issues such as drug addiction continue to be a problem (IBGE 2010). These towns are, beyond the high points of tourist interest, largely depressed rural communities that are very much removed from whatever upticks in fortune Salvador may enjoy due to tourism and recently developed industrial capacity.

Throughout much of the twentieth century, Bahia's elites largely ignored their city and dwelt comfortably in gated high-rises and segregated suburban communities while the mansions abandoned by planters at the turn of the twentieth century continued to fall into disrepair. But, as Collins (2008) writes, in the 1990s, the state of Bahia and the elites of Salvador started to refocus their efforts into renovating these historic buildings. For more than a century, Salvador had been the *mulata velha*, the Black mother of Brazil—but little more. However, with the growing power of cultural movements in Bahia that sought to valorize African heritage and emphasize the important role that Afro-Brazilian cultural traditions had played in making modern Bahia and Brazil, the northeastern tourist industry began taking an interest in marketing Bahia as something more than a place with striking beaches and a tropical climate. The aspects of Bahian society that *a nova cruzada* railed against a century earlier have now become a key component of helping to reinvigorate both Bahia's economy and also to restore the houses of those who once ruled Bahia and its countryside. Pushed forward by state politicians and both national and international cultural heritage agencies (Collins 2008: 279), Salvador has became a site where every last essence of Blackness—religion, music, Yorubacentricity (Capone 2010), contemporary and past connections with Africa (Matory 2005), food (Dawson 2012), dance, carnival, resistance, marronage, and everything in between—in the city is packaged, commodified, and distributed as part of a new moment in the history of global capitalism in Brazil and in the relationship between this city and the countryside that once served as the source of its wealth.

REFERENCES

Anderson, Robert Nelson. "The Quilombo of Palmares: A New Overview of a Maroon State in Seventeenth-Century Brazil." *Journal of Latin American Studies* 28, no 3 (1996): 545–66.

Andrews, George Reid. *Afro-Latin America, 1800–2000*. New York: Oxford University Press, 2004.

Barickman, Bert Jude. "Persistence and Decline: Slave Labour and Sugar Production in the Bahian Recôncavo, 1850–1888." *Journal of Latin American Studies* 28 no 3 (2009): 581–633.

Borges, Dain Edward. *The Family in Bahia, Brazil, 1870–1945*. Stanford: Stanford University Press, 1992.

Calógeras, João Pandiá. 1930. *A Formação Historica do Brasil*. Rio de Janeiro: Pimenta de Mello.

Capone, Stefania. *Searching for Africa in Brazil: Power and Tradition in Candomblé*. Durham: Duke University Press, 2010.

Castro de Araujo, Ubiratan. *Salvador era Assim: Memorias da Cidade*. Salvador: Instituto Geográfico e Histórico da Bahia, 1999.

Collins, John. "But What If I Should Need to Defecate in Your Neighborhood, Madame?: Empire, Redemption, and the Tradition of the Oppressed in a Brazilian World Heritage Site." *Cultural Anthropology* 23 no 2 (2008): 279–328.

Dawson, Allan Charles. "Food and Spirits: Religion, Gender, and Identity in the 'African' Cuisine of Northeast Brazil." *African and Black Diaspora: An International Journal* 5, no 2 (2012): 243–63.

Dawson, Allan Charles. *In Light of Africa: Globalizing Blackness in Northeastern Brazil*. Toronto: University of Toronto Press, 2014.

Doria, Siglia Z. "O Quilombo do Rio Das Rãs." In *Terra De Quilombos*, edited by Eliana O'Dwyer, 3–34. Rio de Janeiro: Associação Brasileira de Antropologia, 1995.

———. "O Processo de Ocupação da Região do Rio Das Rãs." In *Quilombo do Rio Das Rãs: Historias, Tradições, Lutas*, edited by José Jorge Carvalho, 83–114. Salvador: EDUFBA, 1996.

French, Jan Hoffman. "Buried Alive: Imagining Africa in the Brazilian Northeast." *American Ethnologist* 33 no 3 (2006): 340–60.

Freyre, Gilberto. *Casa-grande e senzala: Formação da Família Brasileira Sob o Regime De Economia Patriarchal*. Rio de Janeiro: Maia & Schmidt, 1933.

———. *The Masters and the Slaves: A Study in the Development of Brazilian Civilization*. New York: Alfred A. Knopf, 1956.

Furtado, Celso. *Formação Econômica do Brasil*. Rio de Janeiro: Editôra Fundo de Cultura, 1959.

Galloway, J.H. "The Last Years of Slavery on the Sugar Plantations of Northeastern Brazil." *The Hispanic American Historical Review* 51 no 4 (1971): 586–605.

Graden, Dale T. *From Slavery to Freedom in Brazil: Bahia, 1835–1900*. Albuquerque: University of New Mexico Press, 2006.

Greenfield, Gerald Michael. "Sertão and Sertanejo: An Interpretive Context for Canudos." *Luso-Brazilian Review* 30 no 2 (1993): 35–46.

IBGE. *Censo Demográfico 2010*. Rio de Janeiro: Instituto Brasileiro de Geografia e Estatística—IBGE, 2010.

James, C. L. R. *The Black Jacobins*. London: Secker & Warburg, 1938.

Kraay, Hendrik. "The Politics of Race in Independence-Era Bahia: The Black Militia Officers of Salvador, 1790–1840." In *Afro-Brazilian Culture and Politics: Bahia, 1790s–1990s*, edited by Hendrik Kraay, 30–56. Armonk: M.E. Sharpe, 1998.

Landes, Ruth. *The City of Women*. New York: Macmillan, 1947.

Lavergne, Barbara. "Quilombo Cafundo: Today's Cultural Resistance in Brazil, Struggle against Its Disappearance." *Journal of Black Studies* 11 no 2 (1980): 217–22.

Leeds, Anthony. *Economic Cycles in Brazil: The Persistence of a Total Culture Pattern, Cacao and Other Cases*. Columbia University, Faculty of Political Science, 1957.

Maia, Sylvia M. Dos Reis. "Market Dependency as Subsistence Strategy: The Small Producers in Sapeaçu, Bahia." *Bulletin of Latin American Research* 10 no 2 (1991): 193–219.

Matory, J. Lorand. *Black Atlantic Religion: Tradition, Transnationalism, and Matriarchy in the Afro-Brazilian Candomblé*. Princeton: Princeton University Press, 2005.

Morton, F. W. O. "Growth and Innovation: The Bahian Sugar Industry, 1790–1860." *Canadian Journal of Latin American Studies* 5 no 10 (1980): 37–54.

Nina Rodrigues, Raimundo. *Os Africanos no Brasil*. Bibliotheca pedagogica brasileira. São Paulo: Companhia Editora Nacional, 1932.

Parés, Luis Nicolau. "The 'Nagôization' Process in Bahian Candomblé." In *The Yoruba Diaspora in the Atlantic World*, edited by Toyin Falola and Matt D Childs, 185–208. Bloomington: Indiana University Press, 2004.

Prado Jr., Caio. *Formação do Brasil Contemporâneo*. São Paulo: Editora Brasiliense, 1945.

Price, Richard. "Reinventando a História dos Quilombos: Rasuras e Confabulações." *Afro-Ásia* 23 (1999): 239–65.

Ramos, Arthur. *O Negro Brasileiro: Ethnographia, Religiosa e Psychanalyse*. Rio de Janeiro: Civilização Brasileira, 1934.

Reis, João José. *Rebelião Escrava No Brasil: A Historia do Levante dos Malês em 1835*. São Paulo: Companhia das Letras, 2003.

Romo, Anadelia A. *Brazil's Living Museum Race, Reform, and Tradition in Bahia*. Chapel Hill: University of North Carolina Press, 2010.

Schwartz, Stuart B. *Sugar Plantations in the Formation of Brazilian Society: Bahia, 1550–1835*. Cambridge: Cambridge University Press, 1985.

———. *Slaves, Peasants, and Rebels: Reconsidering Brazilian Slavery*. University of Illinois Press, 1996.

Scott, Rebecca J. "Defining the Boundaries of Freedom in the World of Cane: Cuba, Brazil, and Louisiana after Emancipation." *The American Historical Review* 99 no 1 (1994): 70–102.

Selka, Stephen L. "Ethnoreligious Identity Politics in Bahia, Brazil." *Latin American Perspectives* 32 no 1 (2005): 72–94.

Slenes, Robert W. *The Demography and Economics of Brazilian Slavery, 1850–1888*. Ph.D Dissertation, Stanford University, 1975.

Williams, Eric E. *Capitalism & Slavery*. New York: Russell & Russell, 1961.

9 Abandoned Environments
Producing New Systems of Value Through Urban Exploration

Veronica Davidov

"The oddity of the things and places our society is willing to discard drew me in. The people I have met kept me around. My first illegal trespass was Sand Point Naval Base. I really enjoy the sounds of these places. Most people call it silence, but there is always sounds. Each place has its own strange reality. I mostly explore alone. When I am alone, I mostly go just for the zen time. When other people go too, I am there just to have fun."

"My first experiences with urban exploring were with my father—he used to work at a factory that had closed down, and he got laid off—and when I was thirteen he took me and my brother there, just to look around. All this stuff was left in there—timecards and everything."

"I had a friend who was into photography and he used to go over to Detroit with another one of my friends to drive around and take pictures. Detroit's a little different in that you don't necessarily have to set out to go into buildings; there are plenty of buildings that sit in ruin or wide open. So where they never looked at it as 'going into buildings' or 'exploring;' they just happened upon and inside of some buildings. The other fact is that being Canadian and living across from Detroit; you get this sense of fear and mystery instilled in you about the city. These two facts coupled together; caused me to bother and bother my friends to bring me with them until one cold day I found out about the Fisher and we went there. The next day we went to the Packard; and then it just escalated from there."

"I saw the movie *The Three Faces of Eve* when I was 13 and that sparked my interest in mental health, which led to asylums/mental hospitals. I researched it a bit and found out about the Pontiac State Hospital here in Michigan. Unfortunately, it was demolished before I got a chance to check it out . . . which led to my overall interest in abandoned buildings."

—From interviews with urban explorers affiliated with urbex community Deggi5

INTRODUCTION

Contemporary urban landscapes throughout the world have been dramatically transformed by the ebbs and tides of cultural and economic globalization. Loss of industries, economic reform, new directions in urban planning, and growing and shrinking immigrant diasporas, among other factors, have created both new urban forms and lacunae in the modern cities. And in the wake of these shifts, every urban enclave now has areas not generally considered intentional destinations—areas that may be occasionally visited by development consultants, or happened upon and then hastily exited by a driver who has made a wrong turn. Yet, when no one is looking, small groups of people, who often know each other only by adopted nicknames, intentionally converge in such locations, which are either designated as dangerous or off-limits by their local municipal and state authorities, or are forgotten altogether after decades of decay and disuse, still visible on satellite-generated images, but no longer marked on any mass-produced maps. All of the people present at such gatherings will be dressed in utilitarian and inconspicuous clothing, good for scaling fences, squeezing through small openings, and crawling through waterlogged tunnels. Their backpacks will almost always contain flashlights, gloves, and camera gear, sometimes old maps and asbestos masks, and, occasionally, tool kits including rope ladders and crowbars. They are likely to be of both genders (although the males generally outnumber the females), and they will usually be in their teens, twenties, and thirties, although older explorers are not uncommon. They are likely to run the gamut of socioeconomic classes. They include locals, who usually comprise the first wave of explorers in any "postindustrial" region, often negotiating a different relationship to their local environment than the one constructed in media narratives of "the rust belt" and its down-on-their-luck, abject denizens—the history of the buildings they explore may be entwined with their family history of labor for local industries. These locals are likely to have been affected by the loss of the industry in question. Also among their ranks are affluent professionals, creative or otherwise, who may travel great distances to explore abandonments. An inkling of their diverse motivations is represented in the interview excerpts at the opening of the chapter. One by one they will stealthily vanish into buildings that most would avoid. These people are urban explorers—members of a global urban subculture—who, in one way or another, forge meaningful relationships with the postindustrial detritus left in the path of economic and industrial shifts.

As Hebdige (1979) showed, an analysis of a subculture in context can illuminate the tensions and fractures in the hegemonic constructions of the normative cultural space around it. The existence of a devoted subculture, passionate about *existence* value (or intrinsic value) in urban spaces, challenges and problematizes the limited (and limiting) notion of value tethered to either utilitarian function of these spaces or the institutional discourse of historic preservation frequently grounded in a non-pluralist notion of "heritage." As Schwarzer (1994: 2) writes about the American preservation movement: "[Their campaigns] signify the ongoing struggle on the part of preservationists to combat the abandonment of buildings characteristic of the American transient experience. Using the myth of permanence, they also seek to transcend the social fragmentation resulting from industrialization and the commodification of architecture."

This chapter is grounded in the notion that postindustrial urban space can be conceptualized as a contested site, where various social actors pursue their agendas and enact their identities, and in the process redefine and challenge the normative constructions of heritage and value. I use "postindustrial" as a concept that describes a particular urban landscape that tends to occur after previously central industries close or depart, leaving behind an infrastructure. The "postindustrial" landscapes I describe in this chapter are what Mommaas (2004: 522) calls "decommodified space," such as "former warehouses, monasteries, factories, steel works and coal mines, prisons and hospitals." Where Mommaas describes the urban processes by which such spaces become what he calls "cultural clusters," first occupied by counter-cultural movements of squatters, students, and artists, and then "recom-modified" by being brought back on the real estate market and turned into "apartment buildings ('loft living'), office spaces, halls of events and entertainment and/or places of cultural production and presentation ('cultural incubators')." The activities described in my chapter take place in the same milieus, but either precede the formation of such cultural clusters, or occur in locations that never enter such "re-commodification."

I intend for this chapter to contribute to the growing field of urban ethnography that has engaged with topics related to the subjects and topics I explore in the pages below. Various social studies of urban spaces have taken a "city as a context" approach (Rollwagen: 1980) and concentrated on contemporary processes in "advanced capitalist" or "postindustrial" cities (Bluestone and Harrison 1981; Drucker 1989). A number of scholars and writers address the connections and tensions between urban communities and economic development (Lejano and Wessels 2006), the articulation of neoliberalism in urban space (Brenner and Theodore 2003: 4), urban history as contested territory (Favro 1999), the relationship between historic urban landscapes and public memory (Hayden 1995), and conservation conflicts and negotiations over the meaning of "history" in modern cities (Veitch 1997; White 2006). Steven High's (2003) public history project, concerned with the voices and images of the deindustrialization of North America, is a testament to the importance of urban exploration as a historiographic method. High-profile urban explorers themselves, like Troy Pavia (2003 and 2008) and Julia Solis (2004), have been producing an ever-increasing body of work documenting and representing the different aspects of Urban Exploration (UE). But as urban exploration is a subculture in formation, it remains understudied as an academic subject of inquiry, and it is my intention to contribute to a growing foundation for such studies by theorizing the cultural location and meaning of urban exploration and analyzing some of the categories relevant to understanding it as a social phenomenon.

With that goal in mind, this chapter will attempt to ethnographically engage with "urban exploration" as a praxis of producing alternative knowledge about urban spaces, and redefining the parameters and nature of "value" assigned to these spaces in the changing urban landscape. Frequently abbreviated as "urbex" or "UE," urban exploration is an ethnographically rich subculture, situated in a socioeconomic context characterized by prevailing discursive notions of capitalist market value and use value regarding material infrastructures and cultural distance from objects that have lost such value.[1] The analysis will start by offering an overview of the subculture and the various groups encompassed in the inclusive definition of "urban exploration." Then, in order to place the praxis of this subculture in context, this chapter will focus on the socioeconomic conditions that produce the infrastructure for the subculture's agenda and pursuits. Then the ethnographic focus will shift to the structure of the subculture, with an emphasis on the shared values and the production of meaning and identity.

OVERVIEW

In her work on the tensions within the twentieth-century city, Boyer (1994) identifies three dominant ways of "mapping" a city: city as a work of art, city as panorama, and city as spectacle. In a sense, an actively engaged, praxis-oriented subculture that operates at the intersection of these three discourses has the ability to subvert and challenge the normative categories of value assigned to urban spaces.

Henri Lefebvre's (1991: 73) work on spatial practices invokes Marx in suggesting a methodology for "insights into the structure and the relations of production of all the vanished social formations out of whose ruins and elements [bourgeois society] built itself up, whose partly still unconquered remnants are carried along with it, whose mere nuances have developed explicit significance within it," and builds upon that idea to argue that social space is "itself the outcome of past actions, what permits fresh actions to occur, while suggesting others and prohibiting yet others. . . . Among these actions some serve production, others consumption. Social space implies a great diversity of knowledge."

Lefebvre's notion of the diversity of knowledge in social space is a useful frame for my research in documenting and analyzing the fringes of that social knowledge, formed around (and within) *disused or marginalized* social space, such as urban spaces in transition (i.e., earmarked for demolition or renovation), squats, and abandoned buildings, the appearance of which often signals a significant change or rupture in the socioeconomic trajectory of an urban community. Subcultures such as urban exploration, emerging from and around these spaces, produce themselves by building social networks around an alternative regime of value, which emphasizes non-capitalist forms of exchange and "self-making" involving urban material infrastructure that has lost its use-value. I propose that the members of these subcultures engage with transforming urban landscapes and generate alternative knowledge about/within social spaces, in a sense exemplifying Lefebvre's theory of visionary *representational space* and the ways in which it can subvert normative ideological *representations of space*, which are "tied to the relations of production and to the 'order' which those relations impose" (1991: 33).

Lefebvre's ideas, in conjunction with Castells' (1974) work on collective consumption and the effect of progressive movements on urban spaces, provides a framework for looking at an emergent global subculture centered around alternative forms of historical knowledge and systems of use-value, which can be read as countercultural in their resistance to the normative praxis of value creation and assessment. One can argue, as D'Andrea does, that countercultures amplify global processes (D'Andrea 2005: 139), and in doing so, enable the production of plural subjectivities and counter-subjectivities. I propose that the global identity of an urban explorer is, in a sense, a performative rejection of the socioeconomic determinism conferred on the subjects of global industrial capitalism. The systematic alternatives to a regime of capitalist use-value, the illumination of marginalized and forgotten knowledge, and the community formation around cultural capital that would be considered useless or marginal by mainstream standards in a sense all engage with the current moment of capitalism, and concretize the anxieties stemming from it in American urban locations where industries have failed or have moved overseas, or in the formerly socialist countries where the capitalist trajectory of development made an entire socioeconomic infrastructure obsolete. In such places, the alternative systems of value and knowledge allow urban residents to subvert the dominant narrative of the worthlessness of their demesnes.

Countercultures or subcultures whose praxis is, in some way, a rejection of capitalist relations based around use-value frequently exist in a compelling relationship to urban spaces that have been marginalized or discarded. Spaces that often exist in a liminal state, awaiting either demolition (as they have lost their use-value) or renovation (through which they can be interpolated back into the mainstream socioeconomic structure)—inscribed in a cycle of value creation and destruction described by Weber (2003: 172). Within "cities as socio-spatial arenas in which the contradictions of capitalist development are continually produced and fought out" (Brenner 2000: 362), these spaces can be theorized as the loci for such contradictions and struggles, spaces where alternative economies of value may arise.

"Urban exploration" or UE^2 is a materially embedded subculture, where community formation happens around specific physical locations, even though as a global phenomenon, it is almost entirely facilitated by the internet, where decentralized cyber-communities can be theorized as the kinds of "social and technical infrastructures . . . that [enable] a form of social production of heritage as the locus of our sense of place" (Giaccardi and Palen 2008: 282). The inception of UE in its current form is attributed to Jeff Chapman (2005), also known as "Ninjalicious," who founded the 'zine "Infiltration: the Zine about Going Places you're not Supposed to Go" and authored "Access All Areas: a User's Guide to the Art of Urban Exploration." But its roots go further back, to such groups as the San Francisco Suicide Club, whose members, influenced by surrealism and Dadaism, staged renegade events in abandoned spaces, the Cacophony club, an anarchic creative urban group associated with culture-jamming, Hakim Bey's (1985) philosophy of TAZ and infiltrating places off-limits to the public, and, last but not least, the French situationists, whose notion of psychogeography and *derive* pivoted around interventions into public spaces designed to induce new radical awareness of urban spaces (Debord 1956).

Currently there are different branches and genres of urban exploration, based in different agendas and philosophies, and hybrid subcultures that combine UE with other pursuits. One cyber-community offers a broad, inclusive definition of the term on their website:

> Generally Urban Exploration or "UE" for short is the exploration of any man made structure though usually places that are rarely seen, abandoned or off-limits. Urban Exploration is an umbrella name for many other activities such as Parkour, Urban Spelunking, Draining, Inflitration. UE includes the exploration, documentation and preservation of abandoned buildings (factories, houses, hospitals, asylums, warehouses, missile silos, grain elevators, pretty much anything abandoned), tunnels (drainage tunnels, transit tunnels, mines, steam tunnels) and even active buildings and rooftops. Anything interesting that people don't normally see is a possible target for UE.[3]

As a definition of urban exploration, the offering above is ethnographically useful in that it explicitly references a network of subcultures that converge around pursuits involving abandoned urban spaces utilized and valued in ways that run counter to the conventional allocation of use-value in a late capitalist city. In that, it confirms Pinder's (2005: 388) observation that the term "urban exploration" is necessarily politically charged. As a category it is broad and inclusive, containing activities that range from self-consciously political to practices that discursively prioritize the aesthetic dimension; from parkour and "free running," which use abandoned spaces for training to move through urban spaces with maximum efficiency and speed, to groups like the *Untergunther*, a clandestine French "team" that restores abandoned or decaying heritage objects in secrecy and anonymity; to groups like Dark Passage and The Madagascar Institute in New

York City, which reclaim abandoned spaces for games, art installations, and performances.

All of these subgroups share a non-profit-oriented value system concerned with locations and material remnants that, in the mainstream capitalist value system are negative spaces around the trajectory of economic and industrial progress. An urban explorer or "urbexer" is, first and foremost, someone who finds and goes into abandoned buildings. The motivation for such excursions, and the frameworks within which such excursions are undertaken vary, as discussed above, but in most cases this is an illegal, or semi-legal activity, often fraught with physical risks, and one that is extremely rewarding for the people involved in this subculture.

THE MAKING OF URBAN EXPLORATION

The common denominator in all "hot spots" of urban exploration is a period of economic decline in the general vicinity, most frequently resulting from the failure or departure of the dominant local industry, but sometimes occurring due to industrial or natural disasters and other events that can alter the economic and demographic fate of a town or a region. In the United States, hubs of "urbexing" are areas that belong to the so-called Rust Belt, with the most famous example being Detroit, where in certain parts of the city close to fifty percent of properties are vacant or abandoned (as one Detroit explorer said to me in personal communication, "it's kind of hard *not to* [go into abandoned buildings] around here. They're pretty much a part of life. I'm just glad I don't have to live in them like a lot of people around here"). Another iconic remnant on the Rust Belt map is Gary, Indiana, originally founded as a service sector city by the United States Steel Corporation. The downtown there has turned into a virtual ghost town with the decline of the city's manufacturing base, and currently contains a charred and overgrown Presbyterian Church, a waterlogged Art Deco post office (Figure 9.1), a boarded-up library, the abandoned theater where the Jackson Five originally performed, and a grid of streets where abandoned houses outnumber lived-in homes three to one. Other examples of economically depressed areas becoming "hubs" for urban exploration throughout the United States include New England old mill towns like Lowell, MA, Pennsylvania steel industry towns like Bethlehem and Allentown, former mining towns in the southwest, and former leisure destinations like the so-called "Borscht Belt" resort towns in the Catskills and the declined Bombay Beach resort area of Salton Sea in Southern California.

Internationally, large-scale abandonments exist all over the world, telling stories of industries long gone or never materialized. Hashima Island (commonly known as Gunkanjima, or "Battleship Island"), an uninhabited island in the Nagasaki Prefecture of Japan, served as a facility for mining coal from the bottom of the sea for nearly a century. The Mitsubishi

Figure 9.1   An Abandoned Post Office in Gary, Indiana (photograph by author)

corporation purchased the island in 1890, and subsequently oversaw its industrial development. At its peak of production, due to the built-up high rise apartment complexes, Hashima had the highest population density ever recorded. In 1974, after coal in Japan was replaced by petroleum, Hashima Island mines, along with the other coal mines across Japan, were shut down (Burke-Gaffney 1996). All the infrastructure remained on the island, and has been slowly collapsing in on itself after decades of disuse. Although travel to the island is prohibited, urban explorers regularly find a way, as evidenced by sets of images and photo essays circulating in cyberspace. Kolmanskop, a ghost town in the desert of Southern Namibia, was developed after the discovery of diamonds in the area in 1908, and abandoned in 1956. Built to resemble a German town, Kolmanskop now contains the abandoned remnants of the colonial industry: a hospital, a ballroom, a power station, a theater, residential housing.[4] One of the richest locations for urban exploration is the former USSR territory, where UE subculture has an especially strong presence among the generation that experienced the rupture in history as the Soviet era gave way to post-Soviet economic reform and geographic fragmentation. This area, rich in abandonments, includes entire towns near the Arctic circle that were built to be centers of industrial production and mining manned by prison labor, state-funded factories that did not survive privatization, networks of Young Pioneer summer camps, and "houses of culture." The "holy grail" of urban explorers worldwide is Pripyat, the town that housed the doomed Chernobyl nuclear station reactor 4, the culprit of the 1986 nuclear plant accident, in the aftermath of which over 300,000 people were evacuated and resettled. Several companies organize tours to the area, but many explorers sneak in by themselves and visit areas the tours do not cover, often with a Geiger counter in hand, seeing for themselves the iconic images that make for compelling photo essays—the eerily festive ferris wheel, the teddy bear in the empty kindergarten room, the Soviet-era newspapers, immediately dated by the trifecta of Lenin, Marx, and Engels pictured by the header.

Former post-socialist European cities are rich in such abandoned locations as well, with Berlin[5] particularly standing out as a place of great interest to urban explorers worldwide, although within Berlin's rich history of *autonomen* squatters collectives and *soziokultur* centers located in renovated abandoned buildings, many of these locations acquired a different kind of second life.

LOCATION SPECIALIZATION WITHIN UE

Within the larger subculture of UE, explorers can be rather sectarian with regard to their activities of choice within their available or chosen geographic area. Certain branches of urban exploration focus on specific types of locations, which themselves frequently encode a history of financial decline or mismanagement preceding the physical decay. For example, exploring abandoned state mental asylums is popular with American New England explorers. These locations tell the story of the budget cuts and lack of funding within the mental health system in New England states like Massachusetts, and the subsequent closing of a number of institutions in the early 1990s. The most notable of these institutions are the so-called "Kirkbrides"—mental hospitals designed and built utilizing the philosophy of nineteenth-century doctor Thomas Kirkbride, who advocated an asylum system called "Moral Treatment." His *On the Construction, Organization and General Arrangements of Hospitals for the Insane* (1880) was a treatise on design, construction, and administration of mental hospitals that emphasized the patients' humanity and dignity, and the benefits of access to a natural environment away from urban centers for improving mental health.

Extravagant in design and expensive to manage, most of the "Kirkbrides" in New England are inactive at this point. Several, like Taunton State Hospital in Massachusetts and Hudson River State Hospital in New York, have succumbed to fires, while others are being torn down and redeveloped. Danvers State Hospital in Danvers, Massachusetts, was recently purchased and converted into a residential complex of luxury condominiums by a private real estate developer, Avalon Bay Communities. Dixmont State Hospital in western Pennsylvania was demolished as a part of a plan to build a new Wal-Mart on the former hospital grounds. Northampton State Hospital in Northhampton, Massachusetts, has been partially demolished, and is being partially converted into residences. It is interesting to note that urban explorers both harbor severe animosity toward such development corporations, whom they perceive as "destroying history for profit," and feel ambivalently about the efforts of preservation groups like Richardson Center Corporation of Buffalo, NY, with a mission to rehabilitate another Kirkbride, Buffalo State Hospital. On one hand, the agents of development are antithetical in their agenda and values to urban explorers: they aim to reincarnate these locations into objects possessing renewed capitalist use-value, in the process dispensing with the aspects of these spaces that, to the explorers, are infused with the inalienable existence value conferred by the very processes of history that had unfolded in its walls. On the other hand, conservation groups may succeed in preserving buildings, but in a way that transforms them from contested sites of pluralistic meaning to fixed objects in the discourse of heritage, in a sense sterilizing, if not erasing, those same historical processes. Neither paradigm engages with the broader scope of values that can be attached to these spaces, built around memory and desire; in fact, these "alternative" values are rarely theorized even within academic and policy debates around these issues, with the notable exception of scholars like Tim Edensor (2005: 34), who illuminates such marginalized possibilities of value in the "adventurous play" section of his work on industrial ruins, and Bradley Garrett (2009), who, in his experimental video article for *Geography Compass*, analyzes UE as a lens through which failures of capitalism are brought into focus in an embodied, phenomenological way.

AN ALTERNATIVE ECONOMY OF VALUE

At the core of the subculture lies a special relationship that participants experience with physical spaces and the material infrastructure left behind by the waxes and wanes of a capitalist industrialized economy. Inherently, urban explorers create a system of value around objects that have been excised out of the economy of value. The value is attached to precisely the same factors that devalue these spaces in the mainstream economy: extravagance to the point of inefficiency, loss of use-value, severe decay. This engagement provides an alternative way of relating to economically depressed urban areas: one in which those surroundings hold something beyond a straightforward narrative of economic decline. In subverting this narrative, UE enables heterodox relationships to history in that it promotes engagement with the messy, unauthored, unarranged, unclassified material bricolage of the past, still *in situ*, in a culture where museums and official heritage sites are the legitimate form of consuming the past. Once factories, hospitals, hotels, or apartment complexes are abandoned, they are, in a sense, relegated to the past; they become dated by the very objects frequently strewn around within their abandoned walls—newspapers and journals that are decades old, long-expired bottles of medications, portraits

of then-current presidents, official records from the first half of the twentieth century, former patients' x-ray films, undeveloped rolls of police mug-
shots, et cetera. The contents of these buildings comprise narratives that are
more often than not destined to be marginalized and forgotten, with occasional artifacts becoming iconic fixtures in museum settings—for example,
the 2007 *Lost Cases, Recovered Lives: Suitcases from a State Hospital Attic*
exhibit in New York State Museum, which resulted from a discovery of
some 400 suitcases of former patients at the abandoned Willard Psychi-
atric Center. But while museum-goers were compelled by the curatorial
final product—the carefully arranged possessions of twelve former inmates,
accompanied by life stories of the owners—narratives and photographs of
the suitcases that *had not* been selected for the exhibit, and remained in
the attic of the former insane asylum, have been circulating among urban
explorers. While the existence of the exhibit makes this a particularly illu-
minating instance of UE engaging with the margins of history, such "rogue"
archiving is common pastime for urban explorers. Many of them regularly
spend hours in basement archives and file rooms of old institutions, behold-
ing and photographing material culture that will otherwise literally never
again see the light of day—intake records of patients from a different era in
psychiatry, weekly menus in prisons, arts and crafts produced by troubled
juvenile delinquents, work logs of factory workers and train operators.
They talk about the locations they infiltrate as places "where time stands
still" or "where time has stopped."

In her article "Clockpunk Anthropology and the Ruins of Modernity,"
Shannon Lee Dawdy notes that urbexers sometimes call themselves industrial archaeologists, "apparently unaware of their academic doppelgang-
ers"—and that "the most prominent urban explorers are artists, who pride
themselves on their ability to see what society has overlooked in these
neglected spaces" (2010: 767). Indeed, art (especially photography, as discussed elsewhere in the chapter) can be a powerful motivator and status
activity in the urbex community, but the pride Dawdy mentions is just as
often entangled with a kind of antiquarianism, infused with the spirit of
grassroots, DIY heritage preservation or public history. Frequently, explorers consider it their duty to document these pockets of time, thus creating a
historical record of information that, in a lot of cases, offers a glimpse into
the institutional cultures of the past, yet will never be officially archived.
For many explorers this motivation is especially urgent when the places
in question are slated for destruction—in a sense, they feel compelled to
engage in the aforementioned alternative, "rogue" archiving. Although in
general there are different attitudes regarding removing materials from a
location, with treasure hunters who explore partially to add to their collection of interesting mementos from various places on one end of the spec-
trum and explorers who subscribe to the "take only photographs, leave only
footprints" attitude at the other extreme, once demolition of a location is
imminent (that is, when the demolition date has been set for the near future,

or demolition has actively started), most explorers believe that it is ethical to remove objects that will otherwise be destroyed.

THE UE GAZE: ENGAGING HISTORY THROUGH A LENS

Riegl (1982: 32) wrote: "It is probably fair to say that ruins appear more picturesque the more advanced their state of decay: as decay progresses, age-value becomes less extensive, that is to say, evoked less and less by fewer and fewer remains but is therefore all the more intensive in its impact on the beholder." It is impossible to theorize the UE subculture without analyzing the import of the photographic medium to the UE "gaze." Photography is integral to the project of passionate, but ambivalent, documentation and representation that characterizes urban exploration. The urban explorer infiltrates liminal spaces as an intervention against invisibility and forgetting—yet, due to a complex of potential legal repercussions and a desire to protect these places from the perils of overexposure, needs to cloak the revelation in obfuscation. In such circumstances the camera allows for representation that is revelatory, yet coded. The desolate spaces frequently become visible as art objects[6]—their decay, their history, their uniqueness aestheticized—but the knowledge is also coded. Details are visible but the locations are either anonymized with vaguely allusive titles like "New England jail" or "Asylum X" or "on the outskirts of Moscow," or pseudonymised with names that mean little to the general public but are a part of a shared cultural knowledge among the explorers, like "Hellview Hospital," "Iron Lung Hospital," or "Chateau de Noisy." It could be argued that the production and circulation of this body of photography is a disruptive "tactical activity" (De Certeau 1984) in its potential to resignify the normative constructions of aesthetics, value, and access in urban space. As a genre, such photography is particularly subversive because, in a sense, it is the heir to the modernist tradition of industrial photography, now documenting the decline of the same subject whose boom it popularized by the likes of Margaret Bourke-White and Lewis Wickes Hine, Germaine Krull, and Bernd and Hilla Becher.[7] Depression-era sociologist Hine's engaged and empathetic photography, driven by his desire to "show the things that had to be appreciated" (Rayner 1977: 4), seems to be a direct predecessor to the loving and detailed documentations of the forgotten decaying space. And although the passage of history has rendered ironic Bourke-White's teleological appreciation for the objects of industry she photographed and described as "they all have an unconscious beauty that is dynamic, because they are designed for a purpose . . . [this idea] reflects the modern spirit of the world," (Webster 1930: 66), her sentiment that "there is nothing wasted, nothing superficial" (ibid.) in a way resonates with the ethos of urban exploration. Krull's (1928) "Metal" portfolio prefigures the popularity of abstracted close-up details of abandoned structures popular in UE

Figure 9.2 A Polaroid Found on the Floor of an Abandoned Steam Plant, Depicting the Plant when it was still Operational (photograph by author)

photography today. And Bernd and Hilla Becher's first photo collaboration featuring German industrial architecture, and their subsequent documentation of plants under the threat of closing, prefigures the spirit of salvage photography against forgetting that is palpable in UE photography today. As Bernd stated in an interview, "When you approach the theme of industry and everything that goes with it in this manner, you make discoveries. Anyway, it so happened that these plants were torn down . . . the foundries began closing. Then one mine after another closed. I felt the need—I don't want to say the duty—to document these things" (in Ziegler 2002: 143). This sentiment resonates with urban explorers' motivations for photographing their decidedly unorthodox subjects, having mainly to do with investment in resisting the erasure of history, and with documenting the continuous life—or afterlife—of disused material artifacts of a vanishing socioeconomic reality. In some ways, the diachronic photo narratives that emerge from the cameras of urban explorers, of abandoned factories and old hospitals passing from season to season year after year, bridges the gap between what Edwards (2005: 28) describes as "disembodied 'history'" and "an experienced past." (Figure 9.2)

COMMUNITY, STATUS, AND PRESTIGE

As with many subcultures, self-making (Hebdige 1988) is an important part of urban exploration. There are several paths to status acquisition, and various achievements can earn someone recognition as a "hardcore" explorer, or a trusted and senior community member.

"Hardcore" explorer status is difficult to achieve without a track record of visits to locations that are considered especially difficult or dangerous to access and explore, including abandoned hospitals that are located on campuses of still-active hospitals, active prisons, or military property. Certain locations confer the status of a "tough" explorer on someone who successfully infiltrates them. This includes unusually hazardous places, such as offshore ship graveyards, buildings that have reached a dangerous level of decay, or buildings that may require scaling walls or crawling through poison ivy to gain access.

Certain skills, such as photography or creative graffiti (tagging), also help gain status. Many urban explorers are amateur, professional, or semi-professional photographers, and most online UE forums have a space dedicated to people sharing and critiquing photographs. Certain locations have "iconic" photographs attached to them—shots featuring a specific composition from a particular angle taken over and over again by different urban explorers. Coming up with original versions, or "new takes" on these iconic subjects in specific locations—the chandelier in the now-demolished Metropolitan State Hospital cafeteria in Waltham, Massachusetts (Figure 9.3), the amphitheater in a particular New England abandoned mental asylum, the remnants of mailboxes in the aforementioned abandoned post

Figure 9.3   A Chandelier on the Floor of the Cafeteria of the Now-Gone Metropolitan State Hospital in Waltham, Massachusetts (photograph by author)

office in Gary, Indiana, the skeleton of the bus buried in the sand at Salton Sea—earns respect and status. Such images maintain the delicate balance between participating in a collective project of pluralistic documentation over time with the location-inspired individual creativity which is prized and rewarded within the subculture.

In general, discursive participation in a particular aesthetic and a proficiency in a shared pool of relevant popular culture references are important parts of social competency for a UE community member. American explorers often invoke the video game (and the subsequent film) *Silent Hill*—set in a ghost town abandoned after a coal seam fire, the same subterranean event that befell the real-life abandoned town of Centralia, PA—in either descriptions of locations or (complimentary) assessments of one another's photographs. In a similar vein, Russian explorers often call themselves "stalkers." The term comes from a popular Soviet-era dystopian science fiction novel by Arkady and Boris Strugatsky (1972), *Roadside Picnic*, later adapted into a cult film *Stalker* by Tarkovsky (1979). Both the novel and the film are set in and around a mysterious forbidden "zone," where decommissioned and abandoned remnants of urban life are reclaimed by nature and strange and dangerous objects and spaces menace visitors. "Stalkers" are for-hire guides who know their way through the Zone. This discursive framework is reinforced in the cybersocial aspect of UE: many Russian explorers have screen handles that are some variation on the word "stalker" or employ other allusions to the novel. The abandoned hydroelectric plant near Tallinn, Estonia, where *Stalker* was filmed in 1979, is a pilgrimage site for explorers who find themselves in the area, and photographs from such visits always generate interest and respect in the community.

Other ways of garnering status in the subculture consist of sharing with peers in a way that reflects awareness about one's own status relative to others, and the strictly observed if not formally codified rules of exchange. Reciprocity is emphasized. "Asking for handouts"—i.e., appearing in a cyber-forum without preexisting social connections and asking about "cool places" or how to get access to a particular location, is a quickly sanctioned *faux pas*. Discretion about shared information is expected. As long as these rules are observed, social ties within the group are constantly established and reinforced through exchanges which sometimes take the form of generalized reciprocity (Sahlins 1972), where people contribute knowledge (maps of locations, legal information about trespassing, tutorials on safe passage through buildings that have suffered a fire, or information about a location's past, gleaned from archival research) to the shared in-group knowledge pool, without keeping track of give-and-take. Instances of balanced reciprocity (ibid.) are also common, where information about specific locations is swapped. Sometimes well-established individual urban explorers or small groups of people who explore together make UE-themed trips to different cities or states. Usually they are shown hospitality by the explorers local to that city, including lodging, transportation, and "tours" of local abandoned sites of interest. Later, such hospitality may be reciprocated on the guests' home turf.

The length of one's involvement in the subculture is also directly correlated to status, both because a long-time explorer has many opportunities to participate in the kind of reciprocity described above, and because newer explorers often never had a chance to explore locations that were legendary in the UE community before they were torn down. Examples of such places include the aforementioned Danvers State Hospital and Metropolitan State Hospital, Byberry State Hospital in Pennsylvania, and the Ambassador Hotel on the Asbury Park Boardwalk in New Jersey. Frequently physical "souvenirs" from such locations function as markers of status and "proof" that this status was legitimately earned.

CONCLUSION

Ultimately, urbex remains a kind of cipher—occasionally, it catches media attention, and is grouped with other subcultures, like parkour, or even steampunk (Dawdy 2010), that are somehow "remixing" or renegotiating ways of relating to space, and to how particular spaces are envisioned to exist within time. It is tempting to compare it to certain forms of "dark tourism" (disaster tourism, nuclear tourism, toxic tourism)—yet largely urbex exists outside of the economy of supply-and-demand that structures tourism enterprises. The subcultural stress on in-group knowledge and reproduction of secrecy protects urbexing, to a degree, from being a commodity or having the visible and transparent public life that the aforementioned forms of tourism all have, in one way or another. The aesthetics and fantasies of urbex may coincide with the ones that drive "dark tourism," and the demographics in question may overlap, but the logics of these practices are fundamentally different.

The subculture of urbex is a fascinating and rewarding subject for ethnographic analysis of production of meaning and value in recontextualized spaces, marginalized and dismissed within the conventional structures of valuation. Further ethnographic research into urban exploration can fill in the gap in the scholarly understanding and in public awareness of a cultural force that is generating a unique body of knowledge and is opening up new possibilities for public memory and perception regarding urban spaces. At its most constructive, urban exploration can exist in an active collaboration with programs of urban preservation and renewal—yet as a subculture it is alternately occluded or marginalized, so the extensive grassroots documentation of urban sites it produces and disseminates remains esoteric knowledge circulated among a self-selecting demographic. Yet the relevance of this evolving and rich subculture extends beyond its membership, as it enables not only the production of social identity and personhood inscribed into an alternative value system, but also an alternative discourse around an entire material infrastructure that has lost its use-value according to the criteria of the mainstream society.

NOTES

1. By "use-value" I mean Marx's definition of the qualitative value as described in Capital: "The utility of a thing makes it a use-value. But this utility is not a thing of air. Being limited by the physical properties of the commodity, it has no existence apart from that commodity. . . . Use-values become a reality only by use or consumption" (1954: 44).
2. The two terms are used interchangeably.
3. From http://www.shatteredshutter.com/faq.html, accessed on April 14, 2013.
4. It has recently been redeveloped as a tourist attraction by Namdeb Diamond Corporation, co-owned by the Government of the Republic of Namibia and De Beers Centenary AG.
5. Among countless other places, Berlin and the surrounding area contain two "landmarks" of urban exploration: *Beelitz-Heilstätten* tuberculosis sanatorium-turned-military-hospital, abandoned in 2000, known for its easily accessible and well-preserved interior, and the abandoned "culture park" *Plänterwald-Spreepark* in the Treptow district of the city, with an intact ferris wheel.
6. While a lot of explorers approach photography of abandoned spaces from a photojournalistic perspective, there is a strong tendency toward art photography that features urban decay as a subject.
7. Who, incidentally, first collaborated on a "salvage" photography project featuring the disappearing German industrial architecture.

REFERENCES

Bey, Hakim T. A. Z. *The Temporary Autonomous Zone, Ontological Anarchy, Poetic Terrorism*. Brooklyn: Autonomedia, 1985.

Bluestone, Barry and Bennett Harrison. *The Deindustrialization of America: Plant Closings, Community Abandonment, and the Dismantling of Basic Industry*. New York: Basic Books, 1982.

Boyer, M. Christine. *The City of Collective Memory: Its Historical Imagery and Architectural Entertainments*. Cambridge, MA: MIT press, 1996.

Brenner, Neil. "The Urban Question: Reflections on Henri Lefebvre, Urban Theory and the Politics of Scale." *International Journal of Urban and Regional Research* 24 no 2 (2000): 361–78.

Burke-Gaffney, Brian. "Hashima: The Ghost Island." *Crossroads: A Journal of Nagasaki History and Culture* 4 (1996): 33–52.

Castells, Manuel. "Advanced Capitalism, Collective Consumption, and Urban Contradictions: New Sources of Inequality and New Models for Change." In *Stress and Contradiction in Modern Capitalism: Public Policy and the Theory of the Stat*, edited by L. Lindberg, 175–97. Lexington: Lexington Books, 1975.

D'Andrea, Anthony. "Deciphering the Space and Scale of Global Nomadism: Subjectivity and Counterculture in a Global Age." In *Deciphering the Global: Its Scales, Spaces and Subjects*, edited by S. Sassen, 139–51. London: Routledge, 2007.

Dawdy, Shannon Lee. 2010. "Clockwork Anthropology and the Ruins of Modernity." *Current Anthropology* 51 no 6: 761–93.

De Certeau, Michel. *The Practice of Everyday Life*. Berkeley: University of California Press, 1984.

Debord, Guy. "Theory of the Derive." In *The Situationist International Anthology*, edited by K. Knabb, 50–54. Berkeley: Bureau of Public Secrets, 1981.

Drucker, Peter. *The New Realities: In Government and Politics, in Economics and Business, in Society and World View*. New York: Harper and Raw, 1989.

Edensor, Tim. *Industrial Ruins: Space, Aesthetics and Materiality*. Oxford: Berg, 2005.

Edwards, Elizabeth. "Photographs and the Sound of History." *Visual Anthropology Review* 21, no 1–2 (2005): 27–46.

Favro, Diane. "Meaning and Experience: Urban History from Antiquity to the Early Modern Period." *Journal of the Society of Architectural Historians* 58 no 3 (1999): 364–73.

Garrett, Bradley L. "Urban Explorers: Quests for Myth, Mystery and Meaning." *Geography Compass* 4 no 10 (2010): 1448–61.

Giaccardi, Elisa and Leysia Palen. "The Social Production of Heritage through Cross-media Interaction: Making Place for Place-making." *International Journal of Heritage Studies* 14 no 3 (2008): 281–97.

Hayden, Dolores. *The Power of Place: Urban Landscapes as Public History*. Cambridge, MA: MIT press, 1997.

Hebdige, Dick. *Subculture: The Meaning of Style*. London: Routledge, 1981.

Hebdige, Dick. *Hiding in the Light: On Images and Things*. New York: Routledge, 1988.

High, Steven. *Industrial Sunset: The Making of North America's Rust Belt, 1969–1984*. Toronto: University of Toronto Press, 2003.

King, Emilie Boyer. "Undercover Restorers Fix Paris Landmark's Clock." *The Guardian*, November 26, 2007. Accessed April 15, 2013, http://www.guardian.co.uk/world/2007/nov/26/france.artnews.

Kirkbride, Thomas. "On the Construction, Organization and General Arrangements of Hospitals for the Insane." *American Journal of Insanity* 37 (1881): 348–51.

Krull, Germaine. *Facsimile of Métal (Metal)*. Paris: Librairie de Arts Decorativs, 1928.

Lefebvre, H. *The Production of Space* (D. Nicholson-Smith, Trans.). Oxford: Blackwell, 1991.

Lejano, Raul P. and Anne Taufen Wessells. "Community and Economic Development: Seeking Common Ground in Discourse and in Practice." *Urban Studies* 43 no 9 (2006): 1469–89.

Marx, Karl. *Capital: Volume 1: A Critique of Political Economy* (B. Fowkes, Trans.). London: Penguin Classics, 1992 (1867).

Mommaas, Hans. "Cultural Clusters and the Post-industrial City: Towards the Remapping of Urban Cultural Policy." *Urban studies* 41 no 3 (2004): 507–32.

Ninjalicious. *Access All Areas: A User's Guide to the Art of Urban Exploration*. Infilpress, 2005.

Nordanstad, Thomas (director). *Hashima: The Island of Grief*, 2006.

Pavia, Troy. *Lost America: The Abandoned Roadside*. West: MBI, 2003.

Pavia, Troy. *Night Vision: The Art of Urban Exploration*. San Francisco: Chronicle Books, 2008.

Penney, Darby and Peter Statsny. *The Lives They Left Behind: Suitcases from a State Hospital Attic*. New York: Bellevue Literary Press, 2008.

Pinder, David. "Arts of Urban Exploration." *Cultural Geographies* 12 no 4 (2005): 383–411.

Rayner, Paul. 'Lewis Wickes Hine: Progressive Photographer.' *OVO Magazine* (winter, 1977): 5–8.

Riegl, Alois. "The Modern Cult of Monuments: Its Character and Its Origin." *Oppositions* 25 (1982): 20–51.

Rollwagen, Jack R. "Cities and the World System: Toward an Evolutionary Perspective in the Study of Urban Anthropology." In *Cities in a Larger Context*, edited by T. Collins, 123–40. Athens: University of Georgia Press, 1980.

Sahlins, Marshall David. *Stone Age Economics*. Piscataway: Transaction Press, 1972.

Schwarzer, Mitchell. "Myths of Permanence and Transience in the Discourse on Historic Preservation in the United States." *Journal of Architectural Education* 48 no 1 (1994): 2–11.

Solis, Julia. *New York Underground: The Anatomy of a City*. New York: Routledge, 2004.

Strugatsky, Boris and Arkady Strugatsky. *Roadside Picnic* (A. Dubois, Trans.). New York: MacMillan Press, 1972.

Tarkovsky, Andrey. (Director) *Stalker*. Soviet Union: Mosfilm, 1979.

Veitch, Jonathan. "Colossus in Ruins: Remembering Pittsburgh's Industrial Past." *Public Culture* 10 no 1 (1997): 115–134.

Webster, E. 1930. "This Daring Camera Girl Scales Skyscrapers for Art." *American Magazine*, 110 (193): 66.

While, Aidan. "Modernism vs Urban Renaissance: Negotiating Post-War Heritage in English City Centres." *Urban Studies* 43 no 13 (2006): 2399–419.

Ziegler, Ulf Erdmann. "The Bechers' Industrial Lexicon." *Art in America* 93 (2002): 143.

10 "There Goes the Neighborhood"

Narrating the Decline of Place in East Berlin

Nitzan Shoshan

" 'Why only now?' he says, this person not to be confused with me." A stern opening already heralds the intricate temporal entwinements, geographical juxtapositions, and alterations of voice with which Günther Grass's 2002 novel *Crabwalk* proceeds to recount the horrific drowning in January 1945 of the passenger ship *Wilhelm Gustloff* by a Soviet submarine, in which thousands of German refugees found their deaths. Grass's dexterous maneuverings, which many critics acclaimed as expressive of his literary brilliance, at once struggle to fabricate a place from which the inarticulable, namely German WWII suffering, might be narrated. Like the warning above, they operate as so many distancing mechanisms that allow the author—if only partially, as evidenced by the controversy that surrounded the book in Germany—to circumnavigate the strong cultural prohibition on self-victimization. Central to these efforts to challenge the taboo while escaping full responsibility for its violation is Grass's deployment of the peculiar figure of an architectural landscape at once uncanny and, across the post-Soviet bloc, all-too-familiar: the socialist-era high-rise residential neighborhood known in Germany as the *Plattenbauten*. It is here that the sinister temporal attachments that motivate the ominous plot and its tragic conclusion blend into a noxious, inflammable brew, as unvanquished longings for totalitarian pasts and deaths not mourned mingle with the inebriated skinheads and earnest young neo-Nazis of post-reunification Germany.

In this chapter, I look at a particular *Plattenbauten* neighborhood on the southeastern outskirts of Berlin where I conducted fieldwork in order to understand the significance that such urban residential settings more broadly have acquired in Germany. For the historical context that permits Grass to effectively invoke such a neighborhood as a literary device for generating temporal and geographical distance from the unspeakable includes the illicit cultural meanings with which the entire class of such residential environments has been invested. At the same time, certain particular places have come to stand as paradigmatic tokens of this general type, condensing and throwing into sharp relief the underside of a supposedly rejuvenated nation. Such places have emerged within the German geographical imaginary as special locations through which recent processes of social decline have been narrated. Operating as elsewheres and elsewhens (Pred 2000), they appear foreign to the national present.

In what follows, I explore how urban marginalization in the former East Germany has been narrated through the figure of the *Plattenbauten* and its linking with a narrative of creeping nazification. No doubt, emergent landscapes of postindustrial disconnection have everywhere been rendered in ominous forms. In Germany, however, they have come to stand for the country's illicit pasts—both National Socialism and state socialism. The narratives I will consider below construe the landscape of one *Plattenbauten* neighborhood as dilapidated and hopeless, but at once as fertile ground for young neo-Nazis. In them, much as in *Crabwalk*, such neighborhoods become narrative devices that operate as a culturally salient chronotope in the Bakhtinian sense (Bakhtin 1998), articulating a word, a place, and a time so as to organize the discursive genre that has provided the dominant frame for understanding postindustrial urban marginalization, especially in the East.

My inquiry proceeds in three stages. Firstly, I place the neighborhood where I conducted fieldwork within the broader history of *Plattenbauten* neighborhoods in the German Democratic Republic (GDR) and of their vicissitudes under the transition to capitalism. Secondly, I return to the neighborhood to consider how this history of urban marginalization has impacted its landscape. I look at its representations in journalistic media to describe how its socioeconomic decline has been linked with a narrative of ghettoization and nazification. Finally, I examine locally produced discourses about the neighborhood. I analyze the chronotopes that emerge in the narratives through which local printed media construe the neighborhood. I then consider the voices of local residents, including young right extremists. I suggest that the narrative genre of nazification through which the neighborhood's downward turn has been represented turns reflexive. Its very salience renders the neighborhood appealing for socially marginalized young nationalists who aspire to make it their home.

A HISTORY OF URBAN DISCONNECTION

Built just shortly before reunification, the *Kosmosviertel* (cosmos quarter) sits at the southeastern edge of the city, its wide, imposing high-rises clearly demarcating its external frontiers and dividing its interior space into several subsections. Many in the district, including its own residents, commonly refer to this GDR-era neighborhood as the Ghetto. The term seems to oscillate between two contrasting semantic valences. For many, it indicates social marginalization, geographical isolation, and the risk of violence. Others, and especially younger persons, use it with a sense of local pride to invoke such qualities as toughness, masculinity, and camaraderie that they associate with the North American ghetto. Following such colloquial usage, where the term *Kosmosviertel* rarely appears, I will refer to the neighborhood as the Ghetto, without, however, intending to suggest any sociological parallelism with its North American cognates.[1]

Entering the neighborhood from the south, one finds a modest commercial area—a couple of restaurants, a travel agency, a drug store, a pharmacy. A path that meanders between the tall buildings through a poorly maintained park leads to a small square known as the *Kugel* (ball) at its northern entrance. Overlooking a parking lot, a discount supermarket, and an elderly home, the *Kugel* is decorated with scribbles and graffiti, including the letters "NPD," the acronym of Germany's most prominent far-right political party. Barring particularly inclement weather, a number of middle-aged men rest at the wooden benches, sipping on beer bottles as they chat. Small groups of young persons, some of them sporting right extremist jewelry pieces and clothing items, share the space, they too drinking beer as they smoke their cigarettes.

As we shall see shortly, such scenes have often been represented as static friezes of an underclass existence without prospects. And yet, as a residential environment, the Ghetto has witnessed dramatic transformations. The last *Plattenbauten* neighborhood to be completed in East Berlin, it was also the conclusion of a prolonged utopian project of immense dimensions. The project addressed housing problems that went as far back as the industrialization processes of the nineteenth century, but which became especially acute following the massive destruction inflicted by aerial carpet bombings in the last years of World War II. The devastation left approximately three and a half million apartments in ruins and some seven and a half million persons homeless (Sebald 1999: 11). Severe housing shortages thus constituted arguably the foremost challenge for both East and West Germany following the war, a challenge compounded by the arrival of millions of German refugees from Eastern Europe and by the diminished capacities of a decimated war economy.

Perhaps precisely for that reason, housing became a scale for measuring and representing the relative merit of the two nascent states and their capacity to make good on their ideological promises. The GDR codified the right to housing in its constitution and treated residential construction as one of its central tasks, adopting a strategy of gradual nationalization and industrialization of virtually the entire construction sector. Centralization and standardization proceeded at all levels, from urban planning through architectural design to construction work. The efforts focused almost exclusively on industrial techniques using prefabricated concrete slabs (hence *Plattenbauten*, literally panel buildings). Public sector involvement in residential projects and industrial construction techniques were central to housing strategies in West Germany as well. And yet there they complemented a robust private sector and a variety of other construction methods, resulting in a far more heterogeneous architectural landscape. In the GDR, meanwhile, an industrialized, state-centralized construction sector defined the built landscape in its entirety, radically transforming rural and urban contexts alike.

The first generation of large-scale residential neighborhoods dates to the fifties and sixties. It was designed to facilitate industrial production by settling workers near workplaces and as housing for the elderly. In 1971, the GDR government announced an ambitious plan that would resolve housing shortages completely by 1990 through the massive erection of vast residential neighborhoods (*Großsiedlungen*). The plan envisioned the construction of some three million apartments over two decades. Currently, about twenty percent of East Germany's population resides in such *Großsiedlungen* (Hannemann 2005: 155). This second generation of *Plattenbauten* construction similarly responded to the growing needs of East German industrial production, which at the time showed encouraging signs of growth. New neighborhoods often served as residences for employees in nearby industries. The Ghetto, for instance, was erected a stone's throw away from East Berlin's international airport, where today the International Berlin-Brandenburg Airport stands, primarily as housing for the workers of Interflug, the GDR's national airline.

Another problem that the plan addressed consisted of the severely deteriorated condition of aging pre-World War II buildings (*Altbauten*), few of which had not benefited from renovation or maintenance since before the war. Their older infrastructure frequently included shared bathrooms and kitchens, coal heating, small residential units, and antiquated water, energy, and sewage systems. Such living conditions were not only unappealing for many of their residents, but also unfit for providing the modern standards upon which the socialist state sought to pride itself. In West Germany, many *Altbauten* were renovated and fitted with contemporary infrastructure, but the centralization and standardization of construction in the East meant that, beyond political will, the very skills and instruments for such restoration works were all but absent. New industrial construction offered a far more cost-effective solution (Hannemann 2005).

Yet above and beyond addressing housing shortages and offering modern living standards, the new *Großsiedlungen* fulfilled a crucial ideological function. They were represented and, at least by some, also perceived as nothing less than the physical incarnation of a socialist vision, at once a grand statement of a utopian promise and the imposing materiality of its ostensible realization. If their locations were calculated to sustain the growth in industrial output, their architectural layout asserted the possibility of new forms of sociability and new kinds of subjects. The building designs and apartment floor plans answered the needs that such subjects would presumably have. Amenities included elevators, centralized heating, modern electricity, water, and sewage systems, private bathrooms and kitchens, extended living space and additional rooms, and reliable central water heating. Equally significant to this ideological vision, however, were the layout of neighborhoods and public spaces. The high-rise, multiple entrance buildings defined a clearly circumscribed area toward the outside, while inwards they were arranged perpendicularly to form rectangular spaces for various public uses, from play-yards and basketball courts to kindergartens, schools, libraries, community centers, shops, or public squares. Such new kinds of public spaces were expected to produce the socialist subject by stimulating new types of human interactions, new patterns of dwelling, and new forms of sociability.

The new neighborhoods were in great demand. Under the state centralized economy, income levels played an insignificant role in allocating apartments next to educational levels, young children in the household, and professional sectors (Häußermann and Kapphan 2002: 68–72). The residents typically came from the middle to upper echelons of GDR society, with significantly higher educational levels than the national average. Allocation by workplace proximity meant that neighbors were often also colleagues. Hence workplace social networks and residential ones, so sharply separated from each other under capitalism, often converged. This, together with the sharing of public spaces and resources, allowed for a certain coherence of community structures.

Such is the irony of history that the 1971 housing plan, which professed to demonstrate the superiority of state socialism and to prepare the foundations for a utopian society, instead concluded with the implosion of the GDR and its annexation by the Federal Republic of Germany (FRG). The *Wende* (literally turn or transition; here the reunification period) and its abrupt integration into a capitalist economy and a liberal democratic political system spelled drastic transformations for East German society, with dramatic consequences for urban social space in general and *Plattenbauten* neighborhoods in particular. The rapid collapse of virtually all East German industry deprived most neighborhoods of any commuting advantage they might have previously held, frequently leaving them cut-off from emerging new hubs of economic activity. The social continuity between sites of production and places of dwelling likewise became disrupted.

As capitalism replaced state-socialist geographical orders with new urban spatialities, especially neighborhoods on the outskirts of cities became resignified as working-class peripheries. Whereas in the East *Plattenbauten* accounted for virtually all new construction and were perceived as attractive, in the West similar residential environments were historically coterminous with public housing projects and underclass ghettos, and hence considered undesirable. Under the newly hegemonic architectural-aesthetic order, then, the very physical landscape of the neighborhoods, previously perceived as harmonious, was recast as oppressively monotonous. Their formerly exclusive amenities quickly became standard, as government subsidies boosted extensive renovation works in older buildings. The extra room they offered, a top privilege at the time, came to appear puny against new scales of luxury now available for those who could afford them.

The capitalist hegemony thus entirely remade the *Plattenbauten* into an emblematic symbol of colossal failure and reckless inhumanity. Yet the sheer quantity of *Plattenbauten* housing units precluded abandoning them entirely. The German government, concerned about the social problems that could develop in them, sponsored their internal renovation and external beautification. Their actual fates have varied widely, depending for example on their location and their social and professional composition. Some have stabilized into solid middle-class quarters. Many others, however, have witnessed rapid processes of social marginalization.

Such neighborhoods found themselves on the losing end of a rapidly widening social polarization. Those who benefitted from the transition moved out, some now able to afford higher living standards, others following job offers elsewhere. Those who coped less well with the changes—colloquially known as *Wendeverlierer* (transition losers)—remained behind. Some secured low-paying positions in the low-skilled service sector, whether as supermarket cashiers, retail venders, or *Tagesmütter*.[2] The less fortunate have sunk into chronic unemployment after losing their jobs, as one workplace after another collapsed in the wake of reunification. The negative migration created severe problems of under-occupancy. Vacant apartments have been marketed to and taken over by low-income families and welfare recipients.

AT THE MARGINS OF SOCIETY

Today's *Plattenbauten*, then, bear the traces of new *conditions of labor and production*, which transfigured their social composition; of new *architectural and aesthetic orders*, which altered how they were perceived and experienced; of new *scales of consumption*, which redefined notions of luxury and need; and of new *spatial configurations*, which reshuffled urban landscapes. Those neighborhoods which, like the Ghetto, have emerged as hotbeds of societal problems, disclose the impact of these large-scale processes. Similar processes have been studied the world over, and have been linked to re-spatializations of political and economic power that have emerged under the sign of neoliberalism (Brenner and Theodore 2002; Harvey 2001; Lefebvre 1996; Smith 2003; Soja 1989). Unlike many other locations, however, where spatial transformations have come under scrutiny (e.g., Los Angeles, New Haven, Liverpool), the Ghetto has not transformed gradually with the shifting geographies of capitalism. Rather, it has morphed out of a radical discontinuity, a traumatic rupture, in the dominant order. Hardly conceived, it has come overnight under a drastically different political hegemony. If it once offered convenient commutes, it has become severed from today's spatialities of production and consumption. Located at the urban periphery, it is now perceived as an isolated enclave. Many of its residents express a sense of isolation. Some report they only leave it to visit welfare offices. Particularly young residents demonstrate a strikingly limited grasp of the city's general geography. Those who are employed complain of long commutes to work. If its public offerings—community centers, educational institutions, and consumption establishments—earlier seemed amply sufficient, today locals perceive them as highly inadequate. And many less well-to-do inhabitants remain excluded from its handful of commercial venues altogether.

Nor do open, public spaces offer much respite. A steep increase in car ownership and high population density has meant that play-yards and grass lawns have metamorphosed into asphalt parking lots. A disproportionately high ratio of adolescents and young adults, the result of an initial overrepresentation of young families in the neighborhood and the heavy in-migration of mostly young residents, has further accentuated the scarcity of outdoor spaces for recreation and leisure. High unemployment rates and a rise in single-income families likewise meant that more people were spending more time at the Ghetto. Small squares like the *Kugel* have become virtually monopolized by long-term unemployed adults and abject youths, both displaying acute alcohol abuse and, especially among the young, a disposition to violence and delinquency. Internal spaces have likewise been affected. High resident turnover and the disappearance of common workplaces, previously a basis for community cohesion, spelled the shift of the *Plattenbauten* from places of familiarity to anonymous mammoths of alienated dwelling (Häußermann and Kapphan 2002: 161–5).

But how have such processes been narrated and represented? And with what temporal values have such representations invested *Plattenbauten* in general, and the Ghetto in particular? Such representations are crucial not only because they may shape the perceptions of wide publics and carry concrete consequences, but also because they circulate among inhabitants of *Plattenbauten* neighborhoods themselves, exercising a powerful sway on the ways in which they imagine and experience their home. Often, the Ghetto receives mention in the media within short notices on racist or violent events: vandalism at the Italian Café, a brutal assault on a resident, racist incidents at local league soccer matches (Berliner Zeitung 2004; Geyer 2006; Nibbrig and Lier 2005). One occasion that brought the neighborhood into the limelight was the September 2006 state elections, in which two extreme right parties, the NPD and the REP, registered unprecedented gains, winning parliament seats in five Berlin municipalities (*Bezirke*). Their strongest support came from a polling booth at the Ghetto, not far from the *Kugel*. Just two days after the elections a major Berlin newspaper published a story about the neighborhood. Titled "At the Margins of Society," it painted a grim underclass existence:

> The inhabitants [of the Ghetto] live not only at the margins of the city, but also at the margins of society: stranded, shoved away, materially excluded, socially bureaucratized. . . . Unkempt lawns, melancholy, boredom . . . few prospects . . . he who gets stranded at the Ghetto has ceased to hope. Worries and financial hardships are drowned in alcohol. (Stengel 2006)

The article cited the political apathy of a resident who professed not to be surprised by the voting results: "the politicians are all just liars, they make promises and then after the elections don't give a damn." It concluded the bleak description of the Ghetto with the words of an election official who, noting the low turnout, warned against stigmatization.[3]

A few weeks later, a second story about the neighborhood attempted a more refined exposition (Köhler 2006). Its heading, "A Neighborhood Fights for its Reputation," already indicated a different posture. It identified two faces to the neighborhood. The first, expounded by the director of a real-estate association and by one of her tenants, highlighted aesthetic improvements to the buildings, well-maintained gardens and courtyards, tranquility, and contented residents. "Ever since [the elections] all the inhabitants of the neighborhood have been labeled rightists and stigmatized by the media," they complain. The second, presented by a street social worker, expands instead on alcoholism and violence, on inadequate public transportation, on unemployment and poverty, and on political resentment and indifference that reflects the total disregard of authorities and political actors: "The people here have experienced how their quarter has been ignored by local politics for years. Only the vote for the NPD has brought them public attention. This signal is fatal."

Both stories tie together poverty and extreme right sympathies, social marginalization and political resentment. Both maintain a safe distance from the voices of poor and extremist locals, instead citing a satisfied resident, a real-estate agent, a social worker, and an elections official. The NPD voters themselves remain invisible specters: we know they're there but we don't see them. We confront only their "habitat" as a rather finished state of affairs.

A similar, though significantly more detailed, newspaper story about the neighborhood appeared after the 2005 federal elections, in which the Ghetto awarded the NPD its second best voting rate in Berlin. Under the heading "Hostile Takeover of a Residential Neighborhood," the article recounts the author's own personal narrative of the Ghetto's decline: its transformation from a safe, hospitable middle-class environment into a threatening, hostile stronghold of neo-Nazis and their intimidating dogs. The author, married to a Vietnamese immigrant, belonged with the Ghetto's first residents. Expecting a baby, like many others, she appreciated her new apartment's additional living space. She narrates how the idyllic neighborhood changed as the neighbors she befriended gradually moved out. A very different kind of residents took over their empty apartments and eventually rendered the Ghetto unlivable for her, forcing her to move out.

> the new neighbors were eternally surrounded by a stench of schnapps. When the German national soccer team played, my apartment became uninhabitable. . . . To counter the depopulation, the residents' society began to market apartments by welcoming dog owners. They would

have been turned down elsewhere. . . . Every weekend young men with short haircuts, leather boots, and leather jackets carried tables and refrigerators for their friends into the houses. . . . The local bank took note of the new residents: because they occupied the area around its ATMs as their meeting place and dog training ground, fewer people came in to deposit money. The bank hired private security. The rightists moved a few meters away. (Mai 2005)

As a literary form, the narrative parallels the American "there goes the neighborhood" genre, which has served to tie together African-American migration with so-called "white-flight" and ghettoization. This particular rendering uses the Ghetto as scenery to narrate socioeconomic decline as hostile takeover by neo-Nazis. A predominant vernacular of the genre that has become commonplace in mass media, academic contexts, political debates, and literary works, it alarmingly represents *Plattenbauten* neighborhoods under the de-facto sovereignty of neo-Nazi hordes (see, e.g., Butterwegge and Meier 2002; Schröder 1997; Staud 2005; Verfassungsschutz Brandenburg 2001; ZDK 1998). Employing terms like *"National befreite Zonen"* ("nationally liberated zones"), *"Angstzonen"* ("fear zones"), or "no-go areas,"[4] such representations have evoked neighborhoods terrorized by skinheads, where none is tolerated who appears different, where the state has lost its grip on public order, and where the threat of violence is omnipresent. Not infrequently, they have talked of neo-Nazi gangs following organized strategic agendas of territorial domination as both a means and an end.

NARRATING TEMPORAL REVERSAL FROM WITHIN

I am less interested here in assessing whether such representations correspond to lived realities (though in my experience they do not), and more in interrogating them as narratives that entail particular senses of time and place, of movement and direction, of process and change. From this perspective, the "there goes the neighborhood" narrative unsettles the rather static frieze that dominated the first two texts. All, however, construe the Ghetto as a chronotope of temporal reversal with respect to hegemonic narratives of material prosperity and political democratization. But how do such chronotopic forms, found on the pages of newspapers, compare with those that emerge in local texts?

Consider the *Treptower Wende-Chronik* (*Treptow Transition Chronicle*), a commemorative booklet the municipal district published in 2000, on the tenth anniversary of reunification (Teske 2000). It recollects the period between the fall of the wall in 1989 and the dissolution of the GDR in 1990 through personal testimonies as well as archival materials. Its language conjures a sense of effective, fast-paced, future-oriented action. The witnesses recount their experiences with verbs that indicate advancement and progress: begin (*beginnen*), start (*anfangen*), organize (*organisieren*), change itself/oneself (*sich ändern*), build up (*aufbauen*), clear up (*abräumen*), remove (*beseitigen*), renovate (*sanieren*), or arrive (*erreichen*). Their narratives recall the foundation (*Gründung*) of organizations, the implementation (*Umsetzung*) of reforms, the transformation (*Umwandlung*) of institutions, the development (*Entwicklung*) of infrastructure, or the renewal (*Erneuerung*) of public space. They describe the period as a new beginning (*Neuanfang*), progressive (*fortschrittlich*), fascinating (*faszinierend*), and constructive (*konstruktiv*).

The temporal rift between long slumber and awakening (*Aufbruch*) appears as a contrast between such forward-looking, high tempo tropes and the terms with which the GDR is portrayed: a static society of stagnation (*Stagnation*), passivity (*Passivität*), scarcity (*Mangel*), deficits (*Defizite*), and restrictions (*Einschränkungen*), its landscape decaying (*verrotete*), neglected (*ungepflegt*), or ailing (*marode*). This is a slow, backward-bent time, its flow marked by the steady deterioration of a society and its objects. In indexing a history of decline, stagnation, decay, and ailment inevitably also suggest a past of movement and health in which buildings were in good repair, streets were clean, citizens were actively engaged, and the economy was booming. The booklet describes such a nostalgic temporality as itself a thing of the past, announcing its replacement with a revolutionary time for which the original moment is 1989 and the future is full of promises.

There is, of course, a third sense of time at play here, namely the nostalgic mood that the booklet itself weaves together. Published a decade later, it portrays the temporal upheaval of the transition period already in a voice of nostalgic longing, reminiscing about a lost moment of emancipation, and regeneration. Its texts proclaim a nostalgia for anti-nostalgia: a longing for a past in which the past itself ceased to be the object of longing, and in which it became eclipsed by the future. Their language of transformation, foundation, and renewal belongs to that era of swift changes and new opportunities, a revolutionary time indeed. And yet, if they posit a temporal discontinuity between the GDR and the transition, they also constitute—though silently—a distance between the transition and the present, on which they scarcely comment. Their rare reflections on the decade that had transpired include brief calculi of pros and cons and invariable affirmations that, all things considered, change has been for the better. Neither the long sleep of the GDR nor the euphoric effervescence of the *Wende*, the present remains amorphous in their narratives, its temporal outline betrayed only by the nostalgic impetus of the booklet itself.

We find a more sobering and less implicit assessment of the present in the Ghetto's monthly newsletter. Its April 2005 cover story, for instance, reports on a town hall meeting to discuss construction in the area: already behind schedule, the completion of a new road has been postponed once more; an elementary school faces the threat of closure; no plans exist yet for the future use of several shut-down kindergartens; adjacent vacant plots designated for residential development have failed to attract any investment interest (Unverfehrt 2005). The front-page displays a black-and-white photograph of the *Investruine*, a dilapidated eyesore that, its broad dimensions surrounded by debris and its windows shattered, has towered over the Ghetto's modest consumption area for many years now. Lack of public resources and private investment still delays its long-awaited demolition, according to the article. The present here puts on exhibit the traces of the recent past: unfinished projects, abandoned kindergartens, derelict landscapes, and economic stagnation. Its language is one of "closure" (*Schließung*), "cancelled" (*gestrichen*), "with no results" (*ohne Ergebnisse*), "difficult" (*schwierig*), and "refuse" (*weigern*).

This chronotope of the Ghetto as a place of abandonment and disconnection finds its converse reflection on the following page, where the newsletter presents the biographical portrait of a resident (Ernst 2005). Here we learn of a picturesque childhood landscape of open fields, where the family garden "provided sufficient playground . . . and homegrown fruits and vegetables guaranteed a healthful nutrition." We follow the resident as he becomes a celebrated architect, winner of the City of Berlin's 1986 Architecture Prize and eventually responsible for all high residential construction in the GDR. Some of his projects, we read, can still be seen in Berlin, although a well-known work "gave way to an expressionless, ugly post-reunification cement block." In this biographical narrative, the past emerges through figures of "building" (*bauen*), "studying" (*studieren*), "leading" (*leiten*), or "working" (*tätig sein*). If the present has come to a standstill, the past appears as movement and direction, production and progress, vision and creativity. Juxtaposing the dreary cover story with the nostalgic biographical portrait reveals a chronotope of temporal reversal, the unraveling of a time that has lost its coherence, whose direction has become vague, whose motion has turned hesitant.

There is, then, a certain analogical correspondence to be drawn between the temporal forms through which the Ghetto is narrated on the pages of printed media of city-wide and national circulation on the one hand, and in the stories that appear in locally produced texts and that are directed at local publics on the other hand. While the manner in which distinct narratives comment about the past (to the extent that they do so at all) may vary, the present appears as a state of stagnation bereft of a meaningful, viable futurity. It is striking, however, that in contrast with virtually all non-local media, local texts tend to represent the Ghetto as a chronotope of socioeconomic hardship and urban disconnection pure and simple, without inscribing it within a narrative of nazification or the reversal of democratization. It would be too simplistic to understand this absence of neo-Nazis from the Ghetto's representations of itself as a form of self-censorship or as a mode of image management. To be sure, and as the protesting voices of residents make plainly evident in one of the newspaper items mentioned above (as they do, too, in personal conversations), inhabitants of the Ghetto resent what they perceive as their unjust labeling in mainstream media and are conscious of the negative consequences that such labeling might carry. Yet, in Germany, the adverse consequences and the negative significations associated with being perceived to ignore or downplay the problem of right extremism are often no less severe. Mainstream media frequently vilify municipalities and communities for their alleged failure to acknowledge or respond to local problems of right extremism and accuse their leaders and members of harboring similar political sympathies. The absence of the motif of nazification from local texts therefore appears to reflect at least as much a different manner of perceiving and narrating the Ghetto as a chronotope of urban marginality.

Consider Anna, for example. In her mid-40s, she works at the youth club in the Ghetto and lives in an adjacent neighborhood. As a youth worker, and much like other municipal service providers in the neighborhood, Anna participates actively in efforts to confront the problem of right extremism in the area: a neighborhood workgroup on right extremism in the Ghetto that brings together youth workers, social workers, educators, police officers, representatives of the local real estate association, and engaged residents; a district-wide coalition against racism and intolerance called into life by the mayor in which schools, NGOs, cultural and youth venues, and public officials collaborate; or special initiatives such as a festival for democracy at a nearby neighborhood that has gained ill-repute as neo-Nazi territory. At the same time, she says she rarely ever notices right extremist presence either at her youth club or in the neighborhood more generally. Once, she recalls, a youth arrived at the club with a stack of CDs from which he played neo-Nazi music, and which she promptly confiscated. "But he was not a neo-Nazi," she explains, "he said he just found them on a bench at the park and didn't know they had such music on them."

Rather than as a process of nazification, Anna structures her narrative of the Ghetto's recent history by anchoring it in the transition as at once a founding event and a temporal rupture. It marks for her, perhaps counterintuitively from the perspective of hegemonic narratives about reunification, the confinement of activities, the dilution of social relationships, and the foreclosing of possibilities. Before, she says, parents let their children play outside, residents of the neighborhood shared their few belongings generously, families would organize street parties together, and children knew they could count on neighbors for help when in need. No more. Nowadays, according to Anna, parents have turned authoritarian, people have isolated themselves in their private spaces, and neighbors have become strangers behind locked doors. And yet, maybe because both she and her husband have numbered among those fortunate enough to remain employed throughout those years and accordingly view themselves as beneficiaries of the transition, she carefully appends to this narrative of loss and longing a second temporal account whose almost precisely opposite form appears as if calculated to counter or compensate for the first: the progressive trajectory of the accumulation of material property. Not all has become worse, she concludes. The scarcity that characterized the GDR, for example, has given way to much improved material conditions. If people share less, this might be so because every household now commands phone lines and cars, which previously few could afford. Anna finds solace for the disintegrating spheres of family and neighborly relations in the progress she identifies in the domain of consumption. Private property here becomes a discursive operator for recuperating a meaningful temporal narrative.

It goes without saying, of course, that not all in the Ghetto are equally capable of invoking consumption as a compensatory narrative in a similar fashion. The older men at the Kugel, for example, complain about recent price-hikes and express longing for a time when, while scarce, commodities were at least affordable. Long unemployed, they seem unable to construct a compensatory narrative that would provide them with solace. Meanwhile Lars, one of the younger regulars at the Kugel, who relocated to the Ghetto with his girlfriend and their newborn son, describes to me the neighborhood as "a socially deprived area, mostly there is just unemployment [here], and there is no place for young people to go, it's a typical *Platte*." For him as for the older men, the Ghetto no doubt appears as a chronotope of marginalization and disconnection, though not necessarily one that frames a narrative of the "there goes the neighborhood" genre.

But it would be hasty to conclude that the latter form distinguishes non-local discourses from local ones per se. Rather, it is the relatively broader range of chronotopic renderings of the Ghetto that we find in the transition chronicle, in neighborhood newsletters, or in the discourses of Anna, Lars, and the older men at the Kugel, and the ways in which such more local renderings are variously anchored in distinct social positions and discursive contexts, that contrasts so sharply with the monolithic dominance of the "there goes the neighborhood" nazification chronotope in non-local media. Consider, for example, how Uta, a former member of the young clique at the Kugel whose parents counted among the original residents of the Ghetto and who has recently relocated to another part of the district, narrates the history of her former neighborhood:

> Well, in the beginning . . . it was a very very very quiet area. It was mostly families that moved in, [people] who thought "ok, let's start something new here." Really quite a lot of families with children my age or my sister's age . . . and one still felt comfortable walking around. People greeted each other. Even in an eleven-story building the neighbors knew each other and got along with each other. And then quite suddenly it started. Some people moved out because they didn't feel comfortable there. Because really, only the riffraff was moving in . . . after a while so many people moved in that it was sometimes really quite nasty. The bums loitered there . . . it just kept getting worse . . . but

earlier it was pretty quiet. People knew each other and parents didn't need to be worried [about their children]. My mother let me walk on my own to school because she had no reason to be afraid. But after a while you didn't feel that comfortable there anymore. The buildings kept deteriorating.

Uta's narration of the history of disconnection of the Ghetto appears not all that different from the one we found in the newspaper item "Hostile Takeover," whose author, however, maybe because of her marriage to an immigrant, seemed far more concerned about the politically right extremist outlook of the riff-raff that had moved in. Such narratives of ghettoization, in other words, circulate across discursive domains, while the motif of nazification seems to gain increasing salience the farther the source of the discourse from the Ghetto.

And nevertheless, such chronotopic renderings of temporal reversal seem to return to haunt the Ghetto with a vengeance. During my fieldwork there, three young neo-Nazis with whom my personal acquaintance was only incidental but whose names were feared throughout the district and well-known to the police decided to move into a shared apartment at the Ghetto because, as their peers explained to me, they considered it a welcoming neighborhood for their type. Within a few weeks the situation at the Ghetto, which had been calm for months, escalated considerably, including vandalism at the Italian ice-cream parlor, brawls at the Turkish restaurant-bar, and assaults in the park. Other young right extremists with whom I was more closely familiar also expressed a desire to move into the neighborhood, which they had come to view as friendly terrain.[5] Put differently, in the case of the Ghetto and arguably of *Plattenbauten* neighborhoods more generally, an ominous plot of nazification appears to operate in hegemonic representations so as to weave together what is ultimately a history of urban disconnection as a narrative organized by a chronotope of temporal reversal. Such a chronotope then circulates widely. It carries with it as one of its adverse effects the potential for a reflexive and self-fulfilling dynamic that end up frustrating, inexorably, the efforts of local mobilizations to curb the extreme right in the neighborhood and to reconfigure the very chronotope through which the Ghetto is publicly narrated.

CONCLUSION

A paradigmatic token of the process of urban disconnection that has since reunification recast many *Plattenbauten* neighborhoods as marginalized peripheries, the Ghetto emerges as the tragic hero of the narrative of temporal reversal through which this process has been understood in Germany. In local discourses about the neighborhood, from printed newsletters to the voices of its residents, one generally finds some version of this narrative, often rendered as nostalgia for better times. And yet, in such discourses, it appears to maintain a certain degree of openness and indeterminacy that allows for distinct renderings of its core temporal form, depending on differences in contexts of representations, authorial voice, and social positions. Indeed, at times the very dominance of this chronotopic formation appears uncertain and other temporalizations gain strength (think of Anna's narrative of material prosperity, for example). In contrast, non-local renderings of the Ghetto, for instance in public media of national circulation, tend to produce a narrower range of narratives that is held more tightly together as a particular genre. This relative uniformity is achieved not only by adhering faithfully to the chronotope of the neighborhood as linked with temporal reversal, but also by its inscription within a "there goes the neighborhood" plot of creeping nazification. It is that particular chonotopic form that has dominated an entire narrative genre through which post-reunification processes of urban disconnection in *Plattenbauten* neighborhoods has been publicly represented. And it is that very predominance of this chronotope of nazification, its seemingly irresistible compulsion, that has endowed it with illocutionary force, with a certain reflexive capacity that would seem to fold this narrative back into the Ghetto itself.

Günther Grass ends his novel with another warning, this time about the reiterative circularity with which the National Socialist past returns inexorably to violently haunt the German present. "It doesn't end. Never will it end," he writes (2002: 234). In invoking and exploiting the clichéd chronotope of the *Plattenbauten* neighborhood as a narrative device, however, he at the same time authorizes and propagates it and thereby unwittingly reinforces its self-fulfilling reflexivity.

ACKNOWLEDGMENTS

Parts of this chapter were originally published as Shoshan (2012). "Time at a standstill: Loss, accumulation, and the past conditional in an East Berlin neighborhood." *Ethnos* 77(1): 24–49, reprinted by permission of Taylor & Francis Ltd., www.tandfonline.com.

NOTES

1. Indeed, from the racial dimension of the North American ghetto or its frequently inner-city spatial location to the degree of socioeconomic misery to which its residents are subject or the level of criminal (and police) violence to which they are victims, the differences are both numerous and palpable.
2. Literally "day mothers," or women who run small daycare businesses in their own apartments.
3. Indeed, participation rates for Berlin, the district of Treptow-Köpenick (where the Ghetto lies), and the polling booth near the *Kugel* were respectively 58 percent,

57.5 percent, and 27 percent. The NPD's 37 votes at the polling booth thus represented nearly 20 percent of the total ballots (for Berlin and Treptow-Köpenick 0.7 percent and 5.3 percent, respectively).

4. Each of these terms, of course, comes with its own political genealogy. "Nationally liberated zones" has been a key phrase in the rhetoric of certain right extremists for some years, while "fear zones" harks back to feminist discourses and "no-go areas" to the language of urban warfare.

5. Elsewhere, for example, I discussed the case of young Elsa, an intimate of the more militant circles of right extremists in the district, who, under pressure from her parents to move out, looked at the Ghetto and its surrounding neighborhoods as her top choice locations, this despite their remoteness and their poorer transportation infrastructure and consumption and leisure offerings (2008).

REFERENCES

Bakhtin, Mikhail. "Forms of time and of the chronotope in the novel." In *The Dialogic Imagination: Four Essays*, edited by Michael Holquist, 84–258. Austin: University of Texas Press, 1998.

Berliner Zeitung. "Rechte schlugen Vietnamesen krankenhausreif." *Berliner Zeitung*, April 7, 2004, http://www.berliner-zeitung.de/archiv/jugendliche-wollten-bier-anschreiben-lassen---weil-der-imbissbetreiber-ablehnte--zertruemmerten-ihm-die-taeter-das-gesicht-rechte-schlugen-vietnamesen-krankenhausreif,10810590,10166654.html.

Brenner, Neil and Nikolas Theodore, eds. *Spaces of Neoliberalism: Urban Restructuring in North America and Western Europe*. Malden, Mass.: Blackwell, 2002.

Butterwegge, Christoph and Lüder Meier. *Rechtsextremismus*. Freiburg: Herder, 2002.

Ernst, Hans-Eberhard. "Ein Altglienicker." In *Der Altglienicker*, 3. Berlin: Red Eagle Design, 2005.

Geyer, Steven. "Hier regiert die NPD, nicht der DFB." *Frankfurter Rundschau*, October 12, 2006, http://www.fr-aktuell.de/in_und_ausland/politik/aktuell/?em_cnt=987575.

Grass, Günter. *Crabwalk* (Khrisna Winston, Trans.). Orlando: Harcourt, 2002.

Hannemann, Christine. *Die Platte. Industrialisierter Wohnungsbau in der DDR*. Berlin: Hans Schiler Verlag, 2005.

Harvey, David. *Spaces of Capital: Towards a Critical Geography*. New York: Routledge, 2001.

Häußermann, Hartmut and Andreas Kapphan. *Berlin: von der geteilten zur gespaltenen Stadt?* Berlin: VS Verlag, 2002.

Köhler, Regina. "Ein Kiez kämpft um seinen Ruf." *Berliner Morgenpost*, October 13, 2006, http://www.morgenpost.de/printarchiv/berlin/article104628294/Ein-Kiez-kaempft-um-seinen-Ruf.html.

Lefebvre, Henri. *The Production of Space*. Cambridge, MA: Blackwell, 1991.

———. *Writings on Cities*. Cambridge, MA: Blackwell Publishers, 1996.

Mai, Marina. "Feindliche Übernahme eines Wohnviertels." *Die Tageszeitung*, September 23, 2005, 22.

Nibbrig, Hans H. and Axel Lier. "Neonazis foltern Berliner mit heißem Bügeleisen." *Die Welt*, June 25, 2005, http://www.welt.de/print-welt/article678665/Neonazis-foltern-Berliner-mit-heissem-Buegeleisen.html.

Pred, Allan. *Even in Sweden: Racisms, Racialized Spaces, and the Popular Geographical Imagination*. Berkeley: University of California Press, 2000.

Schröder, Burkhard. *Im Griff der rechten Szene: ostdeutsche Städte in Angst*. Reinbek bei Hamburg: Rowohlt Taschenbuch, 1997.

Sebald, Winfried Georg. *Luftkrieg und Literatur: mit einem Essay zu Alfred Andersch*. München: Hanser, 1999.

Shoshan, Nitzan. "Placing the Extremes: Cityscape, Ethnic 'Others,' and Young Right Extremists in East Berlin." *Journal of Contemporary European Studies* 16 no 3 (2008): 377–91.

Smith, Neil. "Remaking Scale: Competition and Cooperation in Pre-National and Post-National Europe." In *State/Space: A Reader*, edited by Neil Brenner, Bob Jessop, Martin Jones, and Gordon MacLeod, 227–38. Malden, MA: Blackwell Pub, 2003.

Soja, Edward W. *Postmodern Geographies: The Reassertion of Space in Critical Social Theory*. New York: Verso, 1989.

Staud, Toralf. "Auf den Rummel kannste nicht gehen." *Die Zeit*, March 10, 2005, http://www.zeit.de/2005/11/Antifa.

Stengel, Mathias. "Am Rand der Gesellschaft." *Berliner Morgenpost*, September 19, 2006, http://www.morgenpost.de/printarchiv/berlin/article104621022/Am-Rand-der-Gesellschaft.html.

Teske, Günter, ed. *Treptower Wende-Chronik*. Berlin: Bezirksamt Treptow, 2000.

Unverfehrt, Viola. "Baugeschehen in Altglienicke." *Der Altglienicker* 156 (2005): 1–2.

Verfassungsschutz Brandenburg. *ZDK.Bulletin 1998–1. "National befreite Zonen"—von Strategiebegriff zu Alltagserscheinung*. Berlin: ZDK, 1998.

Verfassungsschutz Brandenburg. *"National befreite Zonen"—Kampfparole und Realität*. Potsdam: Verfassungsschutz Brandenburg, 2001.

11 Postindustrial Pathways for a "Single Industry Resource Town"

A Community Economies Approach

Janet Newbury and Katherine Gibson

INTRODUCTION

The City of Powell River in the Canadian province of British Columbia (BC) has been synonymous with pulp and paper production for most of the twentieth century. Situated within the traditional territory of the Tla'amin (Sliammon) First Nation, this mill town on BC's Sunshine Coast is found just 30 kilometers south of the northern end of Highway 101, which hugs the west coast of the United States all the way from Baja, Mexico to Canada. The settlements around the industrial port of Powell River are scattered along a narrow coastal corridor backed by dense forest and rugged topography and, due to the inlets interrupting Highway 101 north of Vancouver, the region is accessible only by ferry or airplane. The deep harbor and energy potential, once the Powell River itself was dammed, were sufficient attractors to industrial investment at the turn of the twentieth century.

With the incorporation of the Powell River Company and the opening of an industrial capacity mill in 1909, a mill town was established and grew rapidly as workers and their families arrived from other parts of the country and overseas, especially Italy (Powell River Diversity Initiative 2010; Townsite Heritage Society of Powell River 2013). From the end of World War II until the mid-1970s, the mill was the backbone of Powell River's formal economy: in the 1950s (when it became part of MacMillan Bloedel) it was reputedly the largest newsprint mill in the world; and in 1974 it employed its peak of 2,527 people (Hayter 1997: 32). In the 1980s, the mill produced 471,000 tonnes of paper and still supported 2,300 employees, but faced with international competition and financial difficulties, production and employment rates were beginning to drop (Hayter 1997: 31). From the 1990s on, the pulp and paper industry has significantly downsized all over Canada, leaving single industry towns such as Powell River with what many perceive as major material and symbolic challenges. The Powell River Regional Economic Development Society notes that today the mill employs less than 400 of the region's nearly 20,000 inhabitants (2011: 45). Although it still plays an important role in the town's collective identity, the mill is no longer the economic "driver" it once was, and the void left by its downsizing presents a challenge familiar to all single industry resource towns when the long boom is over—what now?

In a valiant attempt to rebrand Powell River, City Council marketed the region to outsiders not on the basis of logging and the paper industry, but as "the Pearl on the Sunshine Coast." A pearl is a rare gem and an accident of the natural world, not entirely unlike Powell River itself, due to its isolated location and temperate climate. There is a great deal of concern for the future of this pearl and how it can continue to produce value for the community. In recent years public debate has intensified about how to respond to Powell River's crisis of economic identity. Some in the community are keen to find "replacement" secondary industries; others are interested in rethinking what constitutes a sustainable "economic base." A new focus on environmental tourism and a low-impact rural lifestyle have led the current City Council to rebrand the region once again, as "Coastal by Nature." This chapter reports on a research interventionaimed at making a contribution to this ongoing public debate.

Co-author Janet Newbury has been a resident of Powell River for seven years and is a founding member of Powell River Voices, a civic organization aimed at widening the debate about Powell River's social and economic future.[1] Co-author Katherine Gibson recently visited Powell River to participate in a "public conversation" around post-capitalist community economy approaches to economic development organized by Powell River Voices. Together we are actively involved in a form of "desire-based research" that "makes room for the unanticipated, the uninvited, the uncharted, and unintended" (Tuck 2010: 641). We are committed to working with community members who are interested in building a resilient economic future for Powell River.

In this chapter, we reflect on the role academics can play as members of hybrid research collectives concerned to experiment with non-linear and uncertain futures. Using the lens offered by Gibson-Graham's research on post-capitalist economic development, we situate the mainstream responses to industry decline advocated by established economic interests within a diverse economy framing. We trace how, at a citizen level, other possibilities that might contribute to different postindustrial pathways are also being actively pursued. We consider how such pathways might enact community economies centered on ethical interconnection, resilience, and the growth of wellbeing for people and the planet.

The first section of the chapter introduces the social and economic setting of Powell River. Drawing on secondary sources, we briefly identify some of the different social groups that comprise the current Powell River "community" and their history of settlement and migration within the context of colonial and capitalist development. In the next section, we discuss the role of hybrid research collectives in creating new futures. We situate our own actions in the context of an emerging method of participant activist research, and we outline the ethical concerns of community economies that we bring to this project. The last section highlights diverse economic practices and organizations already underway in Powell River and discusses how community economy discourse can deliberately engage with current concerns and open space for new directions.

A MILL, AND MORE

Though most commonly recognized as a mill town, Powell River consists of a cluster of scattered settlements separated by tracts of forest. Travelling from north to south, these include the community of Lund; Sliammon (which is a reservation of land that was allotted to Tla'amin people under federal jurisdiction, although the entire region sits on unceded Tla'amin territory); various neighborhoods within the municipality, including Wildwood, Townsite, Cranberry, Westview, and Greif Point, the rural community around Kelly Creek south of town; and Saltery Bay. All these settlements result from a complex history of waves of newcomers arriving for reasons related to colonization, capitalism, and other political and material realities. To more fully convey the nature of Powell River today, it is useful to briefly introduce the main social groups who make this heterogeneous entity into a distinctive place.

The Sunshine Coast has been home to the Tla'amin people for an estimated 5,000 years. As one of the Coastal Salish peoples, this group lived for generations as stewards of an environment that supported their livelihood. With the coming of European settlers and the logging industry in particular, they were forcibly removed from their original village site (where the mill currently sits) and relegated to a small "reserve" of land, just north of what is now formally known as the City of Powell River. By the turn of the twentieth century, waves of disease introduced by European settlers had reduced the population to a small group of some 300 individuals (Sliammon Treaty Society 2013). The damming of what became known as the Powell River destroyed the salmon run, and the Tla'amin people saw their land built over by industrial infrastructure. Today, Tla'amin people live all around the City of Powell River and beyond, but the community of Sliammon, located approximately 7 kilometers north of the mill, is where their cultural institutions are centered. The population had grown to 730 people in 2011 (Statistics Canada 2013). With subsistence livelihoods increasingly threatened, Tla'amin men have paid jobs mainly in logging, fishing, and construction, and women in administration and healthcare (Statistics Canada 2013).

The twentieth century has been a time of great sorrows and challenges for the Tla'amin people, but their fortitude has resulted in the successful and precedent-setting negotiation of a treaty with the Province of British Columbia and the Federal government in 2012, which will move the Nation out from under the jurisdiction of the "Indian Act" to self-government (Canadian Broadcasting Corporation 2012). For the people who have lived through them, these changes have been a long time coming. As these comments by respected Tla'amin elder, Dr. Elsie Paul, illustrate, the Indian Act enforced restrictions on lifestyles, promoted segregation between Aboriginal and non-Aboriginal people, and was frequently accompanied by State violence:

> But things are improving, they are. We can talk to our MLA now. We couldn't talk before. At least we're talking. . . . Police didn't need a search warrant to come kick your door in and search your house. You can't get away with that today. . . . Now I can sit down and have my glass of wine with my dinner if I choose to. (Newbury 2013a: 105)

The treaty enacts increased land ownership and control over land use, and expanded hunting and fishing rights (Sliammon Treaty Society 2013). This long overdue recognition of Tla'amin sovereignty will potentially usher in significant changes for the fortunes of Aboriginal people in the Powell River region.

While the newly settled treaty signals future change, the downsizing of the Powell River mill has also had a massive and ongoing impact on the region over the last twenty years. For over ninety years, a single pulp and paper mill shaped daily lives and generational expectations for many in Powell River, and for older residents and the established business sector it is hard to imagine a future for the city that is not connected to the mill. In the early part of the twentieth century, the Powell River Company built a "company town" to house its workers. This aspect of capitalist colonization set up a longstanding distinction between mill workers and other inhabitants in the region. The three founders of the company, who moved from Minnesota to establish the mill town, were convinced by current philosophical ideas about the civilizing influences of aesthetics and the environment (Townsite Heritage Society of Powell River 2013). The townsite was pre-planned and laid out according to the principles of the Garden City Movement, which placed emphasis on ensuring a humane environment for industrial workers largely via the inclusion of nature in the form of home yard gardens, parks in the city, and green belts to buffer residential areas (Howard 1902). The original houses for millworker's families were built in the Arts and Crafts style that valued quality building and aesthetic designs. Single-family dwellings with spacious gardens were built along well laid-out tree-lined streets arrayed parallel to the coast.[2] The employment hierarchy of the mill was written into the landscape. Managers occupied more ornate and larger mansions along the first tier of streets with views of the ocean and the mill, and workers were allocated to houses according to rank, with engineers in streets behind managers, foremen behind technical staff, and unskilled workers in the streets furthest from the coast.[3]

Spatial proximity to the mill meant that its rhythms of work permeated the consciousness of workers, wives, and children, as John Campbell recalls:

> Growing up in the townsite, the mill was always part of your life. Your life ran by the mill whistle. You always knew what time it was because

the whistle would let you know when it was time to go for supper, or when it was time to go for lunch at school. (Levez 2002: viii)

Roma Urquhart's memories are of the comforting presence of the mill:

> Something that I can remember . . . is that I used to love to fall asleep. We lived in the front row [of houses] . . . right above the mill. To hear the saws cutting the logs, it was such a nice sound. I felt so comforted by that sound, and I've never forgotten it. (Levez 2002: viii)

But it was not only work and housing that the Powell River Company provided; it was involved in all aspects of people's lives. Roger Taylor, a 91-year-old former carpenter who started working in his teens, remembers with fond pleasure the paternalism of this resource company before World War II:

> They were a darn good company to work for. It didn't matter what it was, they'd donate for this and donate for that. If a sports team was going away, they'd sponsor them. On Halloween they'd put on a big party at the Dwight Hall for the whole community. Every kid would get a present. It didn't matter how many kids there were. Christmas was the same. They would put on a huge do there in the Dwight Hall. (Bolster 2012)

As the mill and town grew in size after World War II, what is now the neighborhood of Cranberry (a close walk to the mill) became its first suburb, followed shortly thereafter by the development of Westview, which was itself incorporated as a village in 1942. In 1955, Townsite, Cranberry, Wildwood, and Westview were amalgamated to create the municipality (Powell River Historical Museum and Archives 2011). Today remaining and former mill workers live all over Powell River, and the company-built houses are privately owned and no longer occupied exclusively by mill employees.

Given the generational attachment to a single industry and a single company, the decline of the mill has shaken the foundations of the Powell River community. While job losses associated with technical change and rationalization of production began to occur in the 1980s (Hayter 1997), until relatively recently the mill was still the provider of many of the most stable jobs in the region. A former mill worker recalled to one author how, when he heard that he had won a job at the mill in the 1980s and was to move to Powell River, he and his wife felt they were "set for life." The wealth of the community was remarkable and, as this man commented, "There was no value put on education because at 17 you could walk into a well-paying job in the mill—people wanted for nothing, they could buy anything they wanted."

It was not just mill families who enjoyed the wealth that flowed from the mill; schools and other infrastructure were built by the mill in earlier years

(Powell River Historical Museum and Archives 2011), and industry taxes have provided what has been considered an important economic base for the community. It should be noted that this stability can no longer be taken for granted, however, with a forty percent tax reduction having been granted to Catalyst (the current owner of the mill) in 2010, meaning a $2.25 million drop from 2009 to 2010 (Dobbin 2011). Given this recent history, many of the mainstream responses to the downsizing of this industry have focused longingly on finding a sizable industrial replacement.

In addition to the two mutually implicated histories of Tla'amin First Nation and the influx of mill workers beginning in the early twentieth century, there is also a more recent history of socio-demographic changes in the Powell River region. Subsequent migrations have seen the settlement pattern spread to the north and south of Sliammon and the old mill town. In the 1960s, the conservative working class community of Powell River experienced a wave of in-migration in response to the American draft. By this time, the mill was no longer the global force it had once been. Small-scale agriculture had now become a significant part of the Powell River economy, as had fishing. During the Vietnam War, young draft avoiders escaped the United States and flocked into Canada. A good number ended up in Lund, just north of Powell River, developing collective homes and farms in the bush both north and south of the municipality. This influx of "hippies" contributed to an emerging counterculture in the otherwise relatively staid community.

After the early twentieth century wave of Italian immigrants who arrived to work in the mill, there was another wave of international newcomers beginning in 1947, followed by those who arrived to avoid the American draft in the 1960s. In more recent years immigration rates have declined (attributed to the slowing down of mill activity), with approximately 14.7 percent of Powell River citizens arriving from outside of Canada in 2006 (Powell River Diversity Initiative 2010: 6). The relative proximity to Vancouver and low housing prices, however, have drawn people from other parts of BC to buy property in the region for both vacation and retirement purposes. These migrant retirees and the aging mill workforce mean the population is now significantly older than the rest of the province. In 2011, the median age in Powell River was 50.1 years, in comparison with a median age of 41.9 years in the rest of the province (Statistics Canada 2012). The number of young children also continues to drop, and the size of the population has not changed significantly in the last five years (Statistics Canada 2012).

The face of the town has thus changed drastically. Despite its still current industrial image, Powell River is already a postindustrial city. By 2011, as many people were employed in the mill (some 340) as in the education sector (320), and social services was the next biggest employer, providing jobs for 204 people (Powell River Regional Economic Development Society 2011: 45). Many residents derive their income from outside the region, including a contingent of men who fly off on a regular basis for work in resource industries elsewhere.

From this description, it is clear that Powell River is a heterogeneous entity both socially and economically and has been in a constant state of becoming under the influences of colonialism, capitalist industrialization, and other internal and external dynamics. The most formative, productive, and environmentally disruptive influence on the region has been the mill, but it is no longer in the "driver's seat." While those traditionally in political power in the region have reflected the values and interests of the old industrial identity, there is increasing involvement of other, less industrially identified groups in the public sphere. This is an important juncture in which Powell River's future is being hotly debated, and as such offers a context in which to engage in discussion about a range of postindustrial pathways.

PARTICIPANT ACTIVIST RESEARCH

The research upon which this chapter is based draws on insights generated from a mix of methods. As mentioned in the Introduction, the site of this inquiry is the hometown of one of the authors. As an "insider," albeit a more recent resident who derives her primary income from outside the region, Janet has for many years been a community participant, activist, and "researcher in the wild," that is, a lay researcher whose observations, reflections, and analyses emerge from immersion in actions around matters of concern (Callon and Rabeharisoa 2003). She has occupied (and continues to occupy) voluntary positions on the Powell River Diversity Initiative (PRDI) board and steering committee, Community Resource Centre (CRC) executive committee, Powell River Child, Youth, and Family Services Society board, and Sunshine Musicfest board. Most recently she co-founded the civic engagement organization Powell River Voices.[4] The experience of these involvements has provided input into a formal postdoctoral research project which she is conducting as a professional academic researcher (or "confined researcher" in the language of Callon and Rabeharisoa) at the University of Victoria, with mentorship from academic colleague (and non-Powell River resident) Katherine Gibson.

We have called this project a participant *activist* research project to denote the difference from a more classic participatory action research (PAR) approach. PAR typically works with vulnerable and marginalized groups and has an emancipatory focus. The object of critique is clear, as is the target for transformation. The mode of participant *activist* research introduced here involves working on matters of shared concern with already mobilized collectives of researchers in the wild to foster emergent possibilities. As academic researchers, we bring to this process an interest in reframing the economy as diverse and proposing post-capitalist development pathways that activate ethical rather than structural dynamics of transformation (Gibson-Graham 2006).

The impact of capital mobility on livelihoods in place has been a longstanding research concern of J. K. Gibson-Graham and members of the Community Economies Collective. Their action research has been conducted with communities experiencing the detrimental effects of economic restructuring who feel that there is no alternative but to be the victims of the business-as-usual capitalist development promise. In the Latrobe Valley of Victoria where, after decades of employment growth in mining and electricity generation, privatization of the state power industry caused massive retrenchments, Gibson and Cameron worked with unemployed youth, single parents, and retrenched power workers to reimagine the people of the Valley, rather than its brown coal, as the primary resource to be mobilized (Cameron and Gibson 2005a). In the rural communities of Jagna and Linamon in the Visayas region of the Philippines, capital investment is largely absent and residents are forced to become contract migrant workers overseas to make ends meet. Here Gibson et al. (2010) worked with unskilled workers, young mothers, and older farming women to mobilize local assets and generate employment in community based enterprises. In the coastal fishing communities of the northeast United States, where the livelihoods of independent fishers are threatened by the overfishing of industrial scale capitalist fishers, St Martin (2005 and 2009) has worked with fishers to map their ocean floor commons and experiment with community-supported fishing, modeled on community-supported agriculture, as a way of strengthening economic and social wellbeing directly. All these projects have employed a language of the diverse economy with which to reposition residents as activated subjects, rather than deactivated victims, in processes of local economic development.

The common conflation of economic development with capitalist, or mainstream, business growth is one of the unexamined "truths" that Gibson-Graham's work has been keen to expose and deconstruct (1996 and 2006). Their contribution has been to rethink economic identity outside of a capitalocentric framework in which capitalist economic relations are taken to be what constitutes and drives a "real economy" while all other economic relations are positioned in relation to capitalism as the same as, a complement to, subordinated by, or contained within (1996: 6). Gibson-Graham's diverse economy framing releases economic diversity from this straitjacket and allows for the imagining of very different dynamics of development and growth (see Figure 11.1). A heterogeneous range of economic practices are seen to contribute to our material wellbeing, not just the production and distribution of goods and services by waged and salaried workers, monetized market transactions, capitalist business, and mainstream finance, all built upon the institution of private property. Taken alone, these activities do not offer a complete picture of a community's economy but are, rather, the tip of the iceberg.[5] When it comes to making decisions about economic futures, public discourse usually limits us to think only of the growth of wage labor, commodity markets, capitalist business, and access to mainstream finance.

Enterprise	Labor	Property	Transactions	Finance
CAPITALIST	**WAGE**	**PRIVATE**	**MARKET**	**MAINSTREAM MARKET**
Family firm	Salaried	Individually owned	Free	Private banks
Private unincorporated firm	Unionized	Collectively owned	Naturally protected	Insurance firms
Public company	Non-union		Artificially protected	Financial services
Multinational	Part-time		Monopolized	Derivatives
	Contingent		Regulated	
			Niche	
ALTERNATIVE CAPITALIST	**ALTERNATIVE PAID**	**ALTERNATIVE PRIVATE**	**ALTERNATIVE MARKET**	**ALTERNATIVE MARKET**
State owned	Self-employed	State-owned	Fair and direct trade	State banks
Environmentally responsible	Cooperative	Customary (clan) land	Alternative currencies	Cooperative banks
Socially responsible	Indentured	Community land trusts	Underground market	Credit unions
Non-profit	Reciprocal labor	Indigenous knowledge	Barter	Govt. sponsored lending
	In-kind		Co-operative exchange	Community-based financial institutions
	Work for welfare		Community supported agriculture, fishing, etc.	Micro-finance
				Loan sharks
NON-CAPITALIST	**UNPAID**	**OPEN ACCESS**	**NON-MARKET**	**NON-MARKET**
Worker cooperatives	Housework	Atmosphere	Household sharing	Sweat equity
Sole proprietorships	Family care	Water	Gift giving	Rotating credit funds
Community enterprise	Volunteer	Open ocean	State allocations/ appropriations	Family lending
Feudal enterprise	Neighborhood work	Ecosystem services	Hunting, fishing	Donations
Slave enterprise	Self-provisioning	Outer Space	Gleaning, gathering	Interest-free loans
	Slave labor		Sacrifice	Community supported business
			Theft, piracy, poaching	

Figure 11.1 The Diverse Economy

This indeed has been the response in Powell River, as it has become increasingly clear that the mill can no longer be relied upon for industrial tax revenue and job creation. The Powell River Regional Economic Development Society (PRREDS) was formed in 2001 after community consultation to "diversify the local economy through new investment attraction, as well as support and strengthen existing businesses and industries" (2011: 2). The diversity mentioned here is sectoral. Instead of pulp and paper, the range of investment possibilities that have been most actively pursued by Powell River's city council include industries such as power generation, garbage incineration, and waste treatment. Like the pulp and paper industry, these activities require abundant water and a measure of pollution tolerance within the community. Somewhat in contradiction, the other industries being courted are tourism, the arts, and retirement villages. PRREDS actively pursues potential investors with such services as its "site selection profile," which highlights opportunities for people- or resource-based capitalist industries to enter the region from outside, and paints a picture of the area as one which is "continuing to grow," and with plenty of room for more growth.

At the same time as pursuing this pro-growth strategy, the City of Powell River contracted the Helios Group management consultants, who advised that cut backs on public expenditure were necessary in order for the City to remain afloat with declining revenue (Helios Group 2011). This dual pronged strategy of making the region more "investment ready" by offering incentives to private capital investment and cutting back on community services that support wellbeing directly, especially for those who are less well off, are highly risky, even as they are well-travelled policy pathways. The era of long term investment and commitment by private corporations to places and labor markets is over. Companies are now looking for quick financial returns and are happy to use state subsidies to bolster their bottom line when poor market performance and bad planning erodes their profits. In addition, there is little modeling of the economic impact on the local economy of maintaining services that support those who are income limited. This region has Canada's highest per capita population of artists, artisans, and craftspeople, and retirees form a major segment of the population (Sunshine Coast Canada, 2013). These groups stimulate the local economy, but their quality of life and allegiance to place is enhanced by having access to what a recent survey identifies as "gap reducing" services, that is those that shrink the gap between rich and poor (Powell River Community Foundation 2011).[6] Such services include the Community Resource Centre, Family Place, Career Link, Food Bank Action Centre Society, Skookum Gleaners, and the Good Food Box program, all of which struggle to stay afloat by seeking funds beyond government support. It seems that there is room for more innovative thinking about how to better grasp the interdependencies that might be stimulated to create a viable and sustainable future for Powell River.

Our participant activist method involves joining hybrid collectives comprised of researchers in the wild and provoking discussion and reflection in such a way as to open up hitherto unthought pathways for economic and social postindustrial development. The approach developed here extends the poststructuralist action research that Gibson-Graham (1994, 1996, and 2006) and colleagues have pioneered in regions where there has been some interest in rethinking economic development pathways (Cameron and Gibson 2005b; Gibson et al. 2010). Central to this methodological approach is reading the landscape for economic difference to see the economy as already more than capitalist. A second research method involves identifying and highlighting examples of existing ethical economic practices that are oriented directly to the growth of wellbeing.[7] We use the language of community economies developed by Gibson-Graham (2006) and Gibson-Graham et al. (2013) to denote these ethical practices as involving negotiation around:

- *surviving* together well and equitably
- *distributing surplus* to enrich social and environmental health
- *encountering others* in ways that support their wellbeing as well as ours
- maintaining, replenishing, and growing our natural and cultural *commons*
- *investing* our wealth so that future generations can live well, and
- *consuming* sustainably.

A third research method involves working with hybrid collectives to initiate discussion about the possible development pathways that might emerge from these two different reading practices. In Powell River, the challenge continues to be that of ensuring that hybrid collectives are truly heterogeneous, thus allowing for democratic discussion. In the next section of the chapter, we present the results of our initial reading exercises and report on ongoing attempts to gather heterogeneous elements of Powell River society into conversations about widening the economic development agenda.

PARTICIPANT ACTIVIST RESEARCH ON RETHINKING DEVELOPMENT IN POWELL RIVER

Among those rethinking development pathways in Powell River there is considerable interest in conducting a full inventory of the diverse economy of the city and region. Clearly the contemporary local economy of Powell River is comprised of much more than the mill and an industrial workforce. People are making livings via a range of modes of work, including paid and unpaid work; a variety of forms of enterprise, including corporate capitalist, family business, self-employment, and artisanal enterprise; and diverse transactions involving formal and informal markets and non-market exchange, such as self-provisioning. We report here on the ongoing practice of reading for economic difference in Powell River.

At present there is a good understanding of the activities and enterprises that comprise the diverse cultural economy of Powell River. Local artist Meghan Hildebrand has represented this diversity in her wonderful "map" of Powell River's cultural capital (see Figure 11.2). In it we see the large number of small businesses, many of them run by self-employed owner-proprietors, in the Creative Cultural Industries and Occupations cluster. This Figure also indirectly points to the huge contribution of volunteer labor to the cultural economy. The Festivals and Events and Community Cultural Organizations, for example, are largely run by unpaid volunteers with some employed administrators. As the footnote to the biennial Kathaumixw Choral festival notes, this event enrolls 560 volunteers for the five-day event and attracts an audience of 14,500 people. In addition to giving insight into the types of labor and enterprise involved in this sector, the "map" also documents the forms of property that support cultural activities. The Spaces and Facilities cluster inventories publically owned facilities like schools, the library and parks as well as individually and collectively owned private property that community members can access, use, and benefit from, such as galleries, studios, and halls.

More detailed research is needed to trace the diverse transactions that knit this cultural economy together and connect it to regional, national, and global flows of value. Certainly all of these activities generate commodity

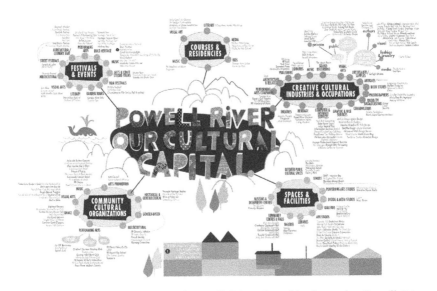

Figure 11.2 A Cultural Map of Powell River (graphic from the Powell River Arts & Culture Initiative Final Report, June 2012; design by Meghan Hildebrand; study funding and support from Tourism Powell River and the City of Powell River)

transactions in formal markets—ticket sales, art and handicraft purchases, hall rentals, wage payments, and so on. Consumers and audiences from outside the region flock to Powell River to purchase the goods and services offered by these cultural activities. There are also a huge number of mostly undocumented gift transactions, payment in kind, barter, cooperative exchange, and state allocations taking place to maintain these activities. The financial backing for this sector would also be very diverse, ranging from family investments in choir members traveling from all over the world to the Kathaumixw Choral festival, to community financed museums, to mainstream insurance for performers and infrastructure.

A similarly complex "map" is yet to be made for the diverse food economy of Powell River, although there have been the beginnings of such a process as part of a larger "Mapping the Heart of Powell River" project (Powell River Diversity Initiative 2013). This has been a year-long participatory arts-based project that engages diverse groups of Powell River citizens to "map" (through experiential and visual collaborations) the multiple narratives of livelihood in the community, including its past, present, and future. With food production being a significant aspect of life for many in the region, one of the maps this initiative produced was a food security map. Participants at 2013's annual *Seedy Saturday* event (a day of seed swapping, seed selling, and food-related workshops) collaboratively constructed this map by identifying which foods they source locally regularly, and where in the region these foods are produced and distributed. This map is useful not only in identifying assets, but in making gaps in food security visible as well.

A full food production inventory would extend this map to include the numerous capitalist food marketing companies which offer wage employment in addition to the many small self-employed and family businesses and farms, and cooperatives such as the Skookum Food Provisioners' Co-op. This is a cooperatively run organization incorporated in 2010 that saw membership rise from 30 to over 130 in the 2011–2012 fiscal year (Skookum Food Provisioners' Cooperative 2013). The Co-op includes a bulk-buying club, fruit gleaning, seed sharing, a community cider press, and runs a variety of workshops about food growing, harvesting, and preserving. The Co-op thus supports practices of individual and collective self-provisioning that take place via nonmarket transactions with the natural environment and local residents.

By broadening the scope of what is taken into economic consideration in these ways, including all activities that fit the definition of "production and distribution of goods and services" (cultural activities, food production, or other initiatives), we gain a more encompassing description of Powell River's economic landscape. Clearly there is more work to be done to complete this task of reading for economic difference. But without completing this inventory it is possible to begin to identify activities that could be seen as building community economies centered on ethical concerns.

The Skookum Food Provisioners' Co-op initiatives, for example, provide opportunities for local consumers to establish ethical trade relations with local food producers that support them through good times and bad with a constancy of commitment. The gleaning and seed saving activities enact responsible relations with the productivity of land now and into the future. The Co-op disperses surplus among local families in need of healthy food, thereby enacting an ethic of care for the survival needs of those beyond the network of cooperative members. The organization also deliberately supports other local services and businesses when it comes to space rentals, catering, web design, and more. In these ways a complex network of interconnections weaves together market and nonmarket transactions, co-op and volunteer labor, capitalist and non-capitalist enterprise, and care for humans and nonhumans alike to produce a resilient economic web that fuels and refuels itself and supports the wellbeing of families, workers, enterprises, and land and plant species.

Volunteer services in the community support various thrift shops, sports teams for youth and adults, extracurricular activities for young people, a vast range of community festivals and events, and ongoing services that provide wellbeing directly to many citizens, such as free church dinners on offer most nights of the week. Including these in our diverse economic framing helps us to better incorporate the often overlooked economic contributions of women in this community. These voluntary initiatives have been relied upon by families for generations, which calls into question the suggestion that "alternative" economic initiatives are driven primarily by newcomers, well-to-dos, or people of particular political allegiances. Opening up our definitions of significant economic activity helps us to see important points of connection in the community that could easily be overlooked, and which serve as potential assets from which we can collectively draw.

The development of a local currency called Powell River Money embraces a notion of "investment" that is not only fiscal, but is also an investment in the future of the community (Powell River Money 2013). Participating businesses accept a percentage of the costs of their goods in PR$, which keeps money circulating in the community. Furthermore, citizens can access PR$ from a number of "cashpoints" in the community, and when they do so a direct contribution is made to a local non-profit organization, making for a doubled benefit of using PR$. This builds a direct link between the business community and the non-profit community, recognizing, once again, that our points of connection are greater than might otherwise be assumed. The "bottom line" for this currency is not growth in terms of profit, but growth in terms of community wellbeing. It does this by adding an ethical option for consumers in the region in a way that *also* supports for-profit businesses.

Currently members of the community are negotiating and struggling to defend commoned property—that is, places that are accessible to all, where people share experiences, ideas, and interconnections that build and sustain community. One group, for example, called "Friends of the Library," has formed to lead a campaign to ensure the library remains a vital and accessible resource for Powell River citizens. The Youth Resource Centre has recently had to reduce its services to one day a week due to financial constraints. Family Place (a family resource center) struggles to stay afloat. And a range of forest areas are being defended from logging.

As a more in-depth example of these commoning practices, a committee (of which Janet is a member) has formed to ensure that the Powell River Community Resource Centre (CRC) can continue its work in the absence of stable government funding. Over the five years since its opening, the CRC has pieced together public grant funds to maintain its operations. Currently it regularly supports 60–100 citizens a day through both direct services (which include legal services supports, healthy food, a range of free workshops, a drop-in café, a community garden, computer access, and laundry facilities, among other things), and important opportunities for socialization and informal connections. These opportunities are particularly significant for the clientele, who are otherwise extremely isolated due to mental illness, physical challenges, poverty, or addictions. Without public investment, the wellbeing of these community members is severely threatened.

The committee has secured core funding for three more years, but is committed to finding ways to ensure the CRC does not find itself in this crisis situation again at the end of that period. To sustain the center's work, they recognize the need to draw together a variety of economic flows apart from grant funding—such things as in-kind donations, volunteer opportunities, and space rentals. They are exploring possibilities for a social enterprise based out of the center which can be both income-generating and capacity-building. Importantly, they are building relationships with a range of existing organizations where partnerships can be mutually beneficial. They are campaigning to raise both awareness and funds at a citizen level and creating a community-driven steering committee to ensure multiple voices are included in future directions and to create pathways for collaboration. The Committee is tapping into a deep understanding among Powell River citizens that the Community Resource Centre is an asset to the community, not a liability. It appears that the work of these organizing groups is shifting the discourse about what matters in Powell River.

Caputo (2000) reminds us that allowing our imaginations and actions to extend beyond inherited discourses *will* alter them. The challenge is to build on and strengthen the practical and discursive movements taking place. When we embrace a performative ontological approach to change (Gibson-Graham 2008), in contrast to a technical-rational one (Blades 1997), we are uniquely positioned as researchers and authors to participate in making some things more "real" than others. The examples of Powell River's diverse economy and efforts to enact ethical community economies that we have offered here convenes a wider set of economic practices on the "economic playing field." Our interest is in engaging more deliberately in public conversations around this emergent community economy that support wellbeing directly. This is not merely an academic exercise; we believe it is in fact something citizenship in a climate changing world demands of us all. We conclude with some reflections on the role of experimental hybrid research collectives in this process.

FROM INVENTORIES TO ACTION: HYBRID RESEARCH COLLECTIVE INTERVENTIONS

In the documentary video *Defining Diversity, Creating Community* produced by the Powell River Diversity Initiative (of which Janet is also a member), Michelle Washington, a Tla'amin woman from Powell River, offers these thoughts about the future:

> You can't just have one plant or one animal and have biodiversity and a healthy ecosystem. For us to have a great community—not just a Tla'amin community and a Powell River community, but a great community together—we need the ideas and different teachings and backgrounds of many, many people. (Powell River Diversity Initiative 2011)

According to urbanist Jane Jacobs, these observations about what constitutes a healthy ecosystem can be applied in the economic realm as well. Economic development, she argues, is connected to the expansion or decline of economic diversity and resilience (Jacobs 2000). When it comes to fostering economic diversity, however, planners usually refer to increasing the number of industrial sectors in a region (Gibson 2012). So in the case of Powell River this means diversifying away from logging and paper and pulp manufacture by attracting investment into tourism, aged care, and possibly waste management. There is little attention given to the diversity of ownership of property or enterprise and who has claims to the surplus generated by business or the benefits bestowed by access to land and resources. Likewise, there is little recognition of the diversity of forms of work and the interdependency of paid work with a wide range of unpaid forms of labor in the community, as briefly outlined above. And the contributions of market transactions are valued while nonmarket transactions are ignored.

A community economies approach to development reminds us that rather than seeking the next big industry, postindustrial communities like Powell River can establish fruitful paths forward by nurturing *multiple* entry-points within a diverse economy. Powell River is well positioned to embrace a more participatory and diversified approach to economic development because of the many grassroots efforts to bolster the community from within that innovative groups of citizens are already actively pursuing. To conclude this chapter we review some of the concrete ways in which we are acting within hybrid collectives of long-term residents, newcomers, the first people of the land, non-human actants (such as old growth forests and fish populations), and multiple others to make real a community economy in Powell River and prepare the ground for greater support from government and non-government institutions.

As we have demonstrated, bringing economic diversity and ethical interconnection to visibility and theorizing their contribution to wellbeing is an important step toward imagining and enacting postindustrial development pathways. The *Powell River Chamber of Commoners* is a celebratory intervention that Janet Newbury along with others initiated to do just this. In most communities the Chamber of Commerce is a well-heard voice in discussions about economic futures. As representatives of private business interests, Chambers of Commerce are keen to highlight the contributions their members make to economic health. The *Chamber of Commoners* is a playful riff on this theme. Rather than an ongoing organization, the *Chamber of Commoners* is an annual event that presents a fun opportunity to connect with and celebrate all the great "hand and heart" work that goes on in Powell River on a regular basis.

There have been four such events so far, the most recent of which explicitly incorporated notions of community economies.[8] It is an all-ages event which involves plenty of time for informal networking over food and drinks, participatory activities, information tables about local initiatives, and an opportunity to celebrate (often unsung) heroes with the "Commoners Choice Awards." These awards are bestowed upon local citizens, groups, organizations, or businesses that contribute a lot to the community, nominated by the public. At the most recent event, Powell Riverites were invited to specifically consider contributors to the "Diverse Economy" for their nominees so that they might better collectively recognize and support that which can so often otherwise gets overlooked. The process of nominating widens the circle of who might initially see themselves as part of the "chamber of commoners." And by inviting key community stakeholders (such as the Mayor and a representative from the local Chamber of Commerce) to present awards, the event has been attracting an increasingly diverse group of attendees each time around.

As we have argued, building a postindustrial pathway toward an uncertain future must involve a truly democratic process of citizen participation, which requires that we learn about the issues that matter to us. The *Chamber of Commoners* is a fun and welcoming way to begin inviting citizen participation. At the center of any community economy is negotiation around how to live together with each other and earth others on this planet. When it comes to the democratic process, voting is just the tip of the iceberg; a true democracy requires civic engagement between elections, and this is at the heart of the community economies approach. In an effort to create opportunities for more in-depth information-sharing and discussion around these kinds of matters, a volunteer group called *Powell River Voices* (noted earlier) has begun hosting a speaker's series, which includes follow-up

dialogues and other activities as well. *Powell River Voices* deliberately partners with different community organizations, institutions, businesses, and
groups. The aim is to provide opportunities for people to become more
informed before the time comes to vote on major issues, and perhaps more
importantly, to find ways to share views before and after voting day. Its
events are advertised widely in an effort to enlarge the circle of who might
choose to populate these events, but the challenge of diversifying this group
remains a real one.

The first event, a talk by Ken Wu of the Ancient Forest Alliance (AFA),
was co-sponsored by both the mill workers' union and the Sierra Club. It
focused on the ecology and history of the region and ways of weaning ourselves off the practice of exporting raw logs. The AFA is committed to ensuring the survival and the thriving of people *and* ecosystems. Wu presented
valuable insights into preserving old growth trees and developing a viable
second-growth forestry industry. This postindustrial pathway would require
investment into building a sustainable forestry industry that treasures the
old growth commons. The event was well attended and led to some exciting
rhizomatic developments. A filmmaker in the community decided to record
the talk and share it widely as an educational tool, the community radio
shared it online, and a list of concrete recommendations for action from the
speaker was published in a free local magazine (Newbury 2013b). Both the
Chamber of Commoners and *Powell River Voices* are experimental hybrid
collective activities that are providing opportunities for new identities, new
visibilities, and new collaborations and negotiations to occur.

The exciting reality that becomes evident at the events described above
is that perhaps the changes needed in Powell River are not as great as initially expected. As these reflections from Tony Culos (a former mill worker)
and Lyn Adamson (director of the local employment services agency, Career
Link) suggest, people have already begun to move on from the belief in the
need for a next "mill":

> I used to believe that the closure of the mill would spell the end of the
> town, but I don't believe that anymore. I have enough evidence in front
> of my eyes to see that the town will keep going, and even growing,
> without the mill. (Tony Culos, Powell River Diversity Initiative 2011)
>
> People used to be really proud that we were a mill town, making
> paper, good jobs. Now, people are really proud that we are no longer a
> mill town. (Lyn Adamson, personal communication 2013)

CONCLUSION

As members of the communities we live in, academic researchers do not
exist outside of our areas of study as purely objective observers. Instead we
can understand ourselves as part of dynamic and emergent hybrid research

collectives. By engaging with(in) our places and subjects of inquiry, we can enhance our capacities to deeply integrate theory and practice through a process we have come to call participatory activist research.

The current chapter is not the culmination of a study, but rather the entry-point into one—keeping in mind of course that the complex processes into which we inquire do not have clear starting or ending points. Although communities are constantly undergoing processes of becoming, this particular community, Powell River, is in a unique transitional moment when it comes to possibilities for postindustrial economic pathways. With the downsizing of its main industry and employer over the past three decades, community members are currently exploring a diverse range of economic possibilities that extend beyond strictly capitalist options. Reading for economic diversity can help us to identify and pursue existing and potential economic pathways that enhance wellbeing for human and nonhuman community members. Knowing that outcomes of such an emergent process cannot be taken for granted, tracking ideas and practices as we have done here is critical for this kind of collaborative research, as it helps to enhance reflexivity and inform decisions.

As conditions continue to change in Powell River, due in part to some of the local activities identified here and in part to broader political, ecological, and economic dynamics, the active elements of the hybrid collective will also continue to change. Our intention, through the participatory research activities described here, is to introduce a community economies approach into this changing landscape in order to see how it may play a part in informing emerging realities.

NOTES

1. Janet is currently engaged in postdoctoral research based in Powell River entitled "Moving Beyond Disciplinary Boundaries: The Symbiosis of Diversified Approaches to Economic Development and Human Service Practices." This research is funded by the Social Sciences and Humanities Research Council of Canada.
2. Designated as a National Historic District in 1995, these streets are one of the best preserved streetscapes of 1910–30s vernacular architecture in Canada (Townsite Heritage Society of Powell River, 2013).
3. This has been a classic feature of resource based company towns the world over and was believed to be a strategy for labor management that maintained micro-class distinctions and provided incentives for promotion. In Australian coal towns built by transnational companies in the 1970s and 80s in Queensland, it was highset and lowset houses that were used to mark management from workers (Gibson, 1990).
4. *Powell River Voices* is a voluntarily run community group, and acknowledges financial support from The Taos Institute.
5. Indeed, we have often used an iceberg image to represent the diverse economy when working with communities (see www.communityeconomies.org/Home/Key-Ideas).

6. The *Vital Signs* report was commissioned by the Powell River Community Foundation to investigate twelve key issue areas regarding the health and vitality of the community. The report indicates that although Powell River's economy as measured by retail sales, tourist visits, family income, and average individual income is lagging in relation to the rest of the province, it is fairly stable (though not growing). The distribution of the wealth in the community, however, is another story. Child poverty, overall poverty, and dependence on social safety nets are all higher in Powell River than most of British Columbia, while high school completion and the average earnings of both male and female workers are lower (Powell River Community Foundation 2011).

7. Clearly there are many activities included in the diverse economy framing shown in Figure 11.1 that are not likely to be seen as desirable, such as slave enterprise, indentured labor, theft, or loan shark lending.

8. See http://prpeak.com/articles/2013/04/26/community/doc51771f711f72577 3958720.txt.

REFERENCES

Blades, David. *Procedures of Power and Curriculum Change: Foucault and the Quest for Possibilities in Science Education.* New York: Peter Lang Publishing, 1997.

Bolster, Chris. "Employees Celebrate Centennial." *Peak Online*, September 12, 2012. Accessed March 27, 2013, http://www.prpeak.com/articles/2012/09/12/news/doc5050c425c4c39858576916.txt.

Canadian Broadcasting Corporation. "Sliammon First Nation Approves First Nations Treaty." *CBC News*, July 11, 2012. Accessed September 15, 2013, http://www.cbc.ca/news/canada/british-columbia/sliammon-first-nation-approves-contentious-treaty-1.1266753.

Callon, Michel and Valalona Rabeharisoa. "Research 'in the Wild' and the Shaping of New Social Identities." *Technology in Society* 25 (2003): 193–204.

Cameron, Jenny and Katherine Gibson. "Alternative Pathways to Community and Economic Development: The Latrobe Valley Community Partnering Project." *Geographical Research* 43 no 3 (2005a): 274–85.

———. "Participatory Action Research in a Poststructuralist Frame." *Geoforum* 36 (2005b): 315–31.

Caputo, John. *Against Ethics: Contributions to a Poetics of Obligation with Constant Reference to Deconstruction.* Indianapolis: Indiana University Press, 1993.

———. *More Radical Hermeneutics: On Not Knowing Who We Are.* Indianapolis: Indiana University Press, 2000.

Dobbin, Murray. 2011. "Letter from Powell River, Catalyst Town." *The Tyee*, July 13, 2011. Accessed September 15, 2013, http://thetyee.ca/Opinion/2011/07/13/PowellRiverCatalyst/.

Gibson, Katherine. "Company Towns and Class Processes: A Study of the Coal Towns of Central Queensland." *Environment and Planning D: Society and Space* 9 no 3 (1991): 285–308.

———. "Economic Diversity as a Performative Ontological Project." In *The Value of Diversity: Biocultural Diversity in a Global Context*, edited by Gary Martin, Diana Mincyte and Ursula Münster, 17–20. Munich: Rachel Carson Centre Perspectives, 2012.

Gibson, Katherine, Amanda Cahill and Deirdre McKay. "Rethinking the Dynamics of Rural Transformation: Performing Different Development Pathways in a Philippines Municipality." *Transactions of the Institute of British Geographers* 35 no 2 (2010): 237–55.

Gibson-Graham, J.K. " 'Stuffed If I Know': Reflections on Postmodern Feminist Social Research." *Gender, Place and Culture* 1 no 2 (1994): 205–24.
———. *The End of Capitalism (As We Knew It): A Feminist Critique of Political Economy.* Cambridge: Blackwell Publishers, 1996.
———. *A Postcapitalist Politics.* Minneapolis: University of Minnesota Press, 2006.
———. "Diverse Economies: Performative Practices for 'Other Worlds.'" *Progress in Human Geography* 32 no 5 (2008): 613–32.
Hayter, Roger. "High-Performance Organizations and Employment Flexibility: A Case Study of *in situ* Change at the Powell River Paper Mill, 1980–1994." *The Canadian Geographer* 41 no 1 (1997): 26–40.
Helios Group. "City of Powell River's General Operations, Service Delivery and Organizational Review: Key Findings and Recommendations." *Powell River Peak*, November 3, 2011. Accessed March 29, 2013, http://www.prpeak.com/media/pdf/news/2012/KeyFindingsandRecommendations%20030812.pdf.
Howard, Ebenezer. *Garden Cities of To-morrow.* London: Sonnenschein and Company, 1902.
Jacobs, Jane. *The Nature of Economies.* New York: Vintage Books, 2000.
Levez, Emma. *People of the White City: Stories from the Powell River Mill.* Powell River, BC: NorskeCanada, 2002.
Newbury, Janet. *Contextualizing Care: Relational Engagement with/in Human Service Practices.* Chagrin Falls: Taos Institute Publications/WorldShare Books, 2013a.
———. "Powell River Citizens Talk Forestry: Democracy in Action." *Policy Note*, April 2, 2013. Accessed August 10, 2013, http://www.policynote.ca/powell-river-citizens-talk-forestry-democracy-in-action.
Powell River Community Foundation. 2011. "Powell River's Vital Signs: Taking the Pulse of Powell River." Accessed March 29, 2013, http://www.prvs.ca.
Powell River Diversity Initiative. "Is It Warm Enough in Powell River?" *Intercultural Parenting Project*, June 30, 2010. Accessed March 29, 2013, http://www.prepsociety.org/PRDI/IPP%20PDFs/IPP%20REPORT%20June%2029%20with%20appendices%201–6.pdf.
———. *Defining Diversity, Creating Community*, Directed and Produced by Tony Papa, 2012, Video Documentary.
———. *Mapping the Heart of Powell River: Community Reflections.* Powell River, BC: Powell River Diversity Initiative, 2013.
Powell River Historical Museum and Archives. 2011. "Powell River Historical Museum and Archives." Accessed September 20, 2013, http://powellrivermuseum.ca/index.php.
Powell River Money Society. 2015. "Powell River money: Community currencies for the Powell River region." Accessed July 11, 2015, http://powellrivermoney.ca.
Powell River Regional Economic Development Society. 2013. "Community Profile and Site Selector Database", Technical report, Powell River, BC.
Statistics Canada. "Focus on Geography Series, 2011 Census." *Statistics Canada*, 2015. Accessed September 15, 2013, http://www12.statcan.gc.ca/census-recensement/2011/as-sa/fogs-spg/Facts-cma-eng.cfm?LANG=Eng&GK=CMA&GC=945.
———. "Sliammon BC National Household Survey (NHS) Profile. 2011 National Household Survey." *Statistics Canada*, 2015. Accessed September 15, 2013, http://www12.statcan.gc.ca/nhs-enm/2011/dp-pd/prof/index.cfm?Lang=E.
St. Martin, Kevin. "Mapping Economic Diversity in the First World: The Case of Fisheries." *Environment and Planning A* 37 (2005): 959–79.
———. "Toward a Cartography of the Commons: Constituting the Political and Economic Possibilities of Place." *Professional Geographer* 61 no 4 (2009): 493–507.

Skookum Food Collective. n.d. "SkookumBlog." Accessed March 29, 2013, http://blog.skookumfood.ca.

Sliammon Treaty Society. 2013. "Who we are." Accessed September 28, 2013, http://sliammonfirstnation.com/treaty/?page_id=43.

Sunshine Coast, Canada. "Arts and Culture." Accessed July 12, 2015, http://www.sunshinecoastcanada.com/play/arts-culture.

Townsite Heritage Society of Powell River. 2013. "Philosophical Foundations." Accessed March 29, 2013, http://www.powellrivertownsite.com/history/townsite_philosophy.htm.

Tuck, Eve. "Breaking Up with Deleuze: Desire and Valuing the Irreconcilable." *International Journal of Qualitative Studies in Education* 23 no 5 (2010): 635–50.

Contributors

Ann Acheson is a Research Associate and Editor of *Maine Policy Review* at the Margaret Chase Smith Policy Center, University of Maine, and Faculty Associate in the Anthropology Department. An applied anthropologist, her recent work has focused on poverty, community development, health, and substance abuse. She has collaborated with her husband, James Acheson, in research on offshore wind power development, on Maine coastal communities, and on the fishing industry. They are co-PIs and co-authors of several articles and reports on these topics. Her other recent publications include several reports and articles on poverty in Maine. Prior to her employment at the Margaret Chase Smith Policy Center, she worked for 15 years in mental health and substance abuse services as a researcher, planner, and in management. She holds a Ph.D. in anthropology from Cornell University.

James Acheson is Research Professor and Professor Emeritus at the University of Maine, where he has been on the faculty since 1968; he has a joint appointment in the Anthropology Department and the School of Marine Sciences. Acheson is an economic anthropologist whose research connects the social, cultural, policy, and environmental components of resource management. He has received three National Science Foundation grants, and is author of over 90 articles, along with five books, including *The Lobster Gangs of Maine* (UPNE 1988) and *Capturing the Commons: Devising Institutions to Manage the Maine Lobster Industry* (UPNE 2004). In 2005, he received the Solon T. Kimball Award for Public and Applied Anthropology from the American Anthropological Association for outstanding achievements contributing to anthropology as an applied science and which have had important impacts on public policy. Acheson holds a Ph.D. in anthropology from the University of Rochester.

Vanesa Castán Broto is a Senior Lecturer at the Bartlett Development Planning Unit of University College London, where she studies the relationships between society, resources, and space. She currently leads an ESRC Future Research Leaders Fellowship to study social and spatial relations in urban energy landscapes. She has recently completed projects on participatory urban planning for climate change in East Africa and on the energy landscapes of post-industrial cities in Bosnia and Herzegovina. She is a co-editor of the volume *Cities and Low Carbon Transitions* (Routledge 2011) and a co-author of the monograph *An Urban Politics of Climate Change* (Routledge 2014).

Veronica Davidov is Assistant Professor of Anthropology and History at Monmouth University. She is an environmental and visual anthropologist whose research focuses on how natural resources are constructed and contested in global and local arenas and the moral ecologies and economies that emerge when nature becomes a commodity. Much of her work explores the various economies of value around space and its various uses. Her main research sites are Ecuador and Russia. She is the author of *Ecotourism and Cultural Production: An Anthropology of Indigenous Spaces in Ecuador* (Palgrave-Macmillan 2013) and the co-editor of *The Ecotourism-Extraction Nexus: Political Economies and Rural Realities of (un)Comfortable Bedfellows* (Routledge 2013).

Allan Charles Dawson (Ph.D., McGill University) is Assistant Professor of Anthropology at Drew University. His research is concerned with issues of ethnicity and identity in West Africa and in the African Diaspora; ethnicity and globalization; identity and violence; religious innovation; chieftaincy; and traditional religious practice in the West African Sahel. Dawson also explores issues of Blackness and Afro-Brazilian identity within the context of the broader Black Atlantic world in his recent monograph *In Light of Africa: Globalizing Blackness in Northeastern Brazil* (University of Toronto Press 2014). Dawson has conducted extensive ethnographic research in Brazil, Ghana, Benin, and Nigeria.

James Ferguson is Susan S. and William H. Hindle Professor in the Department of Anthropology at Stanford University. He also holds honorary appointments at the Department of Sociology and Social Anthropology at Stellenbosch University and the Department of Social Anthropology at the University of Cape Town. He is the author or editor of several books, including *Global Shadows: Africa in the Neoliberal World Order* (Duke University Press 2006). His newest book is *Give a Man a Fish: Reflections on the New Politics of Distribution* (Duke University Press 2015).

Katherine Gibson is a Professorial Research Fellow in the Institute for Culture and Society at the University of Western Sydney and co-founder with Julie Graham of the Community Economies Collective (www.communityeconomies.org). As J.K. Gibson-Graham, the collective authorial presence she shares with the late Julie Graham (Professor of

Geography, University of Massachusetts Amherst), her books include *The End of Capitalism (As We Knew It): A Feminist Critique of Political Economy* (Blackwell 1996, University of Minnesota Press 2006), *A Postcapitalist Politics* (University of Minnesota Press 2006) and *Take Back the Economy: An Ethical Guide for Transforming Our Communities* (www.takebackeconomy.net), co-authored with Jenny Cameron and Stephen Healy (University of Minnesota Press 2013). Her work has been taken up by communities around the world to help them revision and enact economies which sustain people and environments by putting ethical concerns at the center of negotiation about collective futures.

Krista Harper is Associate Professor of Anthropology and the Center for Public Policy and Administration at the University of Massachusetts Amherst. Her research focuses on social movements and mobilizations related to the environment, food systems, and urban public space. An ethnographer who has worked in Hungary, Portugal, and the United States, she is author of *Wild Capitalism: Environmental Activists and Post-socialist Political Ecology in Hungary* (Columbia University Press 2006), co-author of *Participatory Visual and Digital Methods* (Left Coast Press 2013), and co-editor of *Participatory Visual and Digital Research in Action* (Left Coast Press 2015).

Jerry K. Jacka is an Assistant Professor of Anthropology at the University of Colorado—Boulder. His research focuses on the intersection of development, natural resource management, and the political ecology of land use and land cover change. Since 1998, he has worked in communities adjacent to the world-class Porgera Gold Mine in highlands Papua New Guinea examining the differential impacts of mining on social and ecological systems in Porgera. His latest book is *Alchemy in the Rain Forest: Politics, Ecology, and Resilience in a New Guinea Mining Area* (Duke University Press 2015).

Ann Kingsolver is Professor of Anthropology and Director of the Appalachian Center at the University of Kentucky. Her ethnographic work has focused on interpretations of globalization in the U.S., Mexico, and Sri Lanka. Her books include *Tobacco Town Futures: Global Encounters in Rural Kentucky* (Waveland Press 2011), *The Gender of Globalization: Women Navigating Cultural and Economic Marginalities* (co-edited with Nandini Gunewardena, School for Advanced Research Press 2007), *NAFTA Stories: Fears and Hopes in Mexico and the United States* (Lynne Rienner Publishers 2001), and *More than Class: Studying Power in U.S. Workplaces* (editor, State University of New York Press 1998). She has served as president of the Society for the Anthropology of Work and as general editor of the *Anthropology of Work Review.*

Anna Lora-Wainwright is Associate Professor in the Human Geography of China at the University of Oxford. Her research concerns development, health, and environmental issues in rural China. She recently published a special issue of the journal *The China Quarterly* on "Dying for Development: Pollution, Illness and the Limits of Citizens' Agency in China" (2013) and a monograph titled *Fighting for Breath: Living Morally and Dying of Cancer in a Chinese Village* (University of Hawaii Press 2013). Her current work focuses on urbanization and environmentalism in rural China; "cancer villages"; electronic waste; resistance against waste incinerators; rural-urban environmental coalitions; and on the rise of citizen science in rural China more broadly. She has received funding from the British Academy, the Arts and Humanities Research Council, the Social Science Research Council, the Leverhulme Trust, and the Rockefeller Foundation. She holds degrees in Anthropology and in Chinese Studies (SOAS and Oxon) and was the winner of the Philip Leverhulme Prize in Geography in 2013.

Seth Murray is Director of the Program in International Studies and Teaching Associate Professor in the Department of Sociology and Anthropology at North Carolina State University. Since 1999, he has maintained an active ethnographic research project in the Basque region of southwestern France and northern Spain, where he examines the socio-ecological changes associated with mountain farming, particularly those related to European Union agricultural and environmental policies. He is also a principal investigator for a long-term interdisciplinary research project that investigates the evolution of environmental risk-mitigation strategies among cattle farmers in Burgundy, France, especially as they relate to water management and viticulture. He holds a Ph.D. in anthropology from the University of North Carolina at Chapel Hill.

Janet Newbury is a Postdoctoral fellow and Assistant Professor in the Department of Human and Social Development at the University of Victoria, Canada, in the School of Child and Youth Care. Her current research explores the connections between community-based approaches to economic and social development and the wellbeing of children, youth, and families. Through this work, she has participated as a co-founding member of the Post-Growth Institute, a research associate with the Canadian Centre for Policy Alternatives, an associate with the Taos Institute, and a member of the global Community Economies Collective. She is a co-founding member of a local civic literacy group called PR Voices, is vice president of the Powell River Diversity Initiative, and is involved in a number of other community organizations that prioritize intergenerational and intercultural engagement. She has published widely for both academic and popular audiences.

Elena Khlinovskaya Rockhill is an Institute Associate at Scott Polar Research Institute, University of Cambridge. She received her Ph.D. in social anthropology from Darwin College, Cambridge University. From 2004–2007, she worked as a Research Associate at the Department of Social Anthropology, Cambridge University. She was a 2007 Wenner-Gren Hunt Postdoctoral Fellow, and a PI for an ESF-funded international project, "Moved by the State: Perspectives on Relocation and Resettlement in the Circumpolar North" at the University of Alberta, Canada. She teaches part-time at Willamette University, USA and Cambridge University, UK.

Nitzan Shoshan is Professor of Anthropology at the Centro de Estudios Sociológicos at the Colegio de México. He received his Ph.D. in sociocultural anthropology from the University of Chicago. His research interests include nationalism, racist violence, and xenophobia; Europe and Germany after the cold war; social marginality and urban space; memory and temporality in post-socialist and post-Fordist societies; and neoliberal governance. Among his recent publications are "Managing Hate: Political Delinquency and Affective Governance in Germany" (*Cultural Anthropology*); "Time at a Standstill: Loss, Accumulation, and the Past Conditional in an East Berlin Neighborhood" (*Ethnos*); "Post-Fordist Affect: Introduction" (*Anthropological Quarterly*, with Andrea Muehlebach); and "Placing the Extremes: Cityscape, Ethnic 'Others,' and Young Right Extremists in East Berlin" (*Journal of Contemporary European Studies*). He is currently completing a research project on intercultural initiatives in Berlin as well as research on political mobilizations in marginalized neighborhoods of Mexico City.

Ismael Vaccaro is Associate Professor at the Department of Anthropology and the McGill School of Environment at the McGill University. He is a specialist on political ecology and environmental anthropology who has conducted research in Spain and Mexico. He has co-edited *Social and Ecological History of the Pyrenees: State, Market and Landscape* (Left Coast Press 2010), *Environmental Social Sciences: Methods and Research Design* (Cambridge University Press 2010), and *Negotiating Territoriality: Spatial Dialogues between State and Tradition* (Routledge 2014).

Index

Page numbers *in italics* refer to illustrations.

For Product Safety Concerns and Information please contact our EU
representative GPSR@taylorandfrancis.com
Taylor & Francis Verlag GmbH, Kaufingerstraße 24, 80331 München, Germany

www.ingramcontent.com/pod-product-compliance
Ingram Content Group UK Ltd.
Pitfield, Milton Keynes, MK11 3LW, UK
UKHW020941180425
457613UK00019B/491